Fire of Transformation

my life with Babaji...

Fire of Transformation

my life with Babaji...

Gaura Devi

nymet press

Published by

NYMET PRESS
West Leigh, Crediton, Devon EX17 6BL
www.nymetpress.co.uk   email: info@nymetpress.co.uk

Editor: Martin Holyoak
Assisted by: Stuart Wilson and Lili Leicester

Title of original Italian:
Diario Indiano   BABAJI   Il Cielo in Terra
© 1993 J. Amba Editione, Concavagno (AT)

Photographs credited where known
Janki Rani - pages 102, 182   Threesh Kapoor – page 197

First published in the United Kingdom by
Nymet Press 2002

ISBN 0-9541839-0-8

Printed and bound in the UK by
Short Run Press Ltd., Exeter, Devon

CONTENTS

Foreword

by Peter Dawkins

In this book Gaura Devi writes of her personal experiences as a disciple of Shri Hairakhan Wale Baba, the Mahavatar Babaji who appeared publicly in India at the end of the last century and millennium. It is a beautiful account—beautiful in its honesty—and is based upon the diary that Gaura Devi kept during her time with Babaji. As she says herself in her own preface, this diary is intended to be a personal witness to a divine encounter. I always find it very touching, very moving, to hear or read about someone's personal encounter with Babaji, and even more so with Gaura Devi, who was one of the few people in the 1970's to become a disciple of Babaji rather than just a devotee, and to be by Babaji's side during the last crucial years of his public appearance as Hairakhan Baba. This diary concerns Gaura Devi's life and experiences with Babaji as a disciple during the years 1972-1984, and gives a unique insight not only into Babaji and his way of teaching (or one of his ways, as he himself is beyond limitation), but also into the transformational process undertaken by his beloved disciple.

Hairakhan Baba is known as a Mahavatar—a Great Avatar. *Avatar* means 'incarnation or manifestation of God', *Maha* means 'great'. In the Hindu Saivite tradition, Babaji is the Mahavatar of Samba-Sada-Shiva, the Supreme Being who is described as 'He who gives happiness at all times'. When he appeared in 1970 in the Indian foothills of the Himalayas, at Hairakhan, Babaji was recognised as such by many great yogis and saints, who were called to him and who had been preparing for his reappearance. Babaji has many names to describe him, amongst them being the Mahayogi (i.e. the Great Yogi or Yogi of all yogis) and Visva-Guru (i.e. the Guru of all gurus), who gave the world the yogic teachings and who has been with this world from its beginning, manifesting himself whenever appropriate throughout the ages. It is said that such manifestations rarely occur and that when they do it is when a major crisis confronts humanity and the planet, and the world needs greater help than can be given by an ordinary Avatar. Such a time is now, as we move from one Great Age (i.e. a 26,000-year cycle of twelve zodiacal Ages) into a new Great Age, and out of the Kali Yuga or Dark Age that ends each Great Age with a death and purifying, transformational process.

In the Hindu tradition Shiva is the god-name usually associated with that aspect of Deity which brings about death of the old form and transformation (or transmutation) into a new form of expression. However, because this process brings about the birth of each new creation, Shiva is known as the Creator as well as the Destroyer/Transformer. He is also the Maintainer or Preserver of what He creates. In other words, Shiva is the divine Trinity of Creator (Brahma), Preserver (Vishnu) and Destroyer (Rudra). He is often referred to as Samba-Sada-Shiva ('the Ever Holy Shiva'), or as Mahesvara ('the Great Lord'), names that correspond to Jehovah, the Lord God of Hebrew and Christian tradition.

Shiva is that divine Spirit or essence of life, light and consciousness that is everywhere and out of which all things are made. Sometimes it is called the great ocean of life, sometimes the holy breath of life, sometimes the Word or 'Om'. We all share this same essence, and in varying degrees we manifest it consciously and beautifully in our human forms of expression. To the degree that we can understand and truly manifest this divinity we become devotees, disciples, initiates, saints, Adepts, Masters and Great Masters—or, in Hindu terminology, sadhus, jnanis, yogis, Rishis, Sidhas and Avatars. The greatest of these in our world is Babaji ('Beloved or Holy Father'), the Mahavatar and Teacher of all teachers. It is very likely that he is the same great soul as the one known in Western tradition as Idris or Enoch, who is described in Rabbinical literature as the first human being in this world to achieve full enlightenment and rise to the highest level of evolution, to become the supreme Messiah or Christ and the Teacher of all other teachers, Master of all other masters. I believe that this is so; but even this is too limited a viewpoint, as realisation of the Divine is simply the moment in time when we as human souls consciously apprehend and are able to manifest to others our own divinity, which has always existed from the beginning of time.

Although he has chosen to always be in this world, in order to help it, normally Babaji resides behind the scenes, seen and recognised by only a few. It is said that he, as Mahavatar, materialises his body directly when needed and is not born physically of any woman. Normally he maintains his youthfulness even whilst embodied, appearing as the ever-young and beautiful youth; but this is clearly not always the case, as Babaji can do whatever he pleases and sometimes he chooses otherwise. He has appeared young, old, thin, fat, in sequence or simultaneously, in one body or several, to various people. Likewise, as Mahavatar he is said to be immortal even in his physical form or forms, yet this cannot be understood in the ordinary way: death is not always what it seems. Babaji plays a divine drama. He plays with elements. He can appear where and when he wishes, in one or more bodies simultaneously, physical or subtle, and of whatever appearance and age he chooses, and can dissolve them into light or otherwise as and when he decides.

In his last public manifestation — the one in which Gaura Devi was involved and which is the subject of this book — Babaji was referred to as the '1008 Baba'. In this he had an exquisitely beautiful form, but one which he continually changed during the fourteen years of his public appearance. The public manifestation previous to that one (1800-1922), which was referred to by Paramahansa Yogananda in his widely distributed and influential book, *The Autobiography of a Yogi,* was as the '108 Baba'. Both manifestations were as the Hairakhan Baba, for Babaji chose Hairakhan as his place of manifestation, for a specific purpose.

Hairakhan (a name derived from *Hiriya Khand,* meaning 'sanctified area') is a place close to and including a tiny, remote village in the Nainital District of Uttar Pradesh, in the Himalayan foothills of India, twenty-six kilometres east of the market town of Haldwani. The village lies on the bank of the holy river Guatama Ganga, opposite a sacred cave that lies at the foot of the Kumaon Mount Kailash. This mountain is the original Kailash, the physical representation of Mount Meru, the sacred mountain marking the central axis or heart of the world and home of Lord Shiva. It was much more recently in human history that the second Mount Kailash (i.e. the Tibetan Mount Kailash) was 'found' further north in the higher peaks of the Himalayas, on the northern side of Lake Mansarovar, as a kind of substitute for the original. The Guatama Ganga flows underground from Lake Mansarovar and surfaces not far from Hairakhan. The sacred cave, like the Kumaon Mount Kailash, is said to date back to the time of creation, and is described in the Shiva Puranas as a dwelling place of the Gods and the place where Shiva (or Babaji) periodically retreats for meditation and tapasya (ascetic practices).

As '108 Baba', Babaji appeared in about the year 1800 to Hairakhan villagers as a bright light on top of the Kumaon Mount Kailash. Eventually the Mahavatar emerged from this light as a beautiful youth, condensing his body out of the dazzling light. Having stayed at Hairakhan for a few years he then travelled around the Kumaon region, gathering to himself certain devotees and disciples, great saints and yogis, and at times crowds of people came to celebrate festivals with him. In the 1840's he constructed with his own hands and the help of the villagers an octagonal temple (representing Shiva's eight-fold manifest power) on a small hill opposite to and on the other side of the river from the Kailash cave. Besides being at Hairakhan, Babaji was seen by many people in different places, and performed many miracles through the power of his love. Having promised to return again, in August 1922 Babaji went with some of his devotees to the confluence of the Kali and Gauri rivers and, stepping into and then sitting on the surface of the water, he dematerialised into a ball of light in front of their eyes and 'disappeared'. In the following years, however, he appeared to many of his close devotees in dreams, visions or even direct physical form.

The great saint and sidha-yogi, Mahendra Baba, who spent his life searching for and preparing for the return of Babaji, was one of those to whom Babaji appeared physically. Babaji gave him certain signs and a unique, secret mantra by which he, Babaji, could be recognised when he next appeared publicly. Mahendra Baba passed on this knowledge to his disciple, Shri Vishnu Datt Shastriji, who duly recognised and confirmed the reality of Babaji in the Mahavatar's next public appearance. Shastriji subsequently became Babaji's 'priest'. Mahendra Baba also foretold the year, 1970, when Babaji would make his appearance, and prepared the world for this event through his writings, teachings and building of ashrams.

In June 1970 Babaji was duly 'discovered' in the sacred cave at the foot of the Kumaon Mount Kailash. Gradually he drew to himself more and more people, to visit him at Hairakhan, to undergo purification and training under his guidance, and to build an ashram and further temples. After fourteen years of extraordinary activity and demonstrations of divine love, and having foretold the date of the event, he underwent mahasamadhi.

It is said that we all need a guru to help us achieve liberation from mortal attachments and impurity of living, and thus to realise the Divine. *Guru* means 'the remover of darkness'. Sometimes the guru is seen, sometimes not seen. Sometimes he is physically present, sometimes not. Sometimes he is male, sometimes female. At all times he is within us, as we are each part of the Divine, and likewise we are always within the Guru. But we have to gradually realise this and what it means. Several of my friends and acquaintances met the 1008 Hairakhan Babaji in his physical form, and Gaura Devi was one of them. I did not do so: I met the Great Master in another way, and he guides me still. I did not have to undergo the huge shock and lesson of detachment from the Master's physical presence when he left his body in 1984—which is one of the final things that disciples have to learn—but Gaura Devi did. This story of hers is a wonderful story of courage and devotion, and of love shared between two friends, one divine and the other human.

Peter Dawkins
Roses Farmhouse
January 2002

Editor's note

I first met Gaura many years ago, a humble and unassuming person, peaceful yet with a quiet strength. In time I discovered other facets; a very animated person with a playful sense of humour, determined and sincerely dedicated to God. Out of this contact and friendship came the opportunity to be involved with the production of this book. If I had any doubts, they dissolved after reading the text. It is remarkable in its honesty, beauty and intimacy, appearing almost childlike in its innocence; a woman's search for identity and for love, and through her encounter with Babaji and his continuing presence her heart opens to the flowering of divine love.

Gaura's diary is as much a mystical journey as it is a distinctly human story, in which simple everyday events are interwoven with a divine presence that is extraordinary, infinite and mesmerizing, where the tangible is entwined with the intangible. Alongside immeasurable joy there also exists pain, hardships and continual challenge. At times her story is provocative, difficult to understand or accept, sometimes it all appears like a magical fairytale, at other times a heavenly utopia or bizarre drama, yet within the humanity of the events there are echoes in all of our lives, within the words an energy that subtly finds its way to the heart of the reader. The presence of Babaji, felt if not completely understood, increasingly pervades the text and transports meaning beyond the words on the page.

A number of years passed before Gaura considered writing this book, before realizing that the period of time spent with Babaji had also been a preparation for the role of author as well. She recalled that it had been Babaji who, in so many ways, had encouraged her to keep her diary, and when initially asked if she would write her story she replied, 'When Baba tells me to...' The original Italian version was finally published in 1993 and is updated in this English edition by the inclusion of an extra chapter both at the beginning and at the end.

It has been suggested that union with the Divine, whether in form or formless, is the relationship for which the heart of each and every human being truly yearns. Within this book the reader finds that they themselves are travelling on a profound and illuminating journey, one that is truly experiential, at times challenging, not always comfortable and rife with the unexpected; and what emerges so abundantly clearly is that the *Fire of Transformation* which emanates from the essence of Babaji is truly eternal. It is as vibrant, alive, accessible and transformative today as it has always been.

M.H.

Preface by the author

I hesitated for a long time before deciding to write this book, as it is very difficult to speak about Babaji in words. His essence is subtle, occult and can only be grasped by opening oneself to another dimension of consciousness, to the magic of one's heart.

Babaji often taught through a gesture, a smile, an incident. What impressed me most when I first met Him was His great silence and His capacity to communicate through it. Babaji is 'the Presence', the manifestation of the eternal mystery, the other shore of existence. His infinite love is the bridge between us and the great Truth, between the human and the Divine. His physical form is a marriage of heaven and earth.

Many people have been touched forever by His call and our lives have been completely changed. The first word He spoke to me when I met Him, was 'God', and immediately after He added, 'God is love.' From that time on my life has been a search to realize the meaning of these words.

This diary is intended to be a personal witness to a divine encounter, and it is hoped that it will give some understanding of Babaji and His message.

Gaura Devi

[Gaura Devi - from the Sanskrit meaning 'white goddess',
pronounced: *Gor'a Day'vee*]

Community Life

Milan, 15 September 1970

Yesterday evening, for the first time since returning from my summer holidays, I went to Brera. It's an interesting part of the city where artists live and gather together, an old quarter of small streets, elegant buildings and numerous restaurants, in many ways not unlike Montparnasse in Paris. I decided to be truly courageous and wear all my hippie clothes, my long Indian skirt, the elaborate sandals from Amsterdam. People from Milan generally have a decidedly narrow outlook on life, they are bourgeois and look disapprovingly at me when I walk down the street dressed like this. No matter, I have decided that I will be indifferent to their reactions, even going so far as to be provocative if possible, and turn this into my own small, private revolution.

In Brera I met up with everybody again, all my old friends, some of them recently returned from India. They all go around dressed even more outrageously than myself, with multicoloured clothes and very long hair. We eat at Fiorinos, a small, cheap restaurant, just perfect for us. It's as if we take refuge in the small streets of this old quarter of the city because it remains cosy and homely, unlike the rest of the metropolis of Milan, which is grey, cold, hostile and sad. Most people's lives appear to revolve around earning money, just so that they might continue living in a small flat in which they can enclose themselves, as if in a prison; a safe, small prison. People appear afraid of each other, of communication, of love. They are fearful of love and of sex, because love means to open up, to expand, to break through so many barriers. I don't want to end up like them, and that's why I haven't looked for a job yet, even though I'm afraid it could all lead to possible imprisonment.

The radical political movement is also falling apart, the student movement, the revolutionary groups. They have been unable to achieve or even propose anything really new for our society. I feel that the only hope for change and for a new world are the 'hippie' groups that are around, my flower children friends, because they have the courage to search deep within themselves for answers.

I remember Sylvia, my psychoanalyst, telling me that no outside revolution is possible before an inner revolution takes place. It may be that these people smoke dope, take LSD, but it is said that marijuana helps to expand one's consciousness and that LSD is able to open the heart. These experiences can reveal a wider dimension of oneself, a psychic dimension, where one can feel the existence of a divine reality. I have always refused to believe in God, but these days so many magical things are happening to me and realizations are taking place, that it's beginning to break down my insensitive, rational mind. Many of my friends have been to India where they have met spiritual masters, gurus, holders of a forgotten ancient wisdom.

I've met a man called Lorenzo, who wanders around Brera as if he inhabits an Indian temple, dressed in long, orange robes, holding a trident in his hand. Tiziana and Zizi, two capable and independent gypsy women, sit on the pavement knitting and chatting. Zizi has an earring in her nose and she knits rainbow-coloured woollen caps for everybody. A very old friend called Gianni also spends time in Brera. He is a beautiful being with large, green eyes, gentle and ethereal, who is a painter and is presently planning to paint all the bare walls of Milan with designs and messages to change the world. He acts just like a child, thirsty for there to be a magical dimension in his life. Life for him resembles a play and he wants to discover a joyful drama in which we can all take a part, street theatre, a continuous happening. Perhaps we are childish, but what is the purpose of living if we don't search for the real meaning of existence? At least we are prepared to make an effort, to try, rather than ending up little more than wealthy animals only happy with material things; in fact not even that, more likely to be unhappy and greedy.

17 September 1970

Many people visit our community house in 'Via Mayr', especially in the evening. We talk, smoke, make travel plans. It's still summertime in Milan, but the air in the city is polluted, suffocating; nowhere is it possible to find a pleasant, green space. The lyrics of one of our songs says: 'My friend, I have never seen a cemetery so full of life.' At night people want to go out, meet friends, exchange ideas, be loving towards each other.

In the community we try to live in an innovative way by being creative with our daily routine and working together; it's difficult but we are full of enthusiasm. Much of the time we don't seem to be able to maintain a sense of order though, we are lazy, indisciplined, we don't keep the place clean. The other day the sink was full of unwashed dishes and Marco pinned up a piece of paper on the wall with a teaching for us all: 'An unclean house is a house without love.' We are attempting to change our lifestyle and thereby our sense of humanity.

The 1968 student movement failed because the individuals themselves hadn't yet changed and so enable a real transformation; as one of the slogans in France in 1968 prophesied: 'The revolution will be total, or will not be.' There have been many people who have believed in the ideal of communism, but is it really possible to share everything in life, to love and help each other, overcome selfishness, have integrity in everything that we do and also be warriors of truth? Once again the revolutionary groups of 1968 used the outmoded Marxist ideology instead of creating fresh ideals for a possible new world.

Our house is very beautiful, big, with a terrace; it would be cheap to buy, because it's old and hasn't been renovated for a long time, but to us it's already a palace. There is a communal living room, seven metres long, in the middle of which is a decorous yellow brocade tent resembling a theatre stage, our magical show of life. Normally nine or ten people live here, all of us coming from different backgrounds, some involved in politics, while others are psychologists, students, a lawyer. We have open discussions about many things, mainly psychology and revolution and the future of our world. Recently I finished my exams at the University and I am now researching my thesis based on 'Utopia in the history of man', a subject very close to our own experience. We resemble a large, alternative family, looking especially for a quality of love amongst us, our greatest ideal. It is as if we are sharing in an important, historical experiment, unique, new, like explorers of a New Age. We cook vegetarian food, smoke dope, organize parties and workshops, and publish various underground magazines, all the time reading, writing, talking.

The house is not only close to the University but also to Brera and everything that happens there. So many friends come to visit us and sexual relationships are a very important means of expression, our discovery of freedom and love, of contact, union. Even though he knows I'm still quite an atheist, my boyfriend Giuliano has given me some Buddhist books to read, and I do accept that the rational, scientific mind isn't able to know the whole of reality, it can't explain feelings in the heart, can't explain telepathic communication. Science and technology have taken human beings far away from nature, linking people to a reality that is mechanical, robotic, without a soul. Our cities have become stressful and depressing places, people living in isolation from each other, captured by television and the mass media, busily engaged in the pursuit of material toys, like restless children never to be satisfied. In order to earn money, humans are devastating the earth, cheating other people, adulterating food, polluting the natural resources through a lack of awareness, poisoning themselves. In some countries on the earth people waste so many resources, while elsewhere other people still die from hunger; where has humanitarianism gone nowadays?

I know that what we are really seeking is a change in people's hearts, for a revolution of the soul of the earth, and that it is communities like ours which are spiritual research centres. I believe that it is now possible for us to change our society, but only if we create change from inside it, slowly, slowly, with groups of people beginning to live in a different way.

3 October 1970

I am considering the idea of visiting India in order to study Eastern philosophy for a while, maybe it can offer some different answers to the puzzle of life.

Giuliano explained to me that the East and the West have very diverse opinions about life. In the West people pursue all their desires thinking that to fulfil one's desires will bring satisfaction, bring them happiness, whereas in the East people think that desire itself is the cause of all suffering and that peace and real happiness are only found at the end of desire, in Nirvana.

The author 1970

18 February 1971

I have completed my degree in philosophy and my professor had nothing but praise for my thesis about Utopia. Now I would like to organize an experimental kindergarten, because I believe that in order to bring about change in people it is necessary to begin in childhood, when ideas and feelings are first shaped. I no longer have any contact with the political groups, because they have adopted very violent tactics and I don't agree with that approach at all.

Giuliano has spoken to me about Mahatma Gandhi, the great Indian saint and politician, who defeated a mighty country like Britain through a widespread and well organized non-violent movement. Our true strength is spiritual and if we really want to achieve something we should become spiritual warriors because our true power is the power of a new consciousness. We must live truth and show it to the world. Our revolutionary spirit need not die, but we should be able to change reality with new tools. Violence is an old technique and belongs to the past.

10 June 1971

It's summertime again and once more large groups of people meet up in the various haunts in Brera, many returning from India, describing their encounters with Indian gurus and Tibetan lamas. I have met Piero and Claudio, two young men who became Buddhists in Nepal and when they recount their experiences to me I find myself beginning to be really curious about India.

We invade the little streets like a new tribe, with our guitars, posters, outrageous clothes, smoking joints together, similar to the ritual pipe of the Native American tribes. We talk endlessly about India as if we'd discovered a new planet, about our dreams, our longing for an authentic existence, for a distant, mysterious wisdom. Many people have taken LSD and tell of psychic, inner journeys, exploring the deep mystery of the human mind, infinite in its potential. It seems that LSD can open up certain areas of the brain which otherwise remain unexplored, resulting in telepathic, divine experiences, unknown beforehand. It's like sudden enlightenment, a new knowledge of oneself. One has to be ready to risk everything, to die psychologically in order to be reborn in to a new reality, like the hero prepared to combat any peril in order to discover the truth, willing to undergo all manner of darkness in order to find the light.

Conventional members of the public think we are crazy, addicted to drugs, but in fact we prefer to be outsiders and risk ending up in jail or prison, rather than be addicted to television and advertising. Regular society rejects the psychedelic drugs, but readily accepts alcohol, because alcohol makes one oblivious to everything, unconscious, just ready to buy the advertiser's products.

Our movement is becoming an underground organization, virtually secret because society at large is unwilling to accept us, but we work on with a growing awareness of the deep changes happening and the possibility of a different world. Some of my friends have gone to live in the countryside, discovering a simpler way of life close to nature.

I think we can only change others by offering an example. People criticize us, call us freaks, drug addicts, but the psychedelic drugs are a medicine for our minds, a cure against mental rigidity and hardness, they help us to discover our soul, our heart, blocked by the lack of pure love. We begin to feel that life is a cosmic movie, directed by a divine power to which we have been blind for too long.

Sometimes I become afraid, doubts surface, I think I may go mad, but our so-called normal society seems even more insane. Most people take a powerful drug on a daily basis that creates a strong addiction: the television screen, nourishing themselves with contrived fantasies, useless panel games, sport. Some spend thousands on buying a couture dress or a car, while at the same time so many millions are dying in the Third World.

I want to take a risk, to go 'on the road', like a pilgrim, or a beggar. I am thirsty for truth and for real love, but at least at present my life is joyful, full of warmth and friendship, of human exchange, of adventure.

We move around the city wearing our beautifully coloured clothes, endeavouring to give a message to the people, a message of freedom and creativity, of fresh hope. We have plans to construct alternative villages on the planet based on universal love, practical steps, whereas in the past our political movement has just been an act of great passion.

Sometimes there are difficulties to be faced, lazy people in our groups, parasites, people who escape from the responsibility of life into morphine and other heavy drugs, but one day we shall overcome. I know that we are the pioneers for a new world. In the meantime we are learning to help each other, to share everything, money, a house, a job or a business, friends and love, much love, again and again; it's the discovery of a new solidarity, a new human co-operation.

Formentera, 4 July 1971

I am here with Giuliano and Dinni, on this tiny Spanish island where hippies from all over the world have come to find new purpose in their lives. The island is arid, sunny, homely, with wonderful little beaches and the sea turquoise-blue. The landscape is flat and many people move around on bicycles, the houses are small and white, rather like Greece and on some of the walls people have written the forbidden word: 'LSD'. The three of us spend all day by the sea only eating fruits, nourishing ourselves with the energy of the sun and in the evening eating some brown rice. We have decided to take LSD together.

29 July 1971

The experiment with acid has been a huge revelation for me, I have seen all my past lives, or at least I thought I could see them. I had the experience of having been a thousand beings and that now I can be at one with everybody and everything if I can just expand my consciousness. At the end of the experience I saw only light, a blazing, white light enveloping all of reality. I feel a cosmic consciousness breathing through the universe and through myself. Dinni has also undergone a similar experience and Giuliano had visions of certain Christian saints.

We bathe naked on the beach in absolute innocence. Having sex is not so important any more, but we are thirsty for our fantastic, spiritual visions. I sensed an unknown voice talking to me from inside my body and telling me I should leave everything behind and go to India. It frightens me and yet I am also really tempted by the call. This island resembles a laboratory where people experiment with the light of the soul on a high frequency. Suddenly I perceive the magic of a new energy within myself, guiding my life.

Milan, 25 September 1971

On my return home I hurried to Brera once again in the evening to meet everybody and share my new discoveries. Piero and Claudio are visiting the community and have shown me some photographs of their Tibetan teachers, standing close to the snow-covered Himalayan peaks. There is something about the images that is both remote and familiar at the same time. When Piero and Claudio come to visit me in 'Via Mayr' they impress me, because I recognize something very serious and concentrated in them that is not present in other people, a special depth. Piero made love with me the other day in a soft, gentle way, detached, as if it were a strange meditation. They asked me if I would like to go to India with them, soon.

Last week we organized a huge, underground rock concert at 'Ballabio', in the countryside. We gathered all our hopes and all our songs: old revolutionary and anarchist songs, the American ones and our new repertory, Claudio sang *Magic Fly*. The concert turned into a huge gathering of people and in the night fires were lit and sitting around them I saw the new tribe of earth's people: the Indians, the Tibetans, the freaks, the students, the artists, the musicians, the politicians, the journalists, all sitting together, like ancient gypsies looking for a new land. So many friends were present and their eyes were transparent, full of light and love and I sat around the many fires, to talk, or just share the presence, communion on a common path.

15 November 1971

I am working in the experimental kindergarten I organized with Giuliano's help, but I'm finding out that it's not easy for me to work with the children. We want to give them maximum freedom and fantasy, instead of repressing them with an orthodox, heavy-handed authority, but it's a difficult task. The children are very restless and I don't feel mature enough for this job.

I lead a crazy life not regulated by time, never eating or sleeping regularly, always meeting up with friends until late in the night. Gianni now lives with me and has transformed my room into an oriental shop, filling it up with clothes he is buying from Turkey and Afghanistan. Quite often there are four or five other people sharing the carpet on the floor with me to sleep on.

We continue to experiment with LSD and Piero has taught me some Tibetan and Indian prayers, which I have begun to repeat, and I even teach them to the children in the kindergarten. I still feel uneasy about the idea of God, but I have started to have many visions, seeing beautiful mandalas with perfect colours, hearing incredible music and mysterious voices talking to me. Sometimes I am afraid of going crazy, or becoming addicted to drugs, but at other times I feel I have been initiated into a hidden reality only revealed to a few people, to those who have the courage to risk everything, even their own life. What is certain is that we are looking for knowledge and for the mystery of life and death. Our projects take us so far away from the usual pathways of this world.

I have started to think seriously about going to India, to find the masters of the ancient wisdom, to seek an answer to all the many questions that are arising in me. I'm finding it extremely difficult to travel alone on this psychic path and at times even dangerous. Recently I read a Buddhist book about the life of Milarepa, where this Tibetan yogi explains that it's impossible to reach enlightenment without the help of a guru, without his knowledge.

My life here is exciting in many ways, but I've begun to feel very tired and restless. Something is missing; real love is such a difficult thing to realize. I feel that we are still too deeply involved on the physical level in our search and our minds are in no way clear enough to visualize the truth.

I would like to stop running around, to be able to be quiet for a while, even live alone so as to look deep within myself. We are continually meeting up with each other, over and over again making love, touching each other and talking endlessly, but I feel I want to stop this pattern.

During the day I work in the kindergarten, at night I hardly sleep, I experience so many sad moments in Milan and often I feel exceptionally tired. I am sure that an inner journey has begun, an adventure that is without boundaries, capable of taking me anywhere that is required. When I sit with people, often smoking together in a circle, I exist as if in a dream, and the oriental music, sweet, languid, resounding within me, invites my soul to another dimension. We are being called to be sure, maybe by God! Even though the thought of that is still difficult for me to accept, I'm beginning to believe that it's only Him we are searching for, only Him we want to see.

Trip to India

Milan, 5 March 1972

Today I am leaving for India and I'm really frightened. I made the decision all of a sudden when I discovered that Piero and Claudio were going. Gianni wants to come as well so that he can start up some sort of business buying and selling clothes.

A few nights ago we were sitting in the big community room in the commune with the dome of yellow brocade in the centre: Angelo, Tiziani, Serena, Gianni, Zizi and Marco, a group of friends lying on the carpet with a Joan Baez record playing. Angelo started to make sexual advances towards me again and suddenly I felt as if it was an old theatrical performance, too repetitive, leading nowhere, like one of the narrow, dark streets in Brera at night and it annoyed me.

I felt tired, bored, exhausted as well as feeling unable to find truth or experience real love any more; trying to rediscover it through sex, again and again, is exhausting and a pathetic illusion. Also I'd become tired of smoking dope interminably, even my thoughts seemed smoky and I had no peace of mind. What I would have preferred was to have a place of my own, to be able to take a break and stay somewhere where I could be alone for a while, look within myself. I'd also realized that the work I did with the children in the kindergarten couldn't continue the way it was, I was too restless, confused, not mature enough for such responsibility. Then the other day Piero and Claudio showed me the pictures again of Nepal and the Tibetan masters. I imagined a mysterious and magical place, ancient; it felt like a *déja vu* experience looking at those photographs. Piero has a special light in his eyes and I wondered if I should follow him.

So, yesterday evening I left my house to sleep with Gianni in his attic flat, in order to decide definitely what to do. As always we slept close together but like brother and sister, like children, and the next morning I went to the travel agents to buy a ticket to India; I secured the last vacant seat on the plane. Tonight we are travelling to London by train and then we will fly to India, to Bombay. I am afraid and who knows if it will work out! People think I've gone mad, because I am leaving behind my job in the kindergarten where I've worked for six months, my loving relationship with Angelo, my house and my friends. I have very little money, no return ticket, no luggage, but even so it still feels right that I should be leaving in this way, taking nothing with me. All I carry is a bag and one dress, the one Gianni brought me from Afghanistan.

Gian Paolo has given me a book entitled, *Barefoot in India* and whatever the cost to myself I have no doubt that I should just throw myself fully into this adventure. I know I must be extremely courageous to be 'on the road' completely, especially because at times I feel absolutely terrified. Even so I intuitively feel that on the 'other side of the river' I will discover an answer that will make sense of the mystery of my life; that somewhere there is another reality waiting for me. What's the point of living otherwise? Life here in Milan lacks truth and no longer has any meaning for me any more.

The whole situation feels extraordinarily magical as if a wise voice is calling me. In a way it seems that my journey had already begun a few months ago with my first experience of LSD in Formentera. Or maybe it occurred in a more subtle sense with Guiliano in Morocco, sitting on the beach, stringing beads together and watching the gulls flying over the sea. Their flight reminded me about freedom, a freedom that I had forgotten or perhaps never known and now, about to travel to India, I begin to experience those same spontaneous sensations of infinite freedom. I know that I will find the courage to jump into the void and the mystery, to search for and discover some sort of solution, maybe find a teacher.

Last summer in Formentera during my experiences with acid I had visions of many of my past lives as well as a realization of a unified universal consciousness. I envisaged an enormous light comprising of seven perfect colours and saw my soul exiting my body and immersing itself in space. From there I observed the immense flow of life, the lives I have lived, finally realizing that to remain in that state was the all and everything. A voice spoke to me, unequivocally telling me to leave everything behind and depart for India immediately, for a new adventure in consciousness.

The outer journey began by my being in Milan for these last few months; the inner journey involves seeking an answer, perhaps finding a Master.

Mother India

Bombay, 7 March 1972

Our arrival in Bombay was almost too much for me to take and I wanted to run away. Near the airport there are squalid huts, the weather is incredibly hot, the streets overflowing with people. The hotel is exceedingly dirty and full of hippies from Goa, crazy-looking, fascinating people. Outside the streets are teeming with beggars, lepers and children who tease me all the time, calling me a hippie, or shouting 'Hare Ram, Hare Krishna' in a mocking tone. I feel terribly uneasy, with my long dress, my wild hair; it's a completely different world here, a huge, incredible bazaar and I'm scared. Standing in front of the hotel is a strange hippie, a sort of holy man, with long blonde hair and a beard, dressed in dirty, white clothes and I'm afraid of him as well. I found myself thinking that he could take possession of my mind, and I automatically began to repeat a mantra which Piero had taught me, a prayer to the many Indian gods: 'Hari sharanam, Shiva sharanam, Ram sharanam, Prabhu Krishna sharanam...' - my refuge is in Shiva, in Ram, in Lord Krishna...

It's so terribly hot and I have to constantly fight off a feeling of drowsiness. Everybody is smoking dope in our room and it is hard to resist. We drink copious amounts of boiling hot, milky tea and stuff ourselves with sugary sweetmeats that are very greasy, and I feel nauseous. The restaurants are filthy and I don't like the food at all, everything fried and spicy. I try to console myself a little with some fruit juices, but the beggars standing around me with their hands held out take away all my pleasure. I am afraid to walk down the streets alone and Piero and Claudio laugh and make fun of me; Gianni has already lost himself by taking opium and morphine.

Today I saw a snake charmer; and what impressed me the most were the beggar's eyes, ironic, almost happy, smiling at it all. People here seem to live as if in a dream, in a different kind of reality, with the knowledge that everything is relative, some sort of game. In my mind I compare their faces with those sad and pale faces of the wealthy people I used to see in the mornings on the tram in my home city of Milan, so tense and cold.

11 March 1972

Today I met a group of fascinating people from California, the young men dressed in white clothes and having long hair: they appear to be at home in

India, sure of themselves. I also came across Lillo, a young Italian woman who resembles a little magical elf and she encourages me to throw away all of my existing clothes and wear white instead. Then I discovered the 'Rainbow Gypsies', people from every corner of the world, travelling continuously, with little money, almost no luggage and suspect documents. They travel around dancing and singing in the streets; they are very beautiful and rely on the hospitality of others in order to live. There is something magical about the way they live and I find myself enchanted by them.

One of them, Rosa, a striking young Italian woman, walks around with a monkey on her shoulder sucking at her breast, but I am especially attracted to Daniel and Sitaram, two Americans, who even though they are young appear so experienced and wise. I would like to become like them, courageous, fearless, sure of myself and to have the consciousness that they have. I've decided to colour my hair with red henna and have my hand tattooed, I feel it's my first act of courage.

12 March 1972

This morning while sitting in my room there was a knock at the door and in came Carlo. These days he is called Shanti and I hardly recognized him, I hadn't seen him for six years. He still has his childish smile, but that is now mixed with the expression of an elderly, wise man. Also he wears Indian clothes nowadays and his unexpected arrival has made a deep impression on me.

Shanti was one of the first people I knew who left Milan in order to discover the East. He travelled overland through Afghanistan and Pakistan to India six years ago when he was sixteen, in the same way that many other people did at that time. I really admired their courage and faith, travelling 'on the road', practically without any money, risking everything for their search. People tell me that Shanti has been in the company of many Indian gurus during the past few years and that he has now become a guru himself. He speaks in a strange way, slowly, very quietly. I want to stay close to him, because I feel he will be able to show me something.

In 1966, in an old part of the city of Milan, a group of us had our first experience of community in a small, impoverished attic that was freezing cold. That's where we smoked our first joints together and dreamt for the first time about the mystery of the East. Shanti and a few of his friends were among the first long-haired hippies around at that time. People derided and insulted them in the street, calling out: 'Hey layabout, go and get a job!'

I first met him together with Gianni at a restaurant in Brera. I offered them a meal and after that met them frequently. We got involved in all sorts of crazy activities on the streets of Milan, 'happenings' and cultural encounters for which we were eventually arrested a few times. Gianni actually got thrown out of San Vittore after having been attending there for a year and a half, because he was caught in possession of a small amount of hashish and he eventually ended up in jail. Then Shanti suddenly left for India hitch-hiking overland and so I parted company with them. During the time that followed I concentrated on my studies in philosophy at the University and became involved in the student movement of 1968.

For a few years I forgot about the Indian dream and even my old friends, but now Shanti has found me and here we are together again, I can hardly believe it. Shanti starts to tease me, because I am with Piero and Claudio, two people interested in Buddhism. He tells me that Hinduism is a much more advanced yoga, but at the moment I don't really understand the difference. I just feel I should stay close to Shanti, partly because Piero and Claudio are not so willing to take care of me. They are busy with preparations for their trip and I feel lost and alone, particularly because I can't really speak English yet. In the end though I've decided to stay with Piero and Claudio for the time being and attend a Buddhist meditation course in Bombay. It's a Vipassana course, led by a famous teacher, Goenka and even Gianni has decided to give up his morphine and participate.

15 March 1972
Today the course started: never before in my life have I embarked on such an experience and I am really curious about the whole thing. Here everything is clean, orderly, well organized. Half of the people are Westerners, the other half Indians, but the Indian people here are very respectable, mainly dressed in spotless, white clothes and they pay great attention to discipline. I realize that every gesture that they make in their lives, from eating to bathing, is some form of ritual.

I'm also a little frightened and feel rather emotional, because it's the first time I will meet a master, a guru.

17 March 1972
I have been here for three days and it's not been easy for me, it's incredibly hot and the routine hard going.

We wake up at 5 o'clock in the morning, take a shower and try to meditate in silence. We are supposed to concentrate solely on the breath, but for me it's almost impossible to sit on the floor cross-legged and to stop thinking, yet I am still determined to try. Once a day we meet all together in a large hall, seated in front of the teacher, Goenka.

He is a man about fifty years old, with a strong-looking body and the round belly of a Buddha. He emanates an exceptionally quiet energy, peaceful, good, solid and we sing a beautiful song with him. At the end of the singing he repeats this sentence to us in English a few times: 'Love, infinite love for all beings.' It's his teaching every day. He also lets everyone sit in front of him individually for a few minutes in silence, engaging each person in a brief, direct, telepathic encounter. When it is my turn, I become scared. I sit in front of him and am aware of my restless mind, as well as my negative and even aggressive thoughts towards him and am afraid he can see it all. I feel as if I am sitting in front of a mirror and I realize that there are many things that require to be purified within me.

24 March 1972

It's the last day of the meditation course and I am pleased to have completed it. After returning to the hotel I meet up with Shanti again and ask if I could stay with him, because Piero and Claudio want to proceed to Nepal. I have decided I want to leave the city but feel there are many things I have yet to learn about India. I say to Shanti that I would like to meet a guru and he invites me to accompany him to Almora where he has rented a house with his friends, the 'Rainbow Gypsies'. He tells me that a lot of the masters and saints of India live in the mountains and I feel happy about going with him.

25 March 1972

We have been wandering around the bazaar in Bombay, teeming with humanity, people of all colours and types. There is a great pulsing vitality, an expression of love and warmth. The women are so beautiful and I never become tired of looking at them. They are the perfect expression of complete femininity, both harmonious and graceful, their manner chaste and virtuous, the colourful saris they wear absolutely wonderful. India is beginning to fascinate me and I have a strong desire to continue with my adventure.

Today I leave with Gianni and Shanti to go to Rajasthan. First stop on our journey to Almora, which is our final destination, is to find a guru that Shanti knows called Hari Puri who lives near Jaipur in Rajasthan.

New Delhi, 27 March 1972

We arrived in Delhi by plane. It's not as hot as Bombay and seems a little more civilized. We are staying in a very comfortable guesthouse and down in the street we stuffed ourselves with tropical fruits served with ice. I've been told that it is dangerous to consume food prepared in this way but I feel protected by some power and don't want to be fussy. I'm determined to throw myself wholeheartedly into this situation without any holding back in order to try and get to the bottom of it all.

Jaipur, 29 March 1972

Here we are in Jaipur in the state of Rajasthan. We journeyed here by train, travelling slowly, stopping continually, the train overfull, dusty and dirty, the benches and couchettes hard and uncomfortable, made of wood. Fortunately I had some training in enduring this sort of discomfort during my travels in Morocco.

We take a rickshaw to the jungle outside the city to find Shanti's teacher. It's a wild place, full of sadhus who look as wild as their surroundings. They have extremely long hair in dreadlocks that they never comb, their bodies resemble the big cats of the jungle and they smoke hashish all the time. I don't understand a word that they are saying but it makes no difference, they continue to talk to me quite unconcerned, telling us stories about how they kill tigers with their bare hands, and so on. I go to lie down to rest with Gianni and one of them lifts my skirt to see if I have any knickers on. They also insist that I smoke and I am taken aback by their manner, shocked by their behaviour.

Later on they introduce me to the master, who is ill, extremely thin, small in stature and clean-shaven, lying on a bed. He has languid eyes and from him there emanates an incredible love. I'm deeply moved and would like to give him a present. The only thing that I have which is precious to me is a silver bracelet and so I give it to him. Although it is not possible to communicate with him directly, we exchange looks and waves of love pass between us. Perhaps he will die soon because they say he cannot be cured.

2 April 1972

Today we've been to the bazaar to buy material. It is here in the shops that everything comes to a virtual standstill, where you sit, drink tea, chat and tell your life story. Eventually the shopkeepers pull out all the merchandise they have for sale, spread it out and in the end you buy something. The women are never seen in the shops, only the men who sit cross-legged or stretch out on large white beds. It seems as if time stands still for them, as if they are not really waiting for clients but simply living, almost in a state of meditation.

We went to eat in a luxury restaurant in the grand style of the maharajas, waited on as if we were important people. It's incredible to observe the great humility of the Indian servants, who completely identify with the sense of service. I am embarrassed, I feel like an old colonialist, one who is privileged. I think I would rather stay with the poor Indians in their own homes.

Meeting the Great Master, Babaji

Almora, 3 April 1972

This morning we reached Almora, after another interminably long journey. It's a mountain town, at an altitude of about 1800 metres, but the weather is not cold as it would be in the European mountains. The bazaar is filthy, the hotel squalid and it's really difficult for me to drink or eat anything in the small, dirty restaurants that are here. I did not expect to see such poverty, the poorly constructed wooden buildings rotting. Also the hotel is full of fleas, biting us all night; it is terrible.

The mornings are chilly and the water in the shower is freezing. It has all been a very great surprise to me because they had told me it was an idyllic place.

5 April 1972

We are now living in a house in the forest, rented by Shanti and his friends, the 'Rainbow Gypsies'. It is a much more pleasant place to be and the landscape around here is extremely beautiful. Nevertheless it's still uncomfortable and inconvenient; there is no running water, no electricity and no toilets. I have taken on the duty of cooking and washing up the pots and plates, because I feel it is good for me, but I find it extremely tiring doing everything squatting down on the earth the way the Indian people do. They have such agile and supple bodies and are used to working all their lives in this way. Although I admire them, trying to work like this makes me feel awkward and clumsy, but at this moment in time I feel I have to learn to do something for others and be of service.

The 'Rainbow Gypsies' are such lovely people and the two young American men from California who I met in Bombay are here as well with their girlfriends, together with a collection of other people from different parts of the world. Every morning Rosa, the young Italian woman, teaches us some yoga postures to help us become more supple: she moves like a dancer.

Most of the time our diet consists of rice and vegetables and we all eat together sitting on the floor. Shanti helps me a great deal, translating for me and patiently explaining all about the Indian tradition. He takes me around with him and I feel that he is a teacher for me. Daniel often sings some very moving songs accompanying himself on his guitar and I especially love the words of one song: 'We are One, for a universe of love.'

I am slowly getting used to this new rhythm of life and to the simple practical things that need to be done: cooking, washing clothes, cleaning, or just sitting to admire the majestic valley, the green hills and the snow-capped peaks of the Himalayas in the distance. At night the weather turns cold and we all sleep together, close to each other on the floor of one room.

Shanti invites me to accompany him when he visits some of the Indian families he knows in Almora. He introduces me to them with pride, explaining that I am a doctor of philosophy and that my mother is a member of the Italian parliament; it seems that these things are very important in India.

When I see the village women walking along the streets in their long, green skirts, with bundles of grass on their heads, I feel strangely at home, as if I have already seen all this somewhere before.

10 April 1972

Shanti explains to me something of the complicated religious Indian pantheon, but adds that the science of yoga is something different again, it's the knowledge of oneself, an inner discovery. Today I accompanied him on a visit to Tara Devi, an elderly American lady, who has lived in Almora for the last twenty years.

She has invited us to go downtown with her to meet an Indian saint, Babaji, who is supposed to be the present incarnation of another famous yogi from the past, Hairakhan Baba. She tells us that Babaji has overcome death and rejuvenated His body, appearing to be about twenty when in reality He is one hundred and thirty years old. What is more, He exists without eating anything or sleeping: can this be true? I begin to be curious about Him. She says that Babaji had asked her to invite all of the Western people she knows in Almora to come and meet Him, because He is looking for someone amongst them who is His disciple from a previous life. Shanti makes a joke and suggests that maybe I am that person.

The other day, looking at the palms of my hands, he told me that I have the lines of a yogini, the same lines that he has, three united together, which signifies the union of heart and mind. He also said that he feels I am a person who may spend a long time in India, but who can tell if all this is true; sometimes I am very sceptical.

15 April 1972

Today we have been to Almora, to meet Babaji. There were some other Westerners present together with certain important spiritual teachers who live around here: Shunia Baba and Guru Lama, a Tibetan. I must confess that my first thought on seeing Him, with His long, black hair down onto His shoulders, made Him look like a hippie, someone very familiar, one of our tribe, a prophet, an angel of the new world sent here for us.

As soon as I entered the exceedingly crowded room I immediately noticed Him, seated on a raised dais, dressed in white, immobile like a statue. I was enchanted as I watched Him. He is extremely beautiful, radiant like an ancient Christ-like figure, very serious, severe, with sharp, dark, powerful, penetrating eyes. I started to look into His eyes and felt myself becoming hypnotized to such an extent that I began to be afraid of His power. Then suddenly I observed Him lowering His eyes, with such humility and an incredible tenderness. For two, maybe three hours I looked at Him continually, as if magnetized, just like the rest of the people in the room.

Many of those present continued singing religious songs the whole time without any interruption, accompanied by the Indian harmonium and hand cymbals. At one point people began to stand in a queue in order to pranam, to bow down at His feet. Every time a person bowed to Him, Babaji raised His hand in blessing, slightly smiling with compassion. I didn't feel that I wanted to go and pranam to Him, I just sat there staring at His beautiful, perfect form, absolutely still, as if He is not even breathing, like a statue. He doesn't speak, doesn't move, He just looks into everybody's eyes. I have the uneasy feeling that He can read my thoughts, see what I'm thinking, see into my mind, as if He is capable of telepathic communication with me. Silently I spoke to Him inside my heart: 'Please give me the truth.'

Later on, Babaji stood up to leave in order to go to His room. He moves in a fascinating way, like a panther, swift, powerful, precise, with long, slender, brown legs and bare-footed. They called Shanti and myself into the room where He was and with a little reluctance I hesitantly pranamed to Him for the first time. Babaji asked which country I came from and gave me a radiant smile; I felt as if I had received a severe electrical shock, as if struck by a wave of luminous light, and a voice inside me told me that I would see Him again.

I went back to the house where we were staying, deeply affected by this encounter. Even Shanti, who has already met many gurus, also noticed the especial beauty and purity of this Being.

16 April 1972

Last night I had a dream. I was in a dark, deep forest and suddenly Babaji appeared, emerging out of an intense light, surrounded by some disciples. He walked with the help of a stick and He told me: 'I am your guru.'

'What will You teach me?' I asked Him and He replied: 'To wash dishes well.'

I woke up deeply impressed because His message is very clear to me: the importance of learning to accomplish simple, humble tasks, useful to other people. In the past, in the life of our community in Milan, we were continually faced with this problem, nobody wanted to do the washing-up or carry out the simple jobs. People always left dirty plates and other things lying around, out of selfishness, laziness or egotism. I know that it is necessary for me to work through these problems. When I told Shanti about my dream he proposed that I go and visit Babaji where He lives, at His ashram in Hairakhan, and to speak to Tara Devi about it.

Babaji 1972

23 April 1972

We saw Tara Devi, the American woman, and asked her if we could join her on her trip to Hairakhan. She looked me up and down and told me I needed to dress a little better and not to wear these hippie clothes; she added that she doesn't even know if women are welcomed by Babaji in His ashram, since He is a brahmachari, a celibate. Shanti also told me I must be especially careful with my female energy, because the Indian people can easily become hostile and would even kill a woman trying to seduce a brahmachari Baba. I am so surprised by this kind of talk, because to be quite honest sex is the last thing to come into my mind in the presence of somebody like Babaji.

Hairakhan, 26 April 1972

We reached Hairakhan yesterday after an exceedingly long walk and I am exhausted. There were five of us who travelled from Almora, Shanti and myself, a Danish man, an American, Tara Devi and also her Indian cook. We reached a certain point on the road and then began walking through the jungle. The journey seemed to go on for ever. We walked for six hours, barefoot on the hot stones, continuously criss-crossing the Gautam Ganga river, an interminable distance, carrying our luggage on our heads. On more than one occasion I thought that I'd not be able to make it, and because I'm afraid of feeling the cold I had also insisted on carrying a quilt on my head as well.

The jungle here is really charming, the water in the river so pure and transparent one can drink it. Then all of a sudden we caught a glimpse of a white temple on the top of a hill, Hairakhan, a small village, looking as if it belonged in a fairy tale. When we came closer to the temple, we saw Babaji dressed in white coming down the steep steps to welcome us. With great embarrassment I found myself to be the first in line. Babaji took me up the steps with Him and then around the temple in a circle, ringing all the bells. I had the impression I was enacting an ancient, forgotten ritual. Using Shanti as interpreter He asked me if I was a hippie and I answered, 'Yes,' with a certain pride. Then He wanted to know if I smoked dope and when I nodded He told me that here in Hairakhan it was strictly prohibited.

A few minutes later we were approached by an old sadhu called Prem Baba, who took me with him to smoke some hashish and he gave me something strange to eat as well. I sat on the outside wall feeling quite stoned, looking out onto the valley. It is a magnificent place, the landscape archaic and mysterious, the hills covered in terraces, fertile, green with crops and in the background the mountains are covered with pine trees. The movement of the river running through the valley sounds like an exquisite melody and a huge bodhi tree arching its branches down towards the sound completes the scene.

Everybody lives in the open under the trees, the only buildings are the temple and one small hut where Babaji lives, which is open on all sides and has a ceremonial fire-pit at its centre.

While I remained sitting on the perimeter wall, absorbed in my contemplation, Babaji came near me and taking a stone He drew the shape of a small temple on the ground, telling me just one word: 'Dio', God. I felt very embarrassed, since I am still quite an atheist and the idea of God remains difficult for me to accept. Babaji motioned for me to sit with Him in His hut, His dhuni, and said to me in English: 'God is love.' The concept of love is maybe easier for me to accept. His eyes were deep and shining, luminous and He gave me an orange and some nuts to eat. In the evening the people gave us chapatis and a large quantity of halva, a delicious sweetmeat, to eat for our meal.

The temple in Hairakhan

27 April 1972

Yesterday afternoon some of the Indian people wanted to serve us tea, but Babaji shouted that tea is poison and is not permitted in the temple.

I find myself looking at Him all the time, but there remain doubts in my mind and I analyse all His movements, largely because He seldom speaks. He has a magnetic energy, such perfect beauty and Shanti teases me, suggesting that I am merely attracted by His physical presence, but it's not that at all: I feel overcome by a powerful psychic wave, a vibrating light. Sometimes I am afraid of being hypnotized, at other times I receive a deep, exquisite energy within my heart that is overwhelming.

Today, while we were sitting in the dhuni around the sacred fire, some of the village women arrived to visit Babaji. They are very colourful, wearing long, green skirts like myself and when they saw me they laughed. Babaji told them that my name is Lalli, which means 'little girl'. He asked me how old I was, I said twenty-six and He told me that I looked about fifteen.

In the evening, what I witnessed during the ceremony in the temple made a lasting impression on me. Babaji sat motionless, dressed in white, like an exquisite statue, while an Indian man began to sing and lifted a lighted lamp towards His face, which assumed a mysterious radiance. While praying in this way by waving the lamp the man started to cry and I could tell that he felt the presence of a Divine Being. Shanti has also been greatly moved by what he has seen, even if he tells me that I have to be careful not to be led astray by all these rituals.

Prem Baba, the old sadhu, invited us to sit with him around another fire, so that we could all sing together the mantra dedicated to Shiva, 'Om Namah Shivaya', and Shanti laughed at me, commenting that I have so easily become caught in the enchantment of the place. Some of the women were cooking chapatis, Indian bread, on a small improvised fire in the open and everything felt very simple and pure. Tonight we sleep within the temple area, looking up at the dark, tropical sky.

28 April 1972

This morning they woke us up at four o'clock, virtually still night-time. The air was chilly and I went down to bathe in the river. As I descended the steps I met Babaji, already coming back up. I jumped into the river, immersing myself in the cold water, under the bright stars. Later on I sat in a corner of the temple, thinking that I would like to continue being part of this magical story and follow Babaji, but that I would never dare to ask Him; just a few minutes later Babaji called me over to Him and asked me if I wanted to come with Him on a trip to Vrindavan, an extremely ancient city sacred to Lord Krishna. I am more than happy to go, even if I do feel scared about being all on my own and travelling alone, leaving behind Shanti and my friends. First though I must return to Almora to collect my money and my passport. Shanti is a little perplexed by my enthusiasm for Babaji, but I am really fascinated by Him and start thinking that maybe He is my guru.

Vrindavan

Haldwani, 4 May 1972

I am waiting for the train that will take me to Vrindavan. It's the first time I am travelling alone in India, but I have noticed that in the main Indian people are kind and willing to help those of us travelling in their country.

On leaving Almora this morning I observed myself walking barefoot down the road lined with pine trees, dressed in white, carrying a bundle of clothes on my head, all that I have; I possess very little money and no return ticket. For the very first time I really feel alone, 'on the road' in India, going to a guru. It feels like a dream.

Vrindavan, 6 May 1972

I am in Vrindavan and the city is charming, a remarkable place, reminiscent of an image from the pages of a fable. I arrived yesterday by train, which stopped continually on the journey here. Then I travelled by rickshaw through the small streets of the city, nothing less than a vision of paradise to me, remote but somehow known already from some past existence. The houses are all old-fashioned and artistically decorated, with tiny, narrow streets and small, colourful shops selling fruits, sweets and clothes. The people are joyful here, always greeting me with big smiles. Everywhere there are exceedingly ancient temples, thousands of years old, resounding with songs and Sanskrit prayers. Many sadhus, saints and women dressed in white walk around the city in a continual state of prayer, everything existing in an atmosphere that seems timeless.

When I entered Babaji's temple, I caught sight of Him immediately, seated on His dais, dressed in white, always so beautiful, unreal, etheric, radiant. He called an Indian man over and told me to accompany him to the bazaar to drink a large glass of milk taken from a huge terracotta vessel. I am amazed to be in such a wonderful place and I don't feel afraid any more, I feel secure, embraced by Babaji's love and the warmth of the people around me.

In the evening, when I sit in the temple, the Indian women and the children come up close to me and appraise me with great curiosity. They look at me, touch me, they caress me, admire me: to them I am the woman with a white skin and they make me feel very beautiful. Babaji called me over and told me that my name is Kali, the warrioress, the Black Goddess, but then immediately afterwards He changed His mind and said with tenderness: 'No, your name is Gaura Devi,' which means, they told me later, the White Goddess.

I am particularly moved by the music and the songs, by Babaji's splendour and the devotion of the Indian people. They stand in a long queue holding garlands of flowers in their hands as an offering, then place them around His neck before they pranam to Him and receive a gesture from Him, a smile, a word or some prasad, blessed food.

I also stand in line and I feel extremely emotional just by coming in close proximity to Him. An energy of great intensity emanates from Him and I experience an incredible sensation, sensing as well that He can read all my thoughts. His eyes are magnetic, shining, full of love, strength and knowledge. I never become tired of looking at Him and notice that everybody else does the same. For two or three hours Babaji continues to sit virtually motionless. He doesn't speak, doesn't do anything, He just makes Himself visible for us to contemplate and adore; He gives darshan, which Indian people explain to me as being a vision of the Divine in a human form.

The impact of this experience touches everybody in an intimate way; I can see it in people's eyes and from the energy in the temple. People sing continuously, sometimes Babaji's mantra, 'Om Namah Shivaya', sometimes other devotional songs, until late in the evening.

At night we sleep on the roof of a small building constructed next to the temple, lying on a straw mat, the place surrounded by monkeys. It is still dark when we are woken up at four o'clock in the morning as devotional chants begin resounding from all of the temples in the city, more than seven hundred of them. After a shower I meditate in a corner for a short while, then we go to the temple for the aarati, morning prayers. We wait with trepidation for Babaji's arrival, for Him to emerge from His room and be seated on the modest dais prepared for Him. The temple is extremely clean, full of flowers and smelling of sweet incense.

We don't have breakfast or dinner, only a large lunch, as well as pieces of halva and fruit that are distributed during the day. Some people continue singing until late in the morning, other people work, either cleaning, washing, cooking or carrying drinking water from the well that is situated in the square opposite the temple. Babaji often speaks with individual people, just a few words here and there, very quietly, softly. After lunch everybody has a short afternoon nap and at about five o'clock we bathe and meet again in the temple, in order to clean and prepare everything for the evening worship.

In the afternoon many people choose to go to the river to bathe, in the Jamuna, a river sacred to Lord Krishna. In the evening the aarati ceremony is performed again and afterwards people sing until late in the night, beautiful, sweet songs. I don't understand the meaning of the words, but I surrender to the melody, to the feeling of a divine dimension.

It's tremendously difficult for me to adjust to the daily routine and to the strict discipline, to the Indian capacity for hard work, particularly because the weather is extremely hot and it makes me feel tired. The month of May is torrid in India, an especially oppressive time of the year and I often escape to the bazaar to find something cool to drink, even if I know that Babaji doesn't approve of it.

Babaji - '...dressed in white, always so beautiful, unreal, etheric, radiant.'

15 May 1972

I am beginning to find it difficult to withstand the way of life here. The daily routine is tiring, monotonous and some of the young Indian men are very brusque and treat me badly, they don't allow me to work with them and they treat me as if I am a stranger. Babaji always fascinates me, but even He keeps me at a distance, is unapproachable. It is almost impossible to communicate with anybody, since I don't know Hindi and can speak only a few words of English.

In this intense heat I always feel thirsty but the water from the well is tepid and a little salty; it does not quench my thirst. When I bathe in the river, which is cloudy and muddy, it leaves me with a strange sensation and I don't really feel clean after washing. In the morning I have to wait in a queue for an interminable length of time in order to be able to take a shower in the guest-house. In the evening in the temple, everybody is sweating, the temperature rises to more than 40 degrees centigrade, it's sweltering but Babaji seems totally indifferent, not sweating Himself.

In Vrindavan there are hundreds of ageing widows all dressed in white saris, who live all together in various temples. They pray continuously, accompanied by the sound of small cymbals and other instruments. Some of the old women are extremely poor, their saris white-grey, and they ask for alms. It reminds me of a scene from Dante's Purgatory. People explain to me that in India a widow cannot marry a second time; she has to renounce the world, she loses her home, her possessions and spends the rest of her life in prayer. It seems extremely cruel to me and ironically I remember the women's liberation movement in the West. I start to feel restless and a strong sense of nostalgia arises in me to see my Western friends again in Delhi; I ask Babaji if I can go away for a while and He allows me to leave.

New Encounters

Delhi, 18 May 1972

I have started to travel around on my own without any fear or uneasiness. The other day, while waiting for a train in the railway station, I spread a piece of cotton on the platform like the Indians do and I sat down patiently to wait, using the time, as they do, to contemplate life and myself.

Railway stations are meeting places in India, joyful and familiar, and people talk to each other all the time. The Indian people regard me as a curiosity, they ask me where I come from, why I have come to India, what I am looking for. They are surprised that I have left the West, which in their minds is a paradise of material comforts, in order to come here and share their poverty. Some of them ask me if I am looking for mental peace, invite me into their homes, offer me food and shelter, all with a great sense of hospitality and humanity. In India to be hospitable is regarded as a sacred undertaking and people offer it with much warmth, their eyes gentle and full of love.

21 May 1972

I have been in Delhi for a few days and I feel comforted by the city. In old Delhi, in the Crown Hotel, I meet up with my friends again, Piero, Claudio, Shanti and some other people recently arrived from Italy. The hotel is on three floors, old and dirty, but rather grand in its way and from the terrace there's a commanding view of the railway terminus in the old part of the city. It's also the crossing place for numerous roads, the point of departure for numerous destinations, the location of many Hindu temples alongside Muslim mosques. It seems like the meeting place of different civilizations, India, Muslim countries, the West, China, and Tibet. Down on the streets there's a continual movement of people, rickshaws, horses, carriages, cows and cars, there seems no end to it all. Cows are regarded as holy and are shown great respect, so if they decide to cross the road the traffic comes to a standstill.

Many Westerners are camping out on the big terrace as well as occupying the small, hot, humid rooms where they keep the fans on all the time. As in Bombay, people smoke a lot and consume large quantities of fruit juices, tea and sweetmeats, taking numerous showers to fend off the heat. It's not a beautiful or a comfortable place, but it has a certain magical charm despite the dirt and chaos, not least because there are people here like me, searching for truth, ready to risk everything, to suffer, even to go so far as to lose themselves completely for the sake of this spiritual adventure.

People come and go all the time, exchanging news, addresses, tricks for acquiring visas and how to survive in the jungle of the Indian city. Many of them have found Indian or Tibetan teachers and I also talk to them about Babaji and His beauty. I show them photographs of Him and as usual Shanti teases me saying I am only attracted to Him because He is young and beautiful, but it's not like that at all. Later on Shanti proposes that I visit one of his teachers with him, a Dr. Koshik, who is an ordinary man, married with children, but who is very wise and enlightened. He is a disciple of Krishnamurti, who doesn't favour the cult of the guru, or their rituals and mantras; I decide to go.

23 May 1972

Shanti continues to question me and asks what Babaji is teaching me. I have some difficulty in explaining it to him: about singing the mantra I say, and to wake up early in the morning to pray. Suddenly I recall what happened one day in Vrindavan. It was late in the morning, the temple had become empty and I realized that only Babaji and myself remained there, alone together. Immediately I panicked and felt extremely nervous. Then Babaji suddenly called me to sit with Him and we sat in silence. I was aware of my mind continuously active, frenetic, unable to make it stop, when Babaji told me to repeat Om Namah Shivaya. I tried, but even to repeat the mantra seemed impossible, artificial. Then all of a sudden my mind stopped for a few seconds and I experienced a strange calmness; Babaji gave me a broad smile and stood up. In that moment I sensed a silence inside me and realized the completeness of what Babaji had been teaching me. When I recounted what had happened to Shanti, I could see that he was impressed; he told me that, in effect, this experience of silence is what every master tries to impart.

It's incredibly hot and we spend almost all day in the hotel, only going out in the evenings. Living here is incredibly cheap and so we feel wealthy, going out to dine in different restaurants, travelling by taxi, buying clothes. But I am learning to understand many things, including for instance to accept the idea of poverty, which has a dignity over here. It's respected and even appreciated, because it's close to simplicity. In the Western world life is based on competition and arrogance, on the ego, and the poor have no place in society, neither do those who are old or infirm. In India there is room for everybody, including us crazy freaks. India has always had a capacity to accept different religions and traditions with a great deal of tolerance. The caste system is still present, it's true, but it also exists in the West, in a hidden way: the rich and the poor have an entirely different place and role in society. India is open to everybody, like a great mother and it is especially open to the spiritual pilgrim. It's like an ocean where many rivers merge from different civilizations. Here one feels so free that even poverty can be beautiful, colourful, joyful, and any strange behaviour is accepted.

Sonepat, 24 May 1972
I am at Sonepat with Shanti and a large group of his friends, in order to meet his teacher, Dr. Koshik. The doctor is a sweet man, full of love, with a blissful smile like the Buddha, wise and somewhat ironic. We are welcomed by his family with great simplicity and overwhelming hospitality. Like everywhere else in India I've always found that no matter how many guests there may be, they are treated with tremendous hospitality and offered somewhere to sit and an abundance of food.

For most of the time we sit with the doctor in a kind of meditation, talking from time to time, but very quietly and slowly. He expresses a keen interest in me, about my purpose for being in India so far from my home and has introduced me to his neighbours. When I sit with him, I feel immense peace and show him photographs of Babaji and tell him about the temple and my experiences there. I know from Shanti that he is a disciple of Krishnamurti and that he doesn't believe in the use of rituals, mantras and so on, only in self knowledge and self enquiry, but I feel a great respect from him. He talks about the importance of experiencing the spiritual in life and tells us that he attained a certain degree of awareness by simply sitting under a tree for some days, observing his own mind, seeking his own true self with eyes wide open, fully conscious.

After remaining with him for some time, I seem to have the same smile on my face that he has all of the time, a particularly quiet energy engulfing me; the doctor feeds us with Indian sweetmeats and showers us with love and affection.

Delhi, 26 May 1972
I've returned to Delhi again, before leaving for Rishikesh with Piero and Claudio to visit a great Tibetan lama. It feels right for me to know about other teachers and their diverse teachings, so as to deepen my understanding of Babaji and through this comparison come to value Him and His teachings even more.

Rishikesh, 27 May 1972
I have arrived in Rishikesh with Piero, Claudio and some other friends. On the train journey Rosa and I slept together on the same wooden bench.

Rishikesh is beautiful, green, and the water of the Ganges is clean, the river bordered by a wide beach of white sand. We are staying at the small ashram of Swami Prakash Bharti, surrounded by mango trees. The Indian people seem extremely pleased that we have come here and last night we cooked them a delicious feast of Italian rice with tomatoes.

The Swami has large, peaceful eyes, dark and warm. He plays a game with us: to each of us in turn he stares into our eyes to see who can look without blinking for the longest period of time, and he always wins. His eyes resemble the water of a tranquil lake.

The other day an extremely old sadhu arrived here, with exceptionally long hair knotted on his head, his body tall and thin, his skin brown. He walks particularly slowly on some strange wooden sandals and he seldom speaks. The Swami explained to us that he has been in a state of samadhi for one year, for all that time closed up in a cave, without consuming any food and even stopping his heart from beating and halting his breathing. Is that possible? Who knows if it's true, but the sadhu certainly seems like a being from another planet, he is extraordinarily gentle and detached from everything.

The other day Rosa was practising hatha yoga postures in the garden, completely naked. The Swami was embarrassed and laughed awkwardly, but the old sadhu continued watching her with complete indifference. The people here are extremely kind and they offer us food all the time as well as tea to drink, and they often smoke hashish. During the day we frequently take showers under the mango trees, trying to fend off the interminable heat and in the mornings we go to the river Ganges. The river is truly wonderful, the water pure and transparent, with a strong current.

The Swami is teaching me the Indian alphabet and some devotional songs. The other day he placed around my neck a rudraksha mala, a string of seeds from the tree dedicated to Lord Shiva. He told me that he is my guru but I don't feel this to be true. As yet I am not sure whether Babaji is my guru either, but I continually find myself thinking about Him and am surprised how difficult it is to take my eyes off the photograph of Him that I carry. There is a special beauty in His form, a purity that I have never encountered before, the energy of an angelic being.

In India, sadhus, the ascetics, are highly respected since they have dedicated their lives to God. People welcome them, give them food and hospitality. They often travel around the country having renounced a normal life, doing ascetic practices, like living on very little food or sleep, and meditating for long periods of time. Real sadhus are free spirits, beyond every rule and regulation, even if they follow their own spiritual discipline. They look, even physically, different from the rest of the Indian people, they have beautiful, supple bodies, often grow their hair very long and possess special eyes, warm and intense, with a particular light. They maintain a high degree of cleanliness, observing special rules of purity.

Tibetan Initiation - Lama Sakya Trinzin

Mussouri, 1 June 1972

Yesterday, with Piero and Claudio, I travelled from Rishikesh to Mussouri, high up in the mountains. We have come to live in a place called 'Happy Valley', a Tibetan village. Piero and Claudio want to take initiation from Sakya Trinzin, one of the four Dalai Lamas, head of the Sakya order, and they have brought me with them. They told me that this is a serious matter and that I should ask the Lama personally for permission to receive initiation. In the meantime we are staying together in a tiny room in a Tibetan house, sleeping on the floor on some straw mats.

There are only Tibetan people living in this area and I find them extraordinarily beautiful. I am attracted and fascinated by their lovely oriental faces, with high cheek-bones and almond shaped eyes that always express joy. The men often have very long plaited hair usually tied with a ribbon, they are incredibly kind-hearted and some of them even spend time knitting. Otherwise they continuously pray using long rosaries of wooden beads. Unlike the Indian people they don't have an excitable energy, neither do they make a lot of noise or invade the privacy of others. They are quiet, respectful, always smiling, and one feels safe with them. We use their small restaurants because the food is familiar to us Italians, light and without any spices, noodles and vegetable soup much like home, prepared with a mother's care. They also cook momo, a white, soft bread and continually drink salted tea with butter. The women are particularly elegant, clothed in long, traditional dresses, wearing ancient jewellery made of silver, coral and turquoise. On one occasion we went to eat in an elaborate, Western-style restaurant, but I prefer the small simple, Tibetan ones with the welcoming aroma of vegetables. Far away in the distance we can see the snowy peaks of the Himalayas, pure and majestic.

3 June 1972

Today we went to visit His Holiness Sakya Trinzin, in a Tibetan monastery, half-way towards Derhadun. We were permitted to talk with him alone for a few minutes, I felt very shy, particularly because I hardly speak any English. The impression he made on me was of a young man, rather fat and motherly, with a large, rotund face and long hair tied back at the neck, revealing large, turquoise earrings. He symbolizes the perfect integration of both male and female energy in a single human body and has green eyes, very clear, amiable and peaceful. I bowed to him and he placed his hand lightly on my head; small, graceful hands. He smiled softly, encouraging me to overcome my fear and said to me in Italian: 'Dio' - God, which made me feel safe and relaxed.

Then he told me about Mario, the first Italian who ventured up here a few years ago to be with the Tibetan masters. He asked if I wanted to follow the Dharma, the Buddhist path, and I answered that I probably felt more attracted by Hinduism. He nodded. Even so, I still asked him if it was possible for me to take the Buddhist initiation on the following day with Piero and Claudio and he replied that he would be pleased to give me permission. I felt extremely happy and came out from this encounter feeling uplifted, comforted.

Mussouri, 4 June 1972

Today we were initiated by a great Tibetan lama, Sakya Trinzin's teacher. Piero and Claudio have told me that it's a great honour and blessing. In fact I realize that many special things are happening to me, one after the other, as if this trip is invisibly guided.

The three of us were the only Westerners present for the initiation along with a large number of Tibetan monks, dressed in their yellow and dark red robes. The ceremony lasted for eight hours, all day long, and it became almost impossible for me to endure, patiently squatting on the floor cross-legged, experiencing great pain in my legs, not able to understand the language or the meaning of the different rituals. The sound of the tinkling bells and the smell of incense I found quite overwhelming. Tibetan people sing in a particularly unique way, a deep and reverberating tone, in perfect harmony.

The culminating moment of the initiation, when the lama placed a length of red-coloured string around each person's neck, as if sealing the ritual, made a lasting impression on me. He smiled at me, an ancient, wise smile, with a kind of complicity, as if he had known me forever. I came out of the room filled with a new power: something unusual had occurred, an indefinable effect difficult to describe. We have been instructed that we must now meditate and practice the teachings for fifteen days. During this period we can always go to see Lama Sakya Trinzin if necessary, talk with him and ask for further clarification. I feel honoured. From today the three of us are to be confined to our small rooms. The meditation is quite complicated: we should visualize a Buddha, adorned with certain symbols and each time recite a very long mantra with the help of a mala, a rosary.

6 June 1972

The main difficulty is to remain seated correctly and Claudio is teaching me how to sit with my back straight, crossing my legs in the proper way so that they don't feel paralysed. The Western body is used to sitting on chairs and sofas all the time, not seated on the floor, which strains all our muscles. The Indians however are incredibly supple, their joints flexible, both the men and the women quite used to living in close contact with the earth, squatting down, walking barefoot, eating with their hands, sleeping on the floor and cooking and cleaning by crouching down on the ground. The other big problem is to curb the activity of my mind and I try desperately to do that.

We visited the Lama for guidance and I asked him why the Buddha always sits on a lotus flower. He answered that the lotus is the symbol of our soul: as the beautiful lotus opens it's petals, resting on the stagnant, muddy water, so our soul can open to light and knowledge, opening beyond the darkness and ignorance.

Delhi, 20 June 1972

We are in Delhi again and have linked up with all our friends once more. It is strange how we keep meeting up with each other, as if an appointment is arranged through some telepathic message. Soon we will be returning to Mussouri for a further initiation, but I have begun to think about Babaji again. I remain in a dilemma about Him, because He doesn't speak, doesn't give any spoken teachings, doesn't teach meditation. He seems to do nothing and yet there is an inexplicable magic around Him. Every time I look at His photograph I perceive an intense light: maybe it's an hallucination - who knows?

22 June 1972

I have acquired a high fever and so I cannot leave with Piero and Claudio. At the last minute, before they departed, Claudio gave me a small image of Shiva, the deity of Yoga, maybe Babaji Himself. Perhaps I am being called: I begin to think of going to meet Him again in Vrindavan.

Vrindavan, 27 June 1972

I have come back to Babaji with feelings of deep emotion. He called me over to talk with Him by the temple door, touching my bracelets and asking me why I wear all these ornaments. He looked at the tattoo on my hand forming the Om sign and told me in English: 'Full power.' In the evening He had me dancing in front of the Indian people who were present, smiling and telling them that I am a hippie.

Delhi, 30 June 1972

I don't know why but I had to come back to Delhi. I am too restless and the life in the temple is too difficult for me, I am not ready for the discipline especially. I miss my friends, the sense of freedom and comfort that I have here.

Love Story

Delhi, 5 July 1972

As soon as I arrived at the guest-house I came across Sitaram, the young American who I had encountered in Almora with Shanti. I asked him to help me, because there were no other people around and I felt lost in Delhi on my own, especially with my poor grasp of English. Something crazy happened, I don't know how but it did: we are having a love affair after taking an LSD trip together. I don't know whether it will be a successful relationship but we intend to leave for the mountains in order to find a house and live together for a while.

Simla, 7 July 1972

We are in Simla, high up in the mountains, the monsoon has already started and it rains all day. We went around barefoot carrying a large umbrella in search of a house where we could pass the rainy season and now we have discovered a lovely place in the forest with a river and a small lake nearby.

11 July 1972

We've been establishing ourselves in our new home for a few days now and have been busy cleaning, cooking, meditating, taking baths and swimming in a natural pool in the river. When Sitaram travels he carries with him a small suitcase containing inside it a complete temple with representations of many of the Indian deities. He has met many gurus and has learnt a great deal, and now he is teaching me English. It feels good for us to be together, but I also find it impossible to forget Babaji.

Vrindavan, 22 July 1972

Here I am, in Vrindavan again, to kneel at Babaji's feet. This time He talks to me very seriously and tells me that I cannot leave again without His permission. I protest, show Him a photograph of Sitaram and tell Him about our house, but Babaji says that he is not the man for me and that the house is not my home. He goes on to say that in future I'll only be able to live in Hairakhan or in Almora; that is where my home will be. What He says has a tremendous impact on me and I think about it for much of the night. I have decided to try and obey Babaji, but first I must go back to Simla to get my luggage, although I have made a promise to return.

Simla, 25 July 1972

Strangely enough, nothing seems to work out right with Sitaram any more and remembering Babaji has become a kind of obsession for me. Before I left He gave me a painting He had done depicting the temple in Hairakhan, simple, naive, delightful and I keep looking at it.

Return to Babaji

Vrindavan, 29 July 1972

I have returned to Vrindavan, without knowing that today is Guru Purnima, the full moon dedicated to the guru throughout India. This evening Babaji had me dance the whole time in the big temple where we went for the occasion. Every time I looked at Him I saw Him suffused in a brilliant, vibrant light. A young Danish man was dancing with me, trying to catch me, but I always eluded him; I feel light, free.

When I pranamed to Babaji on this occasion, I truly had the impression that He really is the only one to be my guru and that it would be futile to continue wandering around in circles looking for someone else.

Ambaji, 4 August 1972

Babaji took me with Him together with many Indian devotees on a trip to Ambaji, in Gujarat, to visit a famous and ancient temple dedicated to the Divine Mother Amba. It is an incredible place and inside a huge crowd had assembled with hundreds of people standing in line waiting to pranam to Babaji. We all sit for hours on end singing and looking at Him and I ask myself why we do this, why we continue to watch Him all the time, while He just sits and looks back at us. There exists a strange, magnetic attraction, difficult to describe, and in His presence many things are happening inside me, as if He is a powerful catalyst for our collective energy. Everything about Him speaks of harmony and perfection: His gestures, His movements and His form are completely seductive. The mind is brought to another dimension, to a state of peace and inner awareness.

The Indians here adore Him as God manifest on earth and prostrate themselves before Him offering their souls, their humility, their prayers and hopes. I would prefer to be like them, not so intellectual but with greater simplicity and purity. Every time I pranam to Him there is pandemonium in my mind, a turmoil of absurd and conflicting thoughts, at times violent and unpleasant. I feel guilty in His presence and would so much like to be at peace.

10 August 1972

Today we travelled with Babaji to Koteshvar, to an ancient temple in the jungle. The building is constructed of white marble, with all the niches and statues carved out of the stone. Babaji resides here in a small underground room. In the evening I dance in front of hundreds of people, the majority of them coming from the villages nearby and living a simple and extremely basic existence. They look at me, this visitor from the West, the white stranger, as if I am a magical being. They gather around me, touching me, prostrating themselves before me: I must be very careful and pay close attention to my ego.

Datha, 20 August 1972

Today we have moved on to a Maharaja's palace, a real fortress; inside there are many grand rooms decorated with tiger skins. The way in which the women live here has had a considerable effect on me: they live in isolation, never going outside the palace or seeing any man other than members of their own family. They sit together all day long, chatting, or busying themselves with small tasks, reminiscent of a scene from the Middle Ages. Babaji is treated as if He were a great king and suddenly I see Him behaving just like that, sitting on an elaborate throne, dressed in royal clothes and with a regal countenance.

Vrindavan, 25 August 1972

We have come back to Vrindavan and the police have paid me a visit, having discovered that I am living here without a visa, which expired a long time ago. The fact is that I haven't even bothered to do anything about it, following my impulsive anarchistic nature, wanting to stay here without the necessary papers as a matter of principle, an expression of my sense of freedom. But now I am in trouble and the police have told me that I have to leave India within three days.

I run immediately to Babaji, who asks me what I want to do and if I would like to go to Nepal. I agree, since I wish to meet the Tibetan Lamas there and smiling He asks me if I know any Tibetan mantras. He also told me that I could ask a question of Him if I wish, and so I inquire if I should go back to Italy or if I should stay in India. Babaji replied softly: 'You will stay all your life in India at My feet.' I also asked if He could see my past lives and He said that in my previous life I was an Indian woman in Almora with a family and children and before that, a Tibetan queen devoted to Lord Shiva. He told me not to worry, because I have His blessing and that I will come back to India and to Him.

Trip to Nepal

Kathmandu, 5 September 1972

I have come to Nepal accompanied by a kind American man who I'd met occasionally in Delhi. It really feels as if I've embarked on a huge adventure now, particularly because I've almost run out of money. We found a room in a large house outside Kathmandu called the 'White House' predominantly occupied by Americans who have lived in Nepal for long periods of time.

It's a nice place, clean, with a pleasant garden. The small village is called Swayambhu and the people who live in the tiny houses and run the restaurants are mainly Tibetan. At the top of the hill there are both Hindu and Buddhist temples where the people happily worship side by side. Day and night one can hear the sound of different bells and devotional songs. Lamps and candles are lit, there is the smell of incense and groups of monkeys climb about and jump from one temple to the other. To reach the top of the hill involves climbing hundreds of steps of white stone, as if undertaking a long pilgrimage, and then it is possible to circumambulate all of the shrines. I bow again and again to the many deities and Buddhas that I pass, of the past, present and future.

15 September 1972

My experiences in Nepal are fascinating, meeting many interesting people, especially the Americans who seem so accustomed to living here in the East. They have been in contact with various masters from India and Tibet and draw on the teachings they have received. All of them are wealthy and live comfortably, making money by organizing business ventures, trading in Tibetan carpets or artwork and they appear to handle everything easily. They are affluent hippies and some have ended up staying here for years living a life of luxury.

Sometimes at the 'White House', the Americans organize big parties, and all the Western people living in the city of Kathmandu come. There is a lot of hashish circulating as well as LSD and the atmosphere is a little unreal, but also very mystical. Some of the people attract me, they are beautiful, intense and I admire them. In their presence I feel like a small child, a beginner, immature, someone without much experience, and yet I am readily accepted by them.

During the day I eat in the small Tibetan restaurants nearby, cheap and comfortable, the people gentle and friendly and I feel at home with them. I have also discovered the existence of a large colony of Italians, friends of friends, but they are totally different to the Americans, mainly crazy people without any money and some of them take heavy drugs.

20 September 1972

I am involved in so many different sorts of activity and feel really free for the first time in my life, at the centre of everything, in the eye of the storm, able to experiment with everything that I want.

In the morning I wake up early, mindful of Babaji's teaching, then at dawn I climb the many steps up to the temples at the top of the hill. From here Kathmandu looks extremely beautiful, enveloped in a pink mist, still sleeping. Later on I meet up with my friends in a small local cafe for breakfast, then go for a long walk around the city.

Kathmandu is a magical place, the capital of Nepal, a gateway city of an ancient civilization while being close to the border of both India and Tibet. The Nepalese are a quiet people, always smiling, colourful and in this city the Hindus and Buddhists live and worship peacefully together. I visit all the temples, go everywhere, walking again and again through all the tiny streets of the bazaar full of things for sale. I want to discover all I can. In one of the many economical cafes in the city I take lunch but in the evening I generally stay at home with my new American friends, trying to learn something more about their culture. It's true to say that they are a little snobbish and a little too sure of themselves, but they were the first people from the West to uncover the potential of the East, not only discovering all the different gurus but also devising ingenious and profitable ways to do business; they appear to me as if they already know everything.

Sometimes we go dancing in the evening to a discotheque called 'Mushroom Rose'. It's a mixture of both East and West, where one can hear both the music of the Rolling Stones and Tibetan horns. It is like being in a movie, so different, I dance wildly, smoke dope, and feel a tremendous sense of freedom.

25 September 1972

Last night I smoked too much, felt terribly sick and almost fainted. I must be careful not to overdo it, not to become completely distracted. I've been to the Indian Embassy to apply for a new visa, but at the moment they have no intention of giving me one. They have written to Delhi, to the Ministry of Home Affairs, for more information.

Abdullah, a young Moroccan actor with the 'Living Theatre', wants to make love with me, but I don't like him. He gives me no peace and rather scares me, always dressed in black, with enormous dark eyes. He is attractive in a way, having the qualities of a dancer, moving like a cat, sinuous, bewitching, like a magician dancing with a snake.

The other evening I watched his dancing with admiration but I have no desire for a sexual relationship with him. Often I look at Babaji's photograph placed above my bed; He appears white, pure, radiant and I think I would like to become celibate like Him, a brahmachari. At the present time I am so tired of sexual contact.

2 October 1972

I am now completely without any money and this is a new experience for me. In the past I often used to ask myself how Westerners had the courage to be on the road without money. I admired their courage leaving everything to chance and now it is my turn. I know it is a test of faith on the path I have chosen and that I shouldn't be daunted or give up. It doesn't seem right to ask my parents for money especially because they absolutely disagree with the way in which I am living my life and anyway it doesn't seem right to impose on them.

Today I didn't have a single penny left in my pocket not even to buy food, I took the bus without paying the fare, a young man I met by chance offered to buy me lunch and on top of that the rent for my room is due to be paid. This evening I borrowed some money from an Italian friend.

25 October 1972

I have spent long periods of my life aimlessly roaming around in circles, smoking and endlessly talking with so many people. Now I am utterly tired of it.

When I came back home last night, feeling quite exhausted after a busy day, I saw a light on in my room: it was my dear friend Piero, sitting on my bed, with his head shaved and his eyes shining. He told me he wants to become a Buddhist monk. I asked him to take me with him, away from this town, to meet the Tibetan lamas; I am so disillusioned and tired of this kind of life.

Lama Tubten Yeshe

Kopan, 2 November 1972

Piero and I have travelled to Kopan to meet Lama Yeshe, Piero and Claudio's guru. The road to the monastery is extraordinarily beautiful, winding through the middle of rice fields and the green Nepalese hills.

The moment I entered the little room where Lama Yeshe was sitting, it was as if I saw a living Buddha, rotund, joyful, luminous, emanating love and wisdom from every pore of his skin. He laughed loudly when he saw us, a cosmic laugh emanating from his heart and he said: 'Italian people, too much.' I found myself sitting in front of him and I also started laughing, but uncontrollably, conspiratorially, not knowing why, just feeling at one with this wonderful energy and joy, with this laughing consciousness. There is a remembering, an ancient recognition that all is relative, that we are one consciousness.

10 November 1972

I have made the decision to come and live in Kopan for an indefinite period of time with Piero in Massimo's house, a friend of his.

When I spoke to Lama Yeshe for the first time, he said to me: 'Here you will find the Dharma and peace, much confusion in the city of Kathmandu.' It's true, even the thought of it now makes me feel nauseous. I am fed up with hippies, smoking dope, going around in empty circles, sexual games.

I don't have any money, but I'll be able to borrow some from Piero and later I should be able to get some from Italy. Piero and I have moved into our new house and I begin a new routine; we meditate together, cook our food and wash our clothes. It is similar to the routine in an Indian ashram: we wake up at four o'clock in the morning and at five we go to Lama Zopa's room, a younger lama, in order to take the five precepts or vows for the day. They are the five rules that constitute the basis of the Tibetan Dharma: not to kill, not to steal, not to tell lies, not to take any intoxicant, not to have sexual relationships outside of marriage. Piero and I live together like brother and sister, even if I am very attracted by him and his intense light.

26 December 1972

Piero has decided to go to India, to Dharamsala, to become a monk and I have decided to attend a meditation retreat for three months. Yesterday we went together to a Christmas party in Kathmandu, at the 'White House' with the Americans, but we both ended up feeling that we'd had enough of this way of life. I realize that my life as a hippie is completely over now, there's no point to it. The way I've come to feel about it is similar to what persuaded me to leave Milan a few months ago, it's like walking on a path that is leading nowhere. The ingredients are always the same: music, smoking, chatting, sex, mystical fantasies, mind games, all of which seem to waste so much time and energy.

Peace is missing, because the mind always remains in a confused and distracted state, life is gloomy, smoke-filled and clouded by fantasy. I am longing for light and knowledge. Yet so many people in the world don't appear to want the light, they prefer to choose the security of darkness, because the light requires us to take courage and plunge ourselves into the flames of transformation, sacrificing ourselves completely.

20 January 1973

Having commenced on the meditation retreat, I have been living alone in this room for nearly one month now. It's proving to be an incredible experience. The room is so small, there is only enough space for me to either sit or to lie on my sleeping bag and I am only allowed out in the morning in order to visit the bathroom. Even my food is served through a hole in the door. I am going through unexpected experiences. By repeating the mantra day and night, my mind goes into a trance-like state and my body is pervaded by an electrical current, which I can sense especially in my forehead and on the top of my head. After two or three hours of this practice a deep tranquillity fills me and silence envelops my mind. I see a bright, white light within myself and around my body and at times the whole room is suffused with its shining brilliance. Sometimes, if I do go outside, I am hardly able to walk, it almost feels as if I am flying, transported by a powerful energy, my feet barely touching the earth.

Whenever I look out from the tiny window in my room, I am touched by the beauty of the snow-covered peaks of the Himalayas in the distance and the bright colours of the flowers.

22 January 1973

Today I wrote a poetic song for Babaji and Lama Yeshe combined. I feel they are two forms of the same unique Essence, one with an Indian appearance and the other Tibetan. They are both representative of the archetypal Great Master, the Great Divine Wisdom and the Divine Energy, an anchor to hold on to when I feel a little afraid.

Lama Yeshe has initiated me into the precepts of Tibetan Buddhism and given me a Tibetan name: Yeshe Wongmo, which means, 'initiation into transcendental wisdom'. It signifies I should maintain a life both moral and disciplined, just the opposite way of living to that of a hippie, which for me is now finished.

At times I find it difficult to accept the idea of imposed religion, because I still react adversely against my Catholic upbringing, always wanting to be contrary, having my own way of doing things. But this present situation feels different and I realize I've reached a point where I must radically change my life; I am even thinking of becoming a Buddhist nun. Now I see the impermanence and relative imperfections of this world and I am longing to find divine perfection and truth in some other level of reality: 'on the other shore', as the Tibetans say, on the shore of another consciousness.

Lama Tubten Yeshe

15 March 1973

It's the third month of my retreat and I've had some extremely intense meditational experiences. On my altar I always keep Babaji's photograph, with His Christ-like smile full of compassion and tenderness, next to one of the Buddha; I am very much looking forward to seeing Babaji again. The experiences during my retreat have helped me to understand Him and His teachings more clearly, things that I had not been receptive to before. I feel that it is now possible for me to renounce many of my worldly desires and attachments, and be able to walk a spiritual path. I have also cut my hair and amused myself by wearing a Tibetan dress of the same colour worn by Buddhist nuns.

25 March 1973

The retreat is almost over and I have spoken with Lama Yeshe about my meditation experiences. He expressed that he was very happy with my practice and told me that I have had a taste of samadhi, the transcendent state of consciousness, when the mind becomes empty, silent, and can then perceive another dimension. Something radically different certainly occurred within me during my meditations and because of that I now view my time with Babaji from a different perspective. Now I understand the purpose of the hardships, the penance that I experienced while with Him, why part of me was rebelling and wanting to run away. Babaji was teaching me detachment from physical comforts, with the intention of inducing within me a more spiritual level of consciousness.

It seems to me now that what I once regarded as reality is really more like a movie, projected onto my mind as if it were a screen, an illusion, a dream. Our mind resembles a perfect mirror, except that it is covered by the dust of illusions, but when the dust is cleaned away there exists a clear reflection and we can see reality as it is. What impedes our ability to see clearly, causing our blindness, is our attachment to the physical and material world of form, our ego and our desires. Through meditation the mind can return to its original purity, to a state of emptiness, devoid of unnecessary thoughts, fantasies and projections. It's a difficult thing to practise, because the ordinary everyday mind doesn't want to die and it rebels, is continually restless, always wanting to be active, thinking, imagining, desiring and wishing.

I feel now that I want the truth, a truth for which I have always been looking, which I yearned for even when I was young and have sought even when my life has been full of confusion and difficulties. The guru is the one who helps us to get rid of our illusions, because without him we are so trapped by them, so blind that we cannot see. In Sanskrit, guru means, 'the one who gives the light'.

The Tibetan teachings are extremely precious to me, an important school of learning in my development. I even feel that Babaji Himself probably sent me here, to learn something, to prepare me. His method, beyond words, based only on the devotion of the heart, couldn't satisfy my Western mind which is so used to thinking all the time and demanding explanations.

2 April 1973

Now at the end of the retreat I have decided to follow a course in meditation given by Lama Zopa, and Kopan is full of people, more than one hundred, from every corner of the world. It is my second period of involvement on a course about the Buddhist Dharma. Lama Yeshe also participates occasionally, giving some of his wonderful speeches. It's been most interesting, hard at times, because we have to sit and listen all day, which demands tremendous patience. Lama Zopa explains to us, in a precise and scholarly manner, the way in which the mind operates, with all its tricks, what is Karma, what is Dharma, clarifying everything. We also meditate with him collectively for defined lengths of time and there are very valuable periods afterwards when we can debate and discuss things. I had made up my mind to prepare myself for this opportunity. Perhaps for the first time I have found a truth I can trust, my mind has received some spiritual food and I have finally attained a certain clarity.

To have found the Dharma, the Lama says, is to have found the Way. To have found the guru is similar to having found a precious treasure. The spiritual master can guide us on a difficult path, occult, secret sometimes, revealed to those who are heroes and heroines, ready to give up everything for it, for the Light. They invite us, through meditation, to experience by ourselves the existence of a hidden, inner reality, our soul's divinity. It's not an act of blind faith that is requested from us, but instead to experience personally what the science of Yoga can offer us.

I now have many clear, inner visions, which sometimes frighten me and make me feel like running away, but I can't do that any more. I know the Divine has taken hold of me and Babaji is waiting for me in India.

Kathmandu, 29 April 1973

Today I travelled down to Kathmandu after completing my retreat and I experienced a terrible crisis, a rebellion within myself concerning everything that had happened. My whole being seemed to be in total revolt about the sense of control and level of tiredness I have been experiencing. So I gorged myself on lots of greasy sweetmeats which made me thoroughly sick, and now I feel terribly weak-willed and stupid.

Returning to India

Delhi, 2 May 1973

I have unexpectedly received some money from my parents in Italy and returned to India. The Indian Embassy in Nepal refused to renew my visitor's visa only granting me a transit visa, but I remembered Babaji's promise that I would be able to return to India and be with Him. I want to remain with Him in India whatever the limitations of every ridiculous, human law and I am ready to risk everything in order to achieve that. So I lit an incense stick in front of His photograph in my hotel room and then burned my passport. I take pleasure in being courageous and now I am free. After all, I have always been trained for revolution and now I must put it into practice, living life from day to day.

Today I'll travel to Vrindavan and try looking for Babaji there, since He told me that it would be there that I would be reunited with Him; He also assured me that after I returned from Nepal I would remain with Him and there would be no visa problem and so here I am, without any papers at all.

Vrindavan, 8 May 1973

I was in a very tense state when I met up with Babaji soon after I arrived here in Vrindavan. But He wasn't surprised to see me at all, in fact it was as if He had been waiting for me and He immediately asked me about my visa. When I told Him that I had burnt my passport, He said: 'Now I am your visa and your passport.' Then, smiling at my Tibetan dress and the image of the Dalai Lama around my neck, He sent me immediately to the market to buy a white sari and to shave off my hair.

This morning He emerged from His room with a shaved head as well, wearing a golden chain that I had given Him as a gift a year ago. For the first time He applied chandan to my forehead, saying: 'Now I am your Guru.' I am tremendously moved, surprised and stunned: in two or three days' time we are leaving for Hairakhan.

I feel as if it is only now that my path with Him is beginning. It took me more than a year to arrive at an understanding of Babaji that was sufficiently profound to allow me to surrender to Him, to trust Him. I had to learn to give up numerous desires as well as the desire to satisfy them. Yesterday, to my great surprise, I received a particularly strong experience in His presence: I was sitting in front of Him and I suddenly saw an intense light coming from Him and entering my body. Was this an hallucination? Babaji looked at me and said softly: 'You are Me.'

Training at Hairakhan

Hairakhan, 13 May 1973

I have returned to Hairakhan and a strenuous, difficult training, both physically and mentally, has begun: in May it is exceedingly hot and Babaji wants us to undertake a great deal of physical work, all to be carried out at a fast pace. We have to carry numerous buckets of water up the steps from the river, clean and sweep everywhere, cook, haul wood from the jungle and wash the big, black, cooking pots in the river.

At the present time I am the only Western person here, sometimes the only woman and permanent person as well. It falls on me to do all the heavy kitchen work, clean the temple and wash everything. I continually fight with my habitual laziness and often I feel exhausted. In the afternoons Babaji wants me to study Hindi with an Indian teacher who is living here.

15 May 1973

I am surprised at the unexpected change in Babaji since arriving in Hairakhan. He has transformed Himself from the distinctly ethereal form I witnessed in Vrindavan and now manifests as an extraordinarily severe Master, scolding everybody and shouting out orders to people. Everyone here seems afraid of Him and they run around obeying His instructions, myself included.

The Indian people accept quite naturally the idea of being of service to others, humility comes easily to them and they are ready to 'jump into the fire' immediately for Babaji. Quite willingly they surrender totally to Him and with their tremendous faith they obey everything that He says instantly. They work tirelessly, without any resistance or holding back and no act of service is too small for them. It is not the same for myself: I have great difficulty in being like them. I feel myself to be full of resistance and a tremendous inertia engulfs me, but it seems that Babaji is particularly working on those qualities in me.

I have suddenly remembered that even as an adolescent I had difficulties with my laziness, my lack of application, and my studies during the period I was at secondary school were ruined because of my total laziness. Any attempts I made to alter my habits, to overcome my unwillingness to study or improve my concentration, were futile. Now, it seems, I will have to confront my nature, and I am determined to try and change.

The Indians have impressed me greatly with their simple loving actions: serving other people with the same care and devotion they have for Babaji. Almost at once Babaji gave me a teaching about this: yesterday He placed in my hands a large plate of prasad, fruits and sweets, to distribute to others. I immediately felt proud, but He instantly spoke to me sternly, saying: 'Babaji means, be of service to all of humanity.' I know I should be able to learn about love and humility at first hand from the people here, who although they are poor, touch me deeply with their simplicity and goodness.

25 May 1973

Babaji told me that I should discontinue writing to my parents for a few months and should forget everything about my past. Today He placed me with Satya, a young woman from Bombay and told me I should learn everything from her and become like an Indian woman. I have to learn how to dress, to sit, to stand, to walk, all in a different way, to start again from the beginning all that I have ever learnt in my life, as if I was a little girl again. Satya is also a schoolteacher and I will be learning Hindi from her. Babaji insists as well that I should eat and sleep with her, in symbiosis with my new Indian sister.

Satya is a beautiful woman, but has decided not to marry; she wears white clothes all the time, like the Indian women who have renounced the world and she has dedicated herself, body and soul, to Babaji. Satya's name means 'absolute truth'. So, we are committed to the experiment and have started sleeping in each other's arms, very close together on a tiny straw mat by one of the pillars of the temple. We don't have any mattress or blanket, the only covering we have for ourselves is a sari, which we wash every day; I also wear only white now.

An old man called Guard Sahib, a retired railway worker, lives with us here in Hairakhan. Babaji expresses such loving tenderness towards him. Guard Sahib looks a little like Mahatma Gandhi, thin, fragile, walking with the help of a stick. All he ever wears is a strip of cotton material wrapped around his waist, even in winter. Quite often Babaji sits with him in the dhuni, sharing with him words of wisdom and the ancient scriptures of India. It's so moving to see the young Babaji talking to the old man as if he were a little child. I feel that the reason why Babaji loves Guard Sahib so much is because of his great humility. His life is continually concentrated on some kind of service, taking care of the smallest details: a stamp, a few rupees to be counted correctly, somewhere to be cleaned. Babaji talks to him with tremendous sweetness, caressing his back and his shoulders, putting something good to eat in his mouth, just like a mother with a little baby.

2 June 1973

The weather is terribly hot and the days are so busy, passing by in a particularly orderly and precise rhythm. The sound of Prem Baba's trumpet wakes us up before four o'clock in the morning and we leap straight into the river to bathe. In the summer this is the best part of the day, when the cooling breeze of the night still blows softly through the valley. When the moon is full the river sparkles silver in between the white rocks and it seems that the jungle becomes full of life and spirits.

As the last vestiges of the night give way to the morning twilight we finish bathing and then climb back up the steps to the temple. Some of us have the privilege of sitting with Babaji around the small fire-pit in His dhuni. It's a confined space and there is only room for four or five people in the dhuni, but I am always invited to sit, together with Guard Sahib. Babaji places ash on our foreheads and then performs a simple fire-ceremony, making offerings to the fire in silence. There is only the sound of the flames crackling, the wind, and the birds singing to the emerging light of dawn. Automatically my consciousness enters another reality, feeling empty, light.

Babaji in the dhuni

Sometimes it's difficult for me to bear such calmness and I become tense and frightened: I am aware that Babaji is observing me closely. The other day He called me over to sit beside Him and asked me: 'Who are you?' and I had no answer. He told me that my reply to this question should always be that I am

Babaji's disciple. This comforts and reassures me and it is the first phrase in Hindi that I have learnt. On another occasion, without at first realizing it, I found myself alone with Babaji around the fire-pit and I became scared, not able to face Him, so embarrassed. Babaji looked at me with much love and said: 'You can sit, you are My disciple.' This comforted me a lot.

At about eight o'clock in the morning, after aarati, the morning prayers, we start working; breakfast doesn't exist. We carry out the few basic tasks essential for our survival: we collect wood from the jungle, carry water from the river, cut up vegetables, make the dough for chapatis, our daily bread. We eat only once a day, at lunchtime, drinking tea or coffee is not allowed and there is no chai-shop. After lunch we can take a nap and then in the late afternoon we go to the river to take a second bath and wash our clothes. Except for a little bit of cleaning the afternoon is a period of free time, which I use to study Hindi with Satya. I haven't learnt to speak it well yet but from the lesson that she gives me I write down the meaning of the words in a small exercise book in a mixture of Italian and English. In the evening there is aarati again and then we sit in silence with Babaji in the dhuni. We go to sleep very early, before nine o'clock, without any dinner and sometimes I am terribly hungry.

When the weather remains warm in the evenings people sing until late. Babaji says that when we sing, the atmosphere becomes charged with divine energy, which means that it then becomes possible for us to meditate for others as well as ourselves.

5 June 1973

Babaji has scolded me harshly because He wants me to work faster. It seems I have to cart endless buckets of water up from the riverbed: yesterday I carried fifty of them. But it is confusing because at other times, if I move quickly, Babaji tells me to go more slowly. It's difficult to understand exactly what He wants; it's as if I have to succeed in finding a rhythm that is somewhere in-between, harmonious. It's like moving to the rhythm of a dance. I remember when I was asked to dance in Vrindavan it was the same sort of question that was being asked of me, to be able to flow with the rhythm and find movements that were just right, of managing to discover a way of dancing for the Divine.

Sometimes I still have doubts and really question everything, even the existence of God, as well as Babaji's Divinity and whether He's as special as He is depicted. The Indians keep telling me that Baba is Bhagwan, God Himself, but sometimes I think that maybe I've just become mesmerized by it all: I have always been a convinced atheist so what am I doing here, where am I going to end up?

7 June 1973

When I succumb to my old pattern of resistance, even blasphemies come into my mind quite unconsciously, and particularly when I am in close proximity with Babaji I find that quite unexpectedly I want to curse and swear. At those moments I really feel so embarrassed, and am certain that He can also read my thoughts. Yesterday it happened that every time I was going to pranam before Him, a blasphemy came into my mind. When I become agitated like this He doesn't permit me to be in close contact with Him and tells me brusquely, in English: 'You go.' All of a sudden I feel so distant from Him, an unbearable sense of separation.

I remember Lama Yeshe's words in Nepal, when he told me that if when trying to meditate one notices menacing, negative thoughts coming into one's mind: 'It could be a good sign, a sign that the ego is beginning to die and is offering resistance, objecting to change. It does not want to die, so it attempts to protect itself by creating all sorts of negativity.' Perhaps my old atheistic karma is now coming to the surface.

10 June 1973

I feel Babaji demands too much from me, pushing me to the limit, beyond my capabilities. I can never relax, He watches my every movement. In the evening I am tired out, what with the heat and all the physical work that has to be done, so exhausted that I lie down to sleep on the outside wall of the temple, just lying on a small strip of cotton material on the hard stone. The tropical stars are enormous, shining amidst the lush foliage of the banana trees. Before falling asleep I cast one last look up to the top of Mount Kailash which stands before me, the sacred mountain dedicated to Lord Shiva.

Shiva and Buddha: Buddhism is a gentler path, the 'Middle Way' as they call it. Shiva is extreme, violent, revolutionary, but that is precisely why it attracts me. Babaji works a lot on our desires, our attachments, the inertia of the physical body and our resistance to change, through the carrying out of daily, practical activities so as to offer us a training in detachment, an active meditation. The lamas explained to me the complicated existence of karma and the binding effect that desires have for a person, but with Babaji the severing of karmic bonds comes about through the practical everyday activities of life, communal action, a concrete and active meditation; it's like shedding a skin. The rigid routine, the constant effort and intensely physical, hard work carrying heavy loads, automatically brings my mind to the point of emptiness; this happens especially in the evening when I am physically exhausted and immediately after waking up early in the morning.

Sometimes at dawn, bathed in the crystal light of the valley, freshly awakened by the cold water of the river, with the mind still pure from a night's rest, I resemble a small child who has retrieved her lost innocence. I see myself like a tiny bundle wrapped in a blanket seated at the feet of this great Being, mysterious and perfect. I feel like a soul who has stumbled upon a forgotten path and found something wonderful but difficult to understand: the guru. Indian people explain to me that the grace of the guru is everything and that without him it is not possible to obtain true knowledge. They say we should be able to obey the guru blindly, but this authoritarian concept is difficult for me to accept. I have spent my whole life up to this point fighting against all forms of authority, even on the streets in Milan where I also organized a free kindergarten, but at this moment, Milan and my past seem so far way, a distant memory.

15 June 1973

I don't have any money, but I don't worry at all, because I feel completely safe in Babaji's hands: He gives me food and lodging and occasionally one rupee to buy a piece of soap to wash my clothes. I have two saris and each day I wash one of them, I also have a sweater, a blanket, a length of cotton cloth on which to lie when I go to sleep, a few tampax and I have no other needs. I don't have any shoes, Babaji walks barefoot and so do I; having shaved my head I don't need a comb or shampoo, instead of tooth paste I am using some ash from the fire-pit: life has become really very simple and beautiful.

Yesterday a succession of dramas occurred because my menstrual period had begun. I was peeling potatoes in the kitchen together with an old Indian woman and I told her I felt particularly tired, because of my period. She started shouting and dragged me by the arm complaining before Babaji, who also told me that I definitely couldn't stay in the temple. It's another shock for me and I told Babaji that my mother had taught me that the menses are a very natural occurrence; there is nothing negative or bad about it. He answered that Indian mothers have a different way of thinking and told me to put up a temporary awning and sit there in isolation. I feel humiliated, but they tell me that this has always been the Indian tradition: women are considered impure when they have their period and can't go into the temple or in the kitchen for five days. Babaji even told me that I should not come into close proximity to men, or even talk to them. This seems such an exaggerated response to me, as if it involves some sort of sexual impurity, but it appears as if I must accept this as well.

18 June 1973

Today Babaji played a strange game concerning this idea of sexual impurity. I was sitting near Him, crouching down close to the earth in the garden, when I started having sexual thoughts and felt tremendously embarrassed. What is happening to me, maybe another aspect of myself is rebelling? For a few days now I have had sexual thoughts every time I come close to Him, not anything in particular, just an idle curiosity. They have told me that Babaji is a brahmachari, but is this true? Does He ever have sexual desires or even have a sexual organ? I wonder if He desires me or indeed any woman? I feel ashamed of these thoughts, but I can't control them and worst of all I know that Babaji is aware of them. So today, while I was sitting near Him, fighting my sexual feelings, He came and took my hand and placed it on His organ, asking me in

English with an sardonic grin: 'You like?' I felt so awful, distraught at seeing the pettiness and limitations of my human needs, so much so that I wanted to disappear. That would have been bad enough but after a moment, He even added: 'You are a hippie?' So now I see myself as representing a way of life that from the perspective of this culture, together with the impression given by some Westerners, amounts to no more than sex, drugs and rock n' roll.

Indian people regard hippies with contempt. They don't appreciate the lifestyle and have their own ancient traditions and very precise cultural morality: marriage, family life and feminine virtue. The thing that pains me most is to think that I may have projected my Western woman's energy and sexual attitudes onto Babaji, who represents purity. I've had a number of sexual relationships in my life, because in the West we are accustomed to having casual sex, but now I would like to renounce it all. I know it will be difficult but I am determined to try because I no longer want to be so heavily attached to the pleasures of the physical body. The presence of Babaji acts like a strong catalyst, there's a powerful and potent energy emanating from Him giving me strength and encouragement to radically change my life.

Certainly everything that I've experienced during this period of little more than a year that I have spent travelling in India has been extraordinary: from a revolutionary hippie I have now been transformed into a monastic Hindu.

21 June 1973

Babaji has begun His sexual games with me again in a very direct way: last night He gave me an appointment to meet Him down by the river and then started to touch me all over my body, with coolness, without any sensuality or any desire, just mirroring my sexual, romantic projections. I am badly shaken and even doubt Him: maybe He's no different to the typical Indian Baba who just wants sex and money from Westerners, even if a part of me does know that He is only mirroring my desires so that I may overcome them, but it's a difficult medicine to take.

Today at sunset I saw Him coming back from His bath: He was so beautiful, full of light, luminous, fresh from bathing in the water of the Gautam Ganga and with a smile full of compassion. I thought of Jesus, walking by the river Jordan with his disciples; I felt that the sexual game had been played out solely for my benefit, to bring me beyond sexual desire. Suddenly Babaji called me over to Him and said in a very tender voice: 'Gaura, you are My disciple.'

26 June 1973

I am exhausted. This is the hottest time of year in India, when the heat builds up daily before the rainy season begins. The valley is always windy which saps my strength as well; the mornings are cold in spite of the burning heat of the day.

Today I felt utterly miserable, kneeling awkwardly on the floor to sweep, a

69

brush in my hand, with a shaved head, my sari a dirty white. I still cannot wear it properly, nor can I squat down on the ground to clean like Indian women do and when I sit to meditate my legs soon become painful. Prem Baba and the other people are always shouting at me shrilly in this incomprehensible language that I do not understand. I am expected to do all the kitchen work and go to the river after lunch to wash all the heavy, black pots, carrying them on my head.

Sometimes I see Tara Devi who consoles me and teaches me some English words as well as Hindi. Babaji seems so distant from me and the Indians are so noisy and clingy. Satya insists on accompanying me all the time so that now I feel suffocated by her and I resent the fact that I do not have my independence.

Today I felt so tired after having washed all the pots down by the river that I fell asleep lying on the stones on the riverbank. When I woke up, I saw Babaji carrying all the pots up the temple steps. I ran after Him and He said to me in English: 'I help you.' A few simple words from Him is enough to console me and make everything all right.

In the afternoon He told the old man Guard Sahib to teach me some office work. Guard Sahib has an extremely small room, no more than a metre square, which stands in front of Babaji's dhuni. Babaji loves him a great deal and in the morning and evening they often talk quietly together. Guard Sahib works slowly and exceedingly carefully taking care of all of Babaji's correspondence, writing His letters. Now he has taught me how to use glue to paste the stamps on to envelopes, very precisely, so they are perfectly aligned and he has given me the basic teaching: I should never take any thing or any money that belongs in the office, not even the smallest amount, rather give it instead, because honesty is the most important quality.

Babaji has asked that in the morning at five o'clock, after bathing, I should teach some hatha yoga to the Indian devotees. It's clearly a fundamental lesson for me both in humility and how to serve; I am learning to share everything with these simple people.

In the West we speak about poverty, but we don't really know what it is, while here in India the poor really do exist and they are like saints. They are good people here, so humble, simple and spontaneous in their love, they warm my heart.

Babaji loves people indiscriminately, no matter whether rich or poor. He is able to assume a way of behaving that is right for everyone, constantly transforming Himself as the situation demands like a chameleon. Love is the main way in which He affects people and He gives continuously, without asking anything back for Himself, taking care of everyone and everything.

The other day Tara Devi asked Babaji what He thinks about when He meditates alone in His room in the morning and He answered: 'I am thinking of you all, how to take care of all your needs and what you will eat.' Baba unites together the qualities of a great father and a great mother in the angelic form of a young man. His hands are very feminine, long and tapering, soft and His touch on your head or shoulder has a magnetic quality, an electrical energy. His feet are like those of a child, rounded, plump, tender. Everybody tries to touch them, because the Indian scriptures say that the guru's feet carry all the grace. We worship them, because they are the representation of His divine presence on this earth, there to save us.

'They wash Him, dress Him, treat Him like a murti, a holy statue…'

29 June 1973
I can never find a quiet place where I can sit in peace, or meditate. Even when

it is time to sleep every single corner is occupied and I am in the company of other Indian people, or with Satya. Only when I go to the river am I alone. I sit on the bank and merge with the sound of the water running over the rocks. The Gautam Ganga is clear and transparent, sparkling. I enjoy sitting with the sun on my face, alone with the smooth polished boulders, the mountains. Due to the intense heat of the day, I don't go for my bath now until sunset and I often see Babaji taking His bath with the Indian devotees. They wash Him, dress Him, treat Him like a murti, a holy statue; I would like to be near Him, but I know that I am not ready yet. I am still afraid of Him, and because my mind becomes agitated in His presence I get even more confused. I remain full of desires and have the fear of being rejected, of not being accepted or loved.

Only when I am calm and not expecting anything does He present something for me to understand.

For a few days now I have been busy working in the garden and every time Babaji passes by I wish He would see me, take notice of me and appreciate the work I am doing. But every time He does come past, the only thing He asks me is: 'What are you doing?' In the beginning I responded by trying to explain to Him that I was doing this and that, but later on my response was to say that I was doing nothing and I know that He is happy with this answer. It's a lesson for me about ego, because I know one shouldn't be proud of what one is doing, everything is just a duty, nothing is exceptional in the eyes of God.

When I am with him I observe the old man Guard Sahib closely, always humble, being of service in his quiet way. He used to be an inspector on the railways during the British colonial period. He talks extremely softly and has no difficulty in being completely relaxed with Babaji; he probably doesn't have a guilty conscience. I would very much like to emulate him, to speak quietly with Babaji and express humility in service. Babaji scarcely talks to me at all, only gestures and a few words from time to time, but He communicates through glances, His eyes like sparks of light, intense, tender, severe, childish and transparent all at once.

I have always tried to be successful in my life, always wanting to be noticed, on top of any situation, the first in line, but now I have to learn to be inconspicuous, become the last of the last, and I accept the challenge.

Yesterday I felt extremely tired, all morning I had to walk in the mountains with the Indian women collecting cow dung. When I returned I complained to Babaji and told Him through an Indian interpreter that I needed to rest more and have more time for myself. His response was to give me the example of Mahatma Gandhi, who made an English woman clean toilets for many months before he would accept her as his disciple. Asking me if I didn't think I also had some karma to purify, He added that when Babaji comes to this world, out of one million devotees who approach Him only one is able to become His disciple. I am perplexed and ask myself if perhaps I might make the grade and be that unique person, but obviously the answer is no.

30 June 1973

Tara Devi explains to me that there is a great difference between being Babaji's disciple and being His devotee. Of the many devotees who follow Him, who have definite faith in Him, pray to Him, there are few who are disciples, the people to whom Babaji gives yogic initiation, to whom He becomes the guru.

I am proud that Babaji often plays a game with me now, repeatedly asking: 'Who are you?' and I have to answer: 'I am Babaji's disciple.' This short sentence makes me so happy, like a child, I feel accepted by Him. Being with Him I feel like a baby, so small in the presence of His immensity.

2 July 1973

Now I study Hindi every day and Babaji Himself is teaching me all the basic words with much patience: 'Come here, sit, go, bring.' It feels as if I am beginning a new life, as if I had died and have been reborn again. When He speaks to me His voice is both gentle and profound, ancient and youthful all at the same time, and I feel as if I am starting all over again, no more than five years old, about to embark on a fascinating adventure.

The sexual games have stopped abruptly. I think I've understood the teaching and can now feel relaxed. I am determined to become a brahmachari and dedicate my life, my energy and my love to Him, to the Divine. I recall how Christian nuns regarded themselves as the 'Brides of Christ' and I also feel like Babaji's spiritual bride now. Satya also tells me that she feels like Babaji's spouse, that is the spouse of God. When one loves God intensely it is not possible to also adore the physical form and difficult to give one's love solely to another individual human being. Only universal love is left, the same for all, the whole of humanity, men, women and children. Even in Italy I'd become tired of sex, of repeated physical contact, because it seemed so far away from real love. Also my relationship with Giuliano had become more and more spiritual, especially after our experiments together with LSD, when we both felt that the bond between us was beyond that of the physical body. Often we had lain down together, hand in hand, lost in unequivocal mystical visions. The meaning of life is beyond, in the realms of consciousness and of spirit.

3 July 1973

I am often terribly hungry, because we eat only once every 24 hours, no breakfast, no dinner, nothing to drink except fresh water. Babaji's sadhana is extremely rigorous, and even though on the one hand He emanates infinite love, He also demands tremendous effort and a high degree of renunciation from us. We need to learn to live with extremely little, our needs reduced to a minimum, just enough for our survival. He told us that He is giving us this training in order to prepare us for a future war, which will shake the whole world and only those people able to live on two pieces of bread and a few potatoes a day will survive.

In a country as hot as India, a person really requires very few essentials in order to live: one vegetarian meal a day, bread, rice, vegetables and lentils, two pieces of clothing to wear, a mat, a blanket, a lota, a water container - just enough to fulfil our bodily requirements. In fact, we don't have a bathroom, shower or toilet here but have to go down to the river to wash, and for everything else we squat among the stones. Cooking takes place outside on an open fire and we sleep on the floor, tucked up on a mat in any place we can find. There is no need for shoes, for it is better to walk barefoot, nor a suitcase because it's sufficient to wrap one's clothes up in a bundle. Mother India is a great teacher of simplicity. In fact, the essence of Babaji's teaching, which He often repeats to us, is these three words: Truth, Simplicity and Love.

4 July 1973

My mind fights with the mantra that Babaji has told me I should repeat twenty-four hours a day: Om Namah Shivaya, I bow to Lord Shiva. At times I feel that the repetition is too mechanical, a form of trickery, at other times I sense its powerful energy. My mind often reacts adversely against it, my thoughts still stronger than the mantra. Babaji admonishes me, saying in English: 'You repeat, repeat all the time.'

Lama Yeshe told me once that the most powerful mantra is the one without words, the silence of the mind. I know that's a very advanced stage to reach and then maintain, but it's a condition that can be arrived at by first using a mantra. Sometimes I rebel, it feels like a foolish game or a fairy story and I would like all the truth straightaway, all at once; but that is presumptuous of me. Also I don't like the endless devotional singing for hours on end, I don't find it pleasurable, but would prefer instead to close my eyes and meditate. After my experience of meditation in Nepal it seems to me that it is superior and much more beneficial than this ritual.

Then at other times I begin to comprehend the significance of the words of the songs and feel moved by the beauty and the melody of them. One chant in particular touches my heart: 'Oh Shankar, have pity, I am immersed in confusion and suffering, have compassion.' The Lama always spoke about taking refuge in the guru, or in Buddha; all experiments, more or less, lead to some sort of suffering, physical or mental, only through the grace of the guru can we be awakened to the knowledge of why self-delusion is the root cause of all of our unhappiness and ignorance. I have started feeling the importance of the guru, for as the scriptures say, we should take refuge in him because of our ignorance; alone we are unable to see, we continuously cheat ourselves.

The explanation is complex but both Indians and Tibetans believe in karma and reincarnation and according to this theory we keep dying and are reborn again in an infinite cycle, propelled by desires and by the actions we take, in order to satisfy them. We are reborn again according to our past deeds, or to complete a karma, in order to fulfil certain desires, but the action of karma can be seen as both positive as well as negative. The negative aspect always involves the creation of desires and their necessary fulfilment whereas karma can be positive whenever we act to obtain knowledge and liberation from karma itself. At the root of this process is our ego, our need for self-justification, which is the reason for the existence of samsara, the cycle of birth and death, but which in the ultimate analysis is found to be a creation in our own minds, an illusion, similar to that of a dream. The Master incarnates to show us the path to Truth and without Him we remain so entranced with the fantasy created by our own minds that it is impossible to escape from it.

Babaji is considered an Avatar, a divine manifestation. Sometimes I still have doubts about the reality of all these beliefs but at the moment I am following the path of my heart and I know that finally it's a question of faith, as every religion says. From faith, comes revelation, a profound, inner intuition. By now I have received so many magical signs and indications that it is difficult not to believe it is true. The greatest sign is the one Babaji demonstrates to me every day, reading all my thoughts, confirming exactly what my mind is thinking and knowing precisely how I feel at every moment. It is something far greater than rational communication, not just powerful telepathy: isn't it an extraordinarily elevated level of consciousness?

7 July 1973

Yesterday Babaji took me with Him together with a young Indian man, for a long walk. We finally arrived at what is called the old English bungalow, which has stupendous views overlooking the most beautiful part of the valley. Babaji had me stretch out a shawl on the grass and sat down with the young man and myself, looking very softly into my eyes. I felt completely innocent like a child, suddenly entirely quiet inside. I took the courage to ask Him why I should repeat the mantra all the time because it seemed to me like an artificial formula. He began to tenderly sing a song: 'The mantra is amrita, divine nectar, sing, sing, all the time.' I was overwhelmed by the presence of a delightful, transcendent energy and Babaji sang another song: 'One day even Indira Gandhi will go, but Gaura will remain here.' I feel more and more that I belong to Him and to the land of India.

Someone asked Babaji what His message was for the world and He replied: 'Truth, Simplicity and Love.' It seems like a very simple message but that is misleading because what is Truth, what is Love? Every philosopher and all the religions in the whole world have tried to answer these questions, humanists and utopians have attempted to create a society built on these principles, but it has proved to be an impossible task.

Babaji addressed me and asked if I had a degree in philosophy and with a certain pride I said, 'Yes'; to which He responded ironically: 'I am a boy from the mountains, without any education.' In India wisdom is not confined to the rational mind or intellectual knowledge but belongs in reality to the profound intuition of the soul. It is not uncommon to encounter sadhus who live a life of great simplicity but who nevertheless have perceived a sense of the ultimate, developing deep understanding through their practice of yoga. I remember Lama Yeshe saying to me one day in Nepal that when we Westerners talk about the mind we are referring to our heads while mind to a Tibetan means the heart.

Babaji - '…a monastic Japanese Zen Master…'

10 July 1973

Now I feel as if I am becoming a nun, wanting to renounce the ordinary world. Babaji too, with His shaved head, assumes the role of a monastic Japanese Zen

Master, very severe, even if He does play the jester and makes jokes sometimes. In my old life as a hippie I looked for truth through freedom, but now in this new stage of my spiritual life it involves discipline.

The monsoon, the rainy season, is about to start and we will have to go to Vrindavan because there are no rooms here in which to sleep. The day before yesterday it rained heavily for the first time and unable to sleep we huddled around the columns of the temple all night long, soaking wet and singing Om Namah Shivaya. The singing helped to keep us awake and induced a peculiar sort of excitement even if we were all soaked to the skin. It seemed like passing a devotional test. Babaji also had no proper protection from the rain in His little dhuni but people covered it as best they could with some sheets of plastic.

The valley is remarkable, the wind fierce and wild, with thunder in the distance, the river fuller, more turbulent, the current stronger. Last night it rained again and in preparation we had tried to make a temporary shelter in which to pass the night, but the rain came in anyway and we ended up lying in the mud. An elderly lady from Bombay kindly shared her raincoat with me. The weather is suddenly chilly, the mountains have taken on an air of foreboding and all the time the river is becoming more and more swollen.

Almora, 15 July 1973
Today I left with Babaji for Almora and He has arranged for me to spend a few days here at Tara Devi's house. She lives in a lovely place, a cottage built in the Swiss style by her husband, surrounded by a large garden. It's very comfortable and there is a cook and a gardener, I feel like a British colonial. I need to rest because recently I've felt quite weak. Tara Devi has a large library here full of religious and spiritual books, so I have the opportunity to read and study at my leisure, as well as learn more Hindi.

Almora is a town with an ancient spiritual tradition and in the past many saints and sadhus have travelled through here because it is on the pilgrimage route to the Tibetan Mount Kailash. Nowadays various teachers live in the town: lamas from Tibet, Lama Anagarika Govinda who comes from Germany and Shunya Baba who is Danish. Tara Devi knows them all very well and they often come to visit her in her house. She has had the acquaintance of many other gurus and saints over the years and has many interesting stories to tell. I feel at home here with her, she is like my spiritual grandmother, and by sending me here it is as if Babaji has given me a month's holiday from the hard sadhana at Hairakhan.

Experiences in Dina Pani

18 July 1973

Today I met up with Marco and Zizi, my old Italian friends, I can hardly believe it. Babaji is visiting Almora and they had come here to see Him. They were among the first pioneering Italians to travel overland to India on foot in the 1960's as an adventure. I first met Zizi in a small street in Brera. He was sitting on the pavement with dyed hair, dressed like a wild gypsy and with a ring in his nose. With him and Marco I sang my first Indian mantras while we wandered around the city, friends walking in the evening along the dark and misty streets of Milan and seeking like magical fireflies to bring a spiral of light into the gloom of the city, so dismal and distressing. It was due to the two of them that I discovered my first commune where we smoked and dreamt of India as well as of our hopes for the future.

Now they tell me that they are living in Dina Pani, a place in the jungle not far from here, where there are some huts and lovely natural caves in which various Western sadhus are living. I am already tired of my luxury cottage and extremely tempted to join them, so I ask Babaji if I can go there with them until He begins travelling again and He gives me permission.

Dina Pani, 25 July 1973

I have been in Dina Pani for a few days now and live in a small hut in the forest with some other Westerners who spend much of their time around an open fire: Sandro from Italy, Motima from Australia, Uma, an ex-photographic model from Holland, Shivji, a young man from China and Shambo from Canada. They live in the jungle like sadhus, covering their bodies with only a tiny piece of cloth, sitting around the fire-pit contemplating the flames and their minds. Two of them reside in small caves that have been carved out of the rock-face. Their way of life is extremely orderly and governed by strict rules of purity; waking up at dawn, taking a bath in the small river, lighting the fire and picking flowers for the first worship of the day. A mixture of tea, ginger and brown sugar is prepared but they do not eat or drink until first making offerings to the fire, which is considered sacred. They also smoke a ritual pipe together, accompanied by a simple prayer before meditating in silence, just watching the flames. A type of black bread and potatoes are cooked in the hot ashes and we collect vegetables from the chai-shop on top of the hill. Nearby, in a small but delightful lake we bathe naked, as innocent as children, without any sexual energy present at all, as if we were living together in the Garden of Eden. The atmosphere is tremendously pure, intense, like living on another planet.

They have given me a tiny hut in which to live, the most beautiful and civilized habitation of them all, but still only just large enough for my body; at night a small cat sleeps around my neck and they tell me that it's a protection against snakes and scorpions.

The pine forest all around is luxuriant and incredibly green because of the rainy season and the grass grows amazingly tall. We see snakes sometimes, but strangely enough I am not scared, whereas in my childhood I couldn't sleep if there was even a spider in my room. I'm told there are also tigers and leopards in the jungle, but I feel completely protected by Babaji.

We share everything that we have, like true brothers and sisters. These young people live a life that is angelic and transcendent and before now I would have been afraid to disturb the purity of this place with the presence of my female body, but I can see now that Babaji has brought about a profound purification of my energy through His sexual games in Hairakhan. My perceptions about sex have changed, it now seems something ridiculous to me, no longer necessary.

We eat very little, just one small meal a day, practising, like the Indian sadhus, detachment from the physical body, from hunger, heat and cold, sleep and all the other comforts to which we have become accustomed. I am enchanted and spellbound and have also given up wearing my sari and just drape a length of cloth around my neck sadhu style, just the essentials. At night I stretch out on a piece of matting, covering myself with my red, Tibetan blanket. If I feel hungry during the day I go to the chai-shop on the hill to drink a glass of fresh milk. Prem Singh, the old man running the shop has a lot of respect for us all and knowing we are looking for God and without money he often gives us flour and vegetables.

30 July 1973

At sunset today the Himalayas sparkled from the rain, set amidst large, red clouds; the whole of the countryside is rejuvenated, the fields bright, washed clean, made fertile by the monsoon. Flowers and vegetables grow quickly and to a gigantic size in this season and the cows give plenty of milk. It's a period of abundance in India, of water and greenness, and the Indian soil, soaked by the rains, becomes generous, nourishing everybody like a great mother.

At this time of the year yogis and sadhus enter into a meditative retreat, not emerging from their caves or huts for two or three months.

8 August 1973

The period of time I am spending here seems extremely important, particularly because it offers me the opportunity and space to practice meditation. I feel

79

Babaji's presence constantly with me, almost intoxicating, and other people here sense somebody near me as well; for myself, thinking about Him has almost become an obsession. Sometimes I feel as if He is entering inside me, like a penetrating light and I feel as if I am becoming at one with Him, it seems presumptuous but it is also my reality.

A few days ago Shankar arrived, a young Englishman and disciple of Nantin Baba. He also lives and dresses like an itinerant monk, a sadhu, with very long hair knotted on his head. He told us that Nantin Baba is a great yogi and a famous ayurvedic doctor who knows all the healing herbs, the natural medicines. He cures people of their illnesses most especially through diet. Shankar himself lives only on fruits and vegetables and prepares some delicious mixtures of potatoes and apples for us; the only strange thing is that on this diet Shankar is always hungry. Nantin Baba has remained in isolation and meditation in the forest for a number of months and Shankar has also undergone long periods of meditation in different places during the last three years. I feel he must have gained considerably from these experiences because there exists a special glow around him.

30 September 1973

My sojourn here at Dina Pani is about to end and so is the monsoon. The air is clear and fresh, the fields rich with crops and last night we saw the full moon surrounded by a rainbow halo in the autumn sky. I can certainly say that it has been a blissful time and I have learnt many things about sadhana and yoga, especially about simplicity. With these new friends I have experienced a wonderful sense of brotherhood and an unusual degree of purity and peace.

Tomorrow Babaji will come back to Almora and I am going to meet Him.

Almora, 5 October 1973

Babaji has returned to Almora and on the outward journey to meet Him I was overcome with emotion. I feel I have become more purified and am now more able to be with Him.

Today is Divali, the Indian festival of lights, signifying the beginning of autumn. We are with Babaji at Dhanyan, an old farm in the country and He instructs me to light bundles of candles for the occasion placed all around the courtyard. I am reminded of an old Indian song, 'Oh Sat Guru, please light in me the light from your Light.'

A Winter at Hairakhan

Hairakhan, 9 October 1973

Here we are again in Hairakhan, ready to face the challenges of winter. There are only a few of us but we will have to sleep in the open and the cold. Babaji has given me a big, black Tibetan blanket which is very warm and I am deeply moved by His concern.

At the present time I am the only woman as well as the only Westerner living here and once again I am doing all the kitchen work with the help of Prem Baba and Jaimal. During the day the weather is fine, but the nights are already quite chilly and so in the early morning and in the evening we warm ourselves up around the fire in Prem Baba's dhuni. Babaji's own small dhuni no longer exists any more and the beautiful mango trees have also been cut down. In their place a large kirtan hall is being constructed and for Babaji they have built a small room, a kutir, close to the peepul tree. It's a pity, Babaji's old dhuni was delightful, but now many more visitors are expected to come and extra space is needed for them.

Another Indian man has now come to live here permanently, Joshi Baba, a young engineer from Almora who has left everything behind to become a sadhu and stay with Babaji. He is continually in a state of trance or profound meditation and he even stops in the middle of eating in order to pray or lose himself in deep contemplation. Babaji has given him permission to remain completely naked, because he is as innocent as a child and completely unaware of his physical body. Often we sit together around the fire and he asks me if I can remain without any thoughts; one can see that he is trying hard to achieve that.

15 October 1973

In the evening Babaji plays a hilarious game. He calls for Joshiji to come to the kirtan hall and asks him to remove the piece of cloth covering his body and to stand naked in front of the crowd of people. Joshiji obeys Babaji with the innocence of a child while the Indian women and young girls laugh in an embarrassed group and Babaji looks around with a sardonic grin on His face. It reminds me of my nudist grandfather who used to walk around naked in our garden in front of the whole family in order to teach us about the naturalness of the human body. Joshiji is not really conscious of his physical body and at

81

times we see him praying for hours on end, standing naked in the river with clasped hands. He only speaks of God and seeks Him desperately.

24 October 1973

At dawn I watch the flashlights on the temple steps, people descending to or returning from the river, taking their baths in the darkness and the night-time mist as if participating in a secret ritual. I can hear Babaji singing softly while in the water. He is teaching us to be strong and after emerging from the river, He reappears with His body wrapped in a blanket. He emanates an aura of power and courage, encouraging us to overcome the natural elements, to be devoted to a superior energy.

The Hairakhan valley

25 October 1973

Hairakhan is completely different in autumn, so beautiful. After so many days of rain during the monsoon the mountains are emerald green, the sky is crystal blue and the river full of water. The air is exceedingly pure, fresh and stimulating and I don't feel tired the way I did in the heat of summer. Now one can enjoy the vibrational presence of the mountains and the crisp, cold mornings.

Babaji's behaviour has changed again, He is softer than before, more available, approachable and I feel that He is about to initiate a new year of training. I still have to work hard in the kitchen, cleaning and cooking, but I have come to take a pleasure in it. Through this work Babaji is teaching me to be a woman and mother, to serve others, nourishing them. He shows me Himself how to cook chapatis and from all the Indian people I am learning again and again about unconditional service.

It feels as if I am purifying a lot of my past karma, especially my laziness, my impatience and my selfishness. Babaji is a powerful Master, aware of all our inner changes and motivations, yet He primarily works with us through the daily actions of practical life, teaching us always how to keep our minds concentrated on the positive, on what we are doing.

He offers us the example of His own great strength, indifferent to heat and cold, detached from everything, the only clothes He wears being a woollen shirt and a blanket, no sweater. We see Him at three o'clock in the morning, jumping into the Gautam Ganga and sitting in the cold water for half an hour, whatever the time of year.

1 November 1973
Today Babaji came into the kitchen to cook and made a huge round chapati, creating a special kind of pizza with a mixture of everything, pieces of vegetables, spices and turmeric powder; it was delicious. Often during mealtimes He enjoys distributing halva, a sweetmeat, with His own hands, just like a generous, prosperous mother.

4 November 1973
We have been with Babaji to the top of mount Siddeshvar, the highest peak in the immediate area. Setting off in the afternoon we stopped to sleep the night at a farm about half way up. We all sat together around the fire in the small room feeling tired and hungry, except for Babaji who was full of energy, as always, His eyes full of light, sparkling, never sleepy. He continuously offers us love, without ever stopping, an inexhaustible source. We walked for many hours barefoot on the sharp stones both on our outward journey and the return, but one doesn't feel any pain or discomfort near Him, losing all sense of physical consciousness.

After reaching the top of the mountain we spent the whole night sitting around a roaring fire, wrapped in our blankets, with Babaji talking and joking with people all the time. At a certain point I suddenly visualized the whole scene as if it were many thousands of years ago, the great Guru Babaji in the forest with His disciples: it seemed like a distant dream.

15 November 1973
I am learning to obey, to say yes, even if I don't understand why sometimes, learning to trust Babaji, whatever He may ask for. Blind obedience can be a dangerous thing, of course, and I think of Hitler or the story of Charles Manson

in the United States: the followers of these individuals also had blind faith and obeyed them without question: isn't it our challenge to know how to discriminate, not to make the wrong decision? It is a difficult question, but I have decided to let my heart rule and trust my deepest feelings. I am reminded of some words from the New Testament, which say: 'By their fruits you shall know them.'

Babaji teaches us only Truth and Love and He harms nobody. Perhaps it is of little use to live this way, even Babaji makes jokes about this, calling Hairakhan the useless country, where useless people live in a useless village. We are not doing special things for humanity, in fact, we have withdrawn from the world, but we are going through an intense learning process, awakening our consciousness, going deep within our souls, seeking knowledge.

18 November 1973

Every morning and evening I am conscientiously meditating and in between am engaged in hard physical work during the day. The cold morning bath in the now icy river remains a great challenge, but immediately after emerging from the water I experience a wonderful energy in my body and while watching the stars I sing the mantra: Om Namah Shivaya, I bow to Lord Shiva. Babaji, I am in Your hands only.

Then, wrapped in a blanket, I climb the steps and sit at Prem Baba's fire-pit with a few other people. The mind is empty early in the morning, clear like the wind in the valley and I concentrate on the fire, the light the symbol of my soul, the flame that of devotion which I want to nourish in my heart.

Indians talk about the path of devotion as bhakti, the way of the heart, it being our love and longing for the Divine. The Indian tradition says that Shakti is proportional to bhakti, which means that we receive as much divine energy as the devotion we are able to develop. It seems that Babaji's path is very much based on this, on the capacity of the heart to surrender to the Divine, to love Him.

I feel that I am now facing a new fire of inner revolution and I am also aware that I can't resist any more. Babaji has probably manifested in such a beautiful form so as to attract us, to awaken our love and our desire to be with Him, slowly transforming our human love into Divine love, the love of God, as if the whole were an alchemical process, a gradual transmutation.

I now repeat the mantra all the time, not only while meditating, but also when I walk, work, eat or sleep. It's as if the magical charm of the words is taking possession of me, a special energy that I cannot identify, the spirit of Shiva, the great Master of Yoga, Guru of all gurus, Babaji.

1 December 1973

Now in the winter we often sit around the fire-pit and even the kitchen work is pleasant near the heat of the flames. During the day the tropical sun is very warm, as if it were springtime, but at night it becomes quite cold, the temperature dropping dramatically and sometimes I am unable to sleep.

Hairakhan reminds me of the mythical mountains of Shangri-La, as described in the old Tibetan books. As in the myth it sometimes appears as if this area is deserted, only inhabited by the wind and wild horses. The village people are different to those who live on the mountains, quite special, their thin bodies so dried up by sun and wind that they resemble ancient pieces of wood but they are nevertheless unusually strong. The women are particularly hardy and do most of the work. They are resilient and skilful, the epitome of Mother Earth and it is due to their hard work, their labour and effort, always carried out with great love and care, that they are able to offer us the food they produce. India, the mother, one of the poorest countries and yet the most generous one.

Yesterday Babaji saw that I was sleeping in the open, on the bare ground and He built a shelter for me with His own hands, using some pieces of material and bits of wood. He constructed it with fatherly love, an effective and simple design. Here in Hairakhan my relationship with Babaji has changed considerably. He is no longer a faraway statue, seated on a throne, adored by His devotees but impossible to reach. These days He participates in all our daily activities, with a touching humility, just like a dear, close friend, a God incarnated for us, sharing with us the human path and human difficulties.

3 December 1973

There are other people among the group of people living here in Hairakhan, who are teachers of simplicity and dedication, like Jaimal, a poor Brahmin who comes from Haldwani, the nearest town. He works all day long, serving everybody and doing the most humble tasks with happiness, with joy, always content and never asking anything for himself. He doesn't even have a sweater to wear when he works outside in the open and so I gave him a woollen one of mine, which he just wears around his shoulders as protection against the wind. A person like him is ready at any moment to jump into the fire for Babaji, for God. I am continually moved by the faith of these people and ask myself where such faith comes from. In this context the words from the Gospels inevitably come to mind: 'Blessed are the poor in spirit: for theirs is the kingdom of heaven.' It is ironic to experience all of this, particularly for a person like myself who has been brought up to be a complete atheist.

Babaji reminds me more and more of the image of Jesus, because of His simplicity, His teaching, His message of kindness and His daily sacrifice for us, even to the extent of how I imagined Jesus to look. Words and ideas that at one time I thought of as very banal, I now regard as true and see lived out in life.

Probably the original message of every religion is common to all, the meaning so simple and straightforward, but our sophisticated minds complicate everything, especially in the Western world. Our civilization, the one of blind materialism, of violence and of overpowering others through war, lacks discrimination. Here in the Indian jungle, I have found a corner of the world where peace and human love exist; it is real, lived every day, a spark of light.

'Babaji reminds me more and more of the image of Jesus...'

6 December 1973

We eat only one meal a day at lunchtime. Invariably I find this difficult and often feel extremely hungry. Sometimes, especially in the morning without having any breakfast, I feel faint and start to tremble, my legs beginning to shake. Today I spoke to Babaji and told Him how I felt, that I was feeling weak and His answer in response to me was that it's better if I feel weak, so that I remain quiet and don't become too excitable, running around aimlessly in circles: I know that I have to give up every desire. He gave me a small jar of honey and told me that I can take a little sip whenever I feel hungry.

Actually I have noticed that whenever I am around Babaji, a small morsel of food is enough to satisfy my hunger and removes my sense of tiredness completely. In the Indian scriptures there is a song which says that the guru's lotus feet are sacred, and that even by only seeing them and offering a prayer the human soul can resolve every problem and difficulty; it is enough just to take refuge at the feet of the Master and entrust everything to Him.

10 December 1973

Sometimes I feel a neurotic desire for food and it's not to do with hunger, it's something else, it's a strong attachment. Babaji called me over to Him yesterday and gave me a large bag full of cubes of white sugar, which I greedily ate all at once sitting on the riverbank. Afterwards I felt like a small animal, so stupid, weak, attached to a gross thing like food: in this sort of extreme situation we are abruptly confronted by our pettiness and sometimes our human desires can be extraordinarily intense and cause so much misery.

Swamiji, an old Indian man who has renounced the world to come and live in Hairakhan, teaches me Hindi every day and I am making progress. Hindi is a vibrant, musical language with a pronunciation similar to that of Italian and Babaji has a deep, guttural voice, warm, ancient and wise.

Some special Indian devotees now come regularly to Hairakhan, Muniraji from Haldwani and Shastriji, Babaji's elderly priest. They serve Babaji in every possible way, down to the smallest detail, accompanying Him wherever He goes, arranging an asan for Him to sit on, somewhere He can lie down and rest, cooking for Him. Babaji seldom eats, and then mostly fruits and vegetables, not eating any cereals as many Indian yogis do, and He doesn't drink tea or coffee, only pure milk.

In the evening, when everyone is singing in the main hall, I am permitted to sit alone in His room to meditate and later when He returns to His room to rest an Indian devotee massages Him with perfumed oil before it is time to sleep.

15 December 1973

Today at dawn looking down the valley at the first signs of pink light, with the smell of burning wood, the movement of the wind in the air and the only sound that of the tumbling water of the river, it all resembled a place so complete and ancient in its purity. It was as if time had stood still for two thousand years: ancient rituals repeated, archaic prayers chanted, eternal symbols.

Babaji has said to me that I have been with Him during many previous lives and tells me about periods of time I have spent with Him both in India and Tibet. On this particular occasion I reincarnated in the West in order to satisfy certain material desires, but now He has called me back home. In fact, I have virtually forgotten about Italy, all my friends, even my family, I feel as if I have died and been reborn again into a new life; but how long will it last?

One evening Babaji told us that He will not remain here for ever and that one day He will disappear into the jungle again, no longer visible to the public any more and who knows if He will take me with Him. He is also predicting that soon there will be wars and devastating catastrophes around the world and says that He is giving us a precise training for survival, teaching us how to live in a very simple way.

20 December 1973

Yesterday evening Babaji sat with us around the fire in Prem Baba's dhuni and offered us a drink of hot water with ginger together with some large pieces of jaggury to eat; it was intensely cold outside. He talked, joked a lot and recounted to us about the period when He had been in Tibet, describing that country to us in precise detail. He said that the Dalai Lama is the true incarnation of Buddha on this earth and that one day he will be able to go back to Tibet, the land of the gods.

Who really knows where Babaji actually comes from, where He was born? Nobody seems to know anything about Him and no one had ever seen Him before His unexpected appearance here. One day Tara Devi asked Him who His parents were and Babaji answered that every living being is His father and His mother. They tell me that Babaji is the immortal guru, the one of whom Paramahansa Yogananda speaks in his book, *Autobiography of a Yogi*. According to Yogananda, Babaji is a Mahavatar, a manifestation of Shiva Himself, the eternal Master of the Himalayas, who has taken a vow to always manifest a physical body on earth in order to help humanity. There is no need for Him to be born by woman because He can materialize a body through His own will when and however He chooses, and He is also capable of changing it or manifesting a number of different bodies at the same time. The Divine has no limitations and has complete power and mastery over the atoms and cells of material matter. According to tradition Babaji also brought to the world the technique of Kriya Yoga, the science of breath, and through its practice yogis have achieved immortality and all manner of spiritual realizations.

I read in Yogananda's book that on one occasion a disciple went looking for Babaji among the mountain peaks, but before accepting him Babaji asked the man to prove that he was worthy by jumping off a high cliff. The man jumped and died, only for Babaji to resurrect him, accepting him as a disciple because he had passed the test of faith and death. So a few days ago when I was walking towards Babaji in the garden I thought that I would ask Him if this story was true and if He really is the Mahavatar Babaji mentioned by Yogananda. Before I had time to even open my mouth to speak He told me to jump off the high garden wall. I didn't dare to do it, but understood that He had read my mind and that He had given me an answer to my question and confirmed His identity.

22 December 1973

Christmas is quickly approaching but it seems unimportant here in India. In the temple we usually only celebrate Hindu festivals like those in honour of Shiva or Krishna. However, Babaji told Tara Devi that He is at one with Christ and in *Autobiography of a Yogi* Babaji is described as the legendary Yogi-Christ of modern India, the one who can bring the spiritual message to the West. At the present time, other than Tara Devi, I am the only Western person living here, but Babaji has now told us that one day He will call many people to this remote place from all over the world and that He will construct many buildings here at Hairakhan: at the moment the prospect of that ever occurring seems quite unreal.

26 December 1973

Two Swiss people have arrived, a husband and wife with their young child. Babaji has named the woman Parvati, the Goddess of the mountain. She and I have become good friends, accompanying each other to take a bath in the river and working together in the kitchen. Babaji has arranged for them to live in a small abandoned hut in the village. Parvati is beautiful, strong, she does not suffer from the cold and gives me courage for the chilly morning bath in the river. She doesn't complain about the meagre amount of simple food available as I sometimes do. Growing up in Italy I was spoilt as a child and it's still hard to accept the changes in lifestyle here, it takes an enormous effort on my behalf to have to give up the many comforts that I was accustomed to before.

10 January 1974

Last night an incredible thing happened. I went to visit Parvati and her husband in their hut, they offered me a tablet of LSD and I swallowed the small pill without thinking. Its effect was particularly intense and I started to have a series of clear and colourful visions. After a while I experienced a strong sensation that Babaji was calling me. The time was exactly midnight and almost immediately I started walking back along the path through the village. When I reached His room the door was slightly ajar as if He was expecting me, so I went inside. Babaji was sitting on His bed wrapped in a blanket, facing the wall and in deep meditation. I sat silently on the floor and also began to meditate with my eyes closed. I started to pray to Him within myself, asking Him to reveal to me something of Himself, of His true identity. Then I opened my eyes and instead of Babaji's body I saw a huge circular rainbow on His bed, iridescent, blazing with light. I realized that this was the rainbow body of the Divine Beings as the Tibetan teachers describe it, the Essence of Babaji.

I was stunned by this vision. Slowly, I saw His body appearing, taking physical form again and then He stood up and started to put some wood on the fire, softly singing a melodious song. His voice was incredibly lovely, divine, and He smiled, looking at me with infinite love and tenderness, His eyes shining with light. He gestured for me to leave telling me to go for my bath and I went down to the river looking at the bright, winter stars, ecstatic, fulfilled, full of rapture.

15 January 1974

This morning I asked Babaji to give me an initiation and a personal mantra, a guru-mantra and He called me to His room this morning and gave it to me. Now I feel as if I am really His disciple, because I know that the bond between guru and disciple is unbreakable.

I want to prolong my meditations more and more, intensifying the practice, especially early in the morning. Now I can remain sitting peacefully for longer periods of time and sometimes I achieve a few seconds of complete silence in my mind, without any thoughts at all, losing consciousness of my body as well as consciousness of external reality. It is so pleasing to feel this ecstatic sensation in every cell of my body, like an electrical current. When I stop meditating and start walking outside it feels as if I could fly, my feet barely touching the earth and I have difficulty doing practical things. Yet I know that Babaji wants us to be fully aware of external reality, in contact with the earth, linked to the world, active in it, able to function on the human level as well as focus on the Divine. That's why He pushes us to work so much, to attain perfection in all that we do. He wants us to love each other, help others, be altruistic, serve all living beings. When I lived in the West I searched for love for so long, but only now am I beginning to discover it. The nature of my relationship with Babaji is elusive, not an easy thing, because of His purity and being so unattached. He doesn't seek love for Himself, is disinterested, but asks us to search for pure love, non-personalized, only love for Absolute Truth, love for the Divine.

1 February 1974

Babaji has invited everybody to Hairakhan for the first, grand, public fire-ceremony to be held here and people are coming from all over India. No accommodation is available so they are putting up large, military tents along the dry part of the riverbed, a huge campsite with open kitchens. Enormous numbers of people are arriving, including a number of sophisticated, wealthy Indians, elegant women dressed in silk, but they all fit into the tents without any complaint, happy to be with Babaji. He takes care of everything personally: food, transport, blankets, every single thing for our comfort, giving precise instructions with great authority. Everybody is running, eager to do their best for just one of Babaji's smiles; to receive a gesture of His love one is ready to do anything. It's a great collective effort, full of enthusiasm and joy. All the time people are shouting out to Him with one voice, 'Jai', victory, victory to the Divine in all His forms.

The first public fire-ceremony

In the evening the Indian people explode with devotional joy, singing and dancing ecstatically, glorifying in the presence of the Lord, adoring Babaji's beautiful human form. In my mind I inevitably compare this paragon with the Catholic religion which lacks warmth, is sadly so distant from the day-to-day life of the people, our churches cold and empty, dead like museums. In India religion is an integral part of daily existence, it's a celebration and expression of joy for the constant presence of the divine energy.

For the people of India it is quite normal to experience God on earth in a human form, and the Divine has manifested in this country in so many different forms: Shiva, Krishna, Ram, Vishnu, Buddha, etc. God comes on earth in a human form to help humanity to evolve spiritually and to restore the Dharma, the cosmic law, to offer liberation to human beings from the cycle of death and rebirth. People adore Babaji as Shiva Himself, ecstatic and fulfilled to be in His presence at His divine feet, happy to be participating in a mystical communion. I realize that the whole of life is a ritual for Indian people, from the moment they bathe in the morning, singing a mantra, right through until evening, by lighting a stick of incense and a lamp in their houses or by singing a simple prayer. It is ever present, even food is always offered to God before being eaten.

10 February 1974

The celebration is impressive, glorious, but simple. The food is distributed to everyone seated along the dry edge of the riverbed, served on large leaves, rice and lentils with spices and a delicious pudding with dark sugar. All the meals are free of charge and hundreds of people come from the nearby villages with their children. Babaji feeds everybody with immense love and people donate money quite spontaneously, which provides for all that is necessary, it's a natural exchange of energy. How wonderful it would be to live like this on earth all the time. Babaji is showing us a new possibility, a way of living life where everybody shares whatever one has to offer: money, work, spiritual or physical energy.

15 February 1974

Babaji is about to leave Hairakhan on a three-month tour to different places in India and I've decided to stay here to meditate, together with Prem Baba and Joshiji, the sadhu from Almora. I am a little scared and worried, because I have become so accustomed to His presence and energy, and I am afraid of being alone and isolated, even if I know that's beneficial for meditation.

The other day I asked Him if I could come in the evening and meditate with Him in His room. He told me that I could and to come at 2 o'clock in the night. So first I went to the river to bathe and then I entered His room where He was seated in meditation on His bed, as usual; it really seems as if He never sleeps at night. Babaji smiled and asked me in Hindi if I wanted to make love with Him. I was deeply shocked and surprised, because I thought the sexual games were over for good and I answered that I didn't want His body, I wanted His spirit. He appeared happy with my response and I felt He had given me a test which I had passed. Nothing happened between us and He told me that from now on I should meditate in the small room He had just finished building for me. I realized that I still have the desire to meditate in His company, but that this is an attachment and that I have to find God within myself, within my own mind when I close my eyes. In any case I am happy that I passed the sexual test. It makes me feel stronger, more purified.

18 February 1974

Before He left on His tour I asked Babaji again how I should meditate. He pointed to His forehead with His hand and then to His heart, saying: 'Slowly,

slowly, everything will come to your heart, you belong to Me.'

When He was about to leave, down by the river, I touched His feet for the first time. Never before had I dared to do it. They are soft, child-like feet, silky skin, strong and tender and I remembered the words of an Indian song: 'The Lord's feet are like a lotus flower and when we find His lotus feet, we finally find rest and the end of our journey.'

I know, Babaji, I am forever united with You, always in service at Your lotus feet.

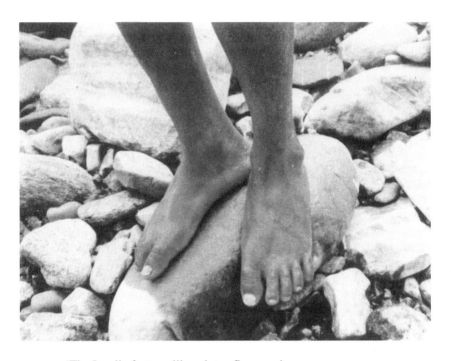

'The Lord's feet are like a lotus flower…'

15 March 1974

It's difficult to live here without Him, even if springtime has arrived once more and Hairakhan is warm again, full of flowers and with beautiful tropical birds singing in the early morning.

I now have a small room all to myself in which I can meditate, but I find it difficult to concentrate, my mind suddenly invaded with so many memories from the past, my life in Italy and my friends there. Yesterday was Shivaratri, the holy night dedicated to Lord Shiva, celebrated all over India with special rituals and prayers. Rather than fast and pray I greedily ate a lump of jaggury, which made me feel sick afterwards. I am restless and worried because to control my mind and eliminate my desires, which is what I want to do, is much more difficult than I thought it would be. It's a particularly difficult undertaking when my attachment to eating, to food, becomes very intense, as if food is the last hurdle to overcome, the last place the child can run to when all the other pleasures have been taken away from me. When Babaji is physically present, with His love, and my mind and all my attention concentrated on Him, it is much easier, but now so many past desires come to the surface again, violent and rebellious.

3 April 1974

It is my good fortune that Babaji has returned early from His travels but I felt embarrassed when I saw Him, feeling guilty, because I wasn't disciplined enough in my meditational practice while He was away. I haven't been strong and He looked at me as if He knew everything, sorrowful but with compassion.

Many people have arrived here and Babaji begins to be more widely acclaimed even if He never publicly demonstrates His power or performs miracles. There are many young Indian men here at present and Babaji takes them with Him when He goes to bathe in the river in the afternoon, as well as taking them for long walks in the hot summer sun.

Sometimes the Indian people are unkind towards me, treating me like a stranger, an intruder, as if I am an impure person, from the wrong caste, not knowing all the rules yet, not Indian enough. The other day the cook didn't want me to enter the kitchen and work there. I felt offended and protested to Babaji, wanting Him to feel protective towards me but He would like me to surrender, to be indifferent, while my nature has always been to rebel. I feel humiliated, isolated.

20 April 1974

Yesterday I had a wonderful surprise: my dear old Italian friend Dinni arrived unexpectedly. She came on a visit to India to try and discover where I had disappeared to and amazingly she discovered this place due to some magical coincidences, it is miraculous. I felt so happy and emotional to be able finally to talk with a personal friend in my own language and to be able to communicate the incredible experiences happening in my life.

Baba is incredibly kind to her and asked her to give a public speech and to dance. We talk for hours: in Milan we went through so many experiences together, going to university, involvement in politics, our first attempts at living in community. Like me she is also searching for something in India, something different not easy to find, but she is afraid of religion and mysticism even if she is fascinated by Babaji. She tries to convince me to return to Italy, to fight for change in the world there, but I tell her that first of all I want to change myself and go more deeply into this adventure of exploring consciousness.

Another person who is travelling with Dinni enquired of Babaji if she could ask Him some questions and to every question that she asked He replied that the answer resided within her own mind. She left the following day.

1 May 1974

Dinni left suddenly and I feel lonely again. Once more it's exceedingly hot and I find it difficult to remain here. Babaji is implacable, His training is hard for me, I still have to wash all the big pots and even go to the jungle with the Indian women to collect great sackfuls of clay. Yesterday I complained to Him, asking if I could have more time for meditation and He looked ironically at me: I know very well that I didn't meditate when I had the opportunity to do so. I have become restless, impatient and I am often obsessed by the desire for food, a kind of neurosis. When I am in this state of mind Babaji completely ignores me, keeping me far away from Him, while He plays the Indian prince with some elegant Indian women who are visiting. Sometimes I feel as if He treats me like the lowest of the low.

Okhaldunga, Madhuvan, Almora

Hairakhan, 1 July 1974

The summer is coming to an end and we've had the first signs that the rainy season is about to begin. Soon we will leave for Vrindavan because when the monsoon starts we have no roof over our heads to protect us from the rain here. Babaji jokingly told me that I would not be able to come but will have to stay in a little village in the middle of the jungle.

Okhaldunga, 4 July 1974

The rainy season has started and yesterday we were walking through the forest towards Haldwani when we stopped about halfway at Okhaldunga, a small village in the jungle and Babaji suddenly told me to stay here for an indefinite period of time. I'm to live in a little hut that is situated close to a tiny, deserted, old temple, dedicated to Devi, the Divine Mother, but which is unattended most of the time. He wants me to do sadhana here, spiritual practice, meditation.

So now I am completely alone, the hut is in ruins, and yet surprisingly, even though I can't close the door or windows of the hut I do not feel afraid. I want to practice my sadhana, want to become strong, and am determined to be successful because I have noticed how easily I become lazy and depressed every time I am left alone by myself. So I clean the small, abandoned temple and for a short time every day I worship there using flowers and incense.

15 July 1974

Yesterday evening a big snake appeared on my open window, but after a few minutes he left of his own accord. When it rains, water pours in through the leaky roof and I have to sleep on the wet floor. But I have started to learn how to collect the rainwater in various metal tins and receptacles so that I can make use of it for cooking and so on. If it pours with rain I'm able to take an improvised shower by simply standing outside the door. Just as it was in Dina Pani I buy flour, potatoes and lentils from the local chai-shop and live on that. The village is extremely poor and the shop has very limited supplies. Sometimes I console myself a little with large pieces of jaggury.

Meditation is still not easy for me, the mind refusing to concentrate;

sometimes I look at the lights of the town shining in the distance and I would like to be there, in the midst of people and nice things, have the consolation of being with other human beings, but probably that's just another attachment.

Vrindavan, 5 August 1974

I became tired of my seclusion and have run away to Vrindavan to meet up with Babaji, but He is inflexible and wants me to continue my practice. He is sending me to meditate in another isolated village called Madhuvan that is not far away. It's an extremely ancient place dedicated to Lord Krishna and his beloved Radha.

I just didn't seem to be able to carry out my practice well in Okhaldunga. Every time I find myself removed from Babaji's presence I become lazy, depressed and my mind won't stop; it is a weakness of mine and I know that Babaji wants me to become strong and independent.

Madhuvan, 7 August 1974

The village here is built around a small lake surrounded by deep steps leading down to the water. The villagers use the lake for everything: they bathe there, wash their clothes and utensils, linger to talk and the children play in the water.

It's an ancient, rural place, exceedingly poor, dusty but very charming, situated on a vast plain, the flat landscape broken up here and there with centuries-old trees. The low houses are made of mud and in the nearby scrub land there are a few small, old temples.

There is also an ancient temple dedicated to Babaji, as well as a dhuni which I have been told has had a fire burning in it for hundreds of years. In the morning I help the local pujari to clean and prepare the temple, then for the rest of the day I am able to sit alone in the small room they have given me there.

15 August 1974

The monsoon is quite intense and the surrounding arid plains begin to come to life again, becoming green. At sunset the clouds are red, full of rain; and I observe a long line of cows and buffaloes accompanied by some women, walking slowly, coming back home to rest.

It's as if time has stood still here in India, each and every day life repeats itself, the same gestures, the same rituals and values. While this can offer a sense of security, an eternal continuum, a part of me is restless and wants to run away from it all. So many memories from my life in Italy resurface again and again in my mind; I have always been a highly motivated and mobile person, involved in the activities of society, so where am I going now? Maybe I should think only of God, I know I ought to repeat the mantra and pray, but where has my sense of humanity gone? Perhaps it is necessary for me to renounce even that, maybe all this is beyond me if everything in this life is Maya, illusion, attachment, but it's so hard.

1 September 1974

Yesterday Babaji came to visit me, accompanied by Swami Kapoor, a famous actor in Indian cinema. Whenever I see Babaji I always feel very emotional. His form is so attractive and every one of His gestures, the way He walks and talks, expresses beauty, perfection, harmony. When He left here the villagers gave Him a large bundle of peacock feathers and He walked away like the young L rd Krishna described in the legends as seductive, mysterious but elusive. Suddenly I felt so distant from Him, an incalculable distance, suffering such an acute pain of separation from a being who I cannot hope to know and understand, and with whom it's not even possible for me to really speak or communicate with clearly. Yet I feel the pain of love, a love-sickness, an immense yearning, distressing yet all-consuming.

Almora, 5 September 1974

The other day, while still in Madhuvan, I had a dream in which I saw Babaji telling me to leave immediately, because the police were after me, since I am travelling without a visa. So I packed my things and left and later on I found out that the day after the dream the police had in fact come, looking for me. I went directly to Babaji in Hairakhan but He sent me away again. He told me I must now go to Dina Pani to continue my meditation practice. I must remain on my own and I have no idea how long I will have to stay there. Babaji told me that I should not go anywhere else, not even come to Hairakhan, until He writes to me. I should meditate, He said, for 14 hours a day and do exactly what He had told me to do before. I'm not allowed to write to anybody, I can't see or speak to anyone, I'm not even allowed to read anything: it is like being in a spiritual retreat.

He told me all this after calling me to His room after aarati on the evening prior to my departure. He was lying on His bed, His face very close to mine, and He was beautiful, like an ancient god, full of love and compassion, emanating divinity from every cell of His body. He asked me if I would prefer to go to Italy for a while, or be alone in the jungle for an indefinite period of time and I told Him I was ready to do anything in order to be able to remain in India with Him. So then He told me that I must first go to Almora by foot, as if on pilgrimage and He sketched a map, showing me the route to take along footpaths.

6 September 1974

I have arrived in Almora after three days of walking barefoot, carrying my luggage on my shoulders. I know this has been a tremendous test of strength and determination for me.

By the evening of the first day after many hours of walking, I had reached the small town of Bhimtal and fortunately I was able to sleep in a Government Guest House. On the second day the path seemed never-ending and I had no idea where I would end up or if I would ever arrive there. Night came and darkness fell without me seeing any sign of a village, then suddenly I saw some lights and a few houses. A farming family welcomed me into their home with much love and gave me food and shelter in a hut. I discovered their family had been devotees of old Hairakhan Baba for many generations in the previous century. On the third day I reached Mukteshvar, so high up in the mountains I could see the snowy peaks of the Himalayas shining majestically in the winter sun. Then, slowly, I walked down towards Almora, tired and exhausted. By the time I reached the town my feet were aching and were badly swollen, but I felt brave and courageous, as Babaji had wanted me to be. I had made it.

Dina Pani, 25 November 1974

I have been living here for about two months now and have not felt much like writing any more, rarely using pen and paper. Except for a break at lunch-time I sit for many hours each day trying to repeat the mantra, to control my mind, but it's so difficult.

I wake up at 5 o'clock in the morning and make a small fire in my room. Next I take a shower using a bucket of water taken from a small, nearby spring opposite the entrance to my hut and afterwards sit to meditate. It is now possible for me to sit perfectly still, not moving for three or four hours. Then I have a break, drink a glass of milk, wash my clothes, clean my hut, or I might collect some wood from the forest. For lunch I cook chapatis, rice and lentils on the fire, my only food, taken once a day. I am determined to become detached from my desire for food and so I am trying to eat the minimum amount necessary for survival. After lunch, I rest for a short time, then in the afternoon study Hindi from a grammar book I brought with me, before meditating again for the rest of the day until sunset. Sometimes I go to the local shop to buy some provisions or take a walk in the forest. In the evening, as it begins to get dark, I re-light the fire and sit contemplating the flames and of course, myself. It's a very regular routine that I follow, this sadhana of mine, my spiritual practice and discipline, but I do find it hard going.

Solitude is the most difficult thing for me to cope with, not being able to talk to anyone, as I've always been used to the company of many friends in my life. Also the desire to eat good things is still quite a challenge. Sometimes I don't want to wake up early in the morning, or I feel too cold because Babaji has forbidden me to wear any woollen clothes, and I can only smear my body with ashes from the fire. Even so the most exacting thing remaining for me though is the challenge to control my mind. I force myself to repeat the mantra, but my useless thoughts are stronger than the mantra: past memories, my friends, life in the West, fantasies about my future, remembrances and nostalgia for Babaji who I miss so much. I miss His presence, His love.

3 January 1975

Sometimes I become extremely restless and think that I am going mad, but at other times I feel a peculiar calmness inside, very quiet and content. At sunset I sit in the doorway of my hut which overlooks a beautiful, green valley. I look at the cultivated terraces, the enormous leaves of the banana trees, the monkeys and the lovely mountain women who I can hear singing in the fields. I wish I could be like them, simple, without any complicated thoughts. Nature is perfect, a mystery of creation, a miracle expressing the vitality of life.

Quite suddenly, at unexpected moments, I experience a sensation of deep peace, as if I'm held in the hands of God. I know I am a soul that belongs only to Him, that I should just surrender, have faith, let go of everything, let go of myself and my petty desires, not wish for anything.

Often my meditation becomes just this kind of contemplation: I look at the rocks and the empty vista before me and I become so immobile that lizards walk over my body. I observe my breath, this simple movement of life, I watch my mind and my heart sings a song: a song to Him, to the guru, to my Lord, to Babaji. This experience of solitude is making me more receptive to His presence.

A leopard came yesterday to drink some water from the small spring in front of the hut and we looked into each other's eyes, but I wasn't afraid at all. I am not scared of death either, it's another step on the path. When I walk barefoot in the forest I feel my body becoming at one with the grass and the pine trees, without any sense of separation. I have seen snakes as well and I wasn't afraid of them either, they are beautiful, a part of the whole.

4 March 1975

For the last few days I have been stubbornly meditating for long periods. I want to experience something that will be able to break through this dark veil that remains inside me when I close my eyes, I would like to know the mind's great secret. On a small number of occasions the darkness disappears and I can see a blazing light dissolving into circles of perfect colour. I can hear a wonderful, subtle melody inside me that is blissful, and I hear a voice talking clearly to me, becoming at one with my own consciousness and awareness: me and Him, Baba, at One for ever. Whenever I am able to make myself empty I receive His energy, His will.

It's so difficult though, so tiring to always maintain this state of being, and the greatest obstacles to this are my laziness and a tendency to remain in ignorance and darkness as if heavily asleep; it's like an obscure but inherent drowsiness that resists any attempt that is made to break through the cycle of inertia, any movement towards the light. Now I understand why Babaji always pushes us to wake up and wants us to carry out a lot of physical work, so as to break out of our inertia, to remove our resistance and the fear surrounding us. It takes so much effort to reach the light, because matter has to be consumed in the fire of transformation and only then will the flames of change emerge, giving us strength, energy and illumination. In India this spiritual practice is called tapasya: they say that when a person burns with the fire of devotion, is consumed by it, a new being is born from the ashes, a light being, reminiscent of the myth of the phoenix.

Hairakhan, 3 May 1975

I am with Babaji again in Hairakhan, after almost one year of seclusion. The period of retreat, of being a recluse, is over: it has been an arduous phase but extremely important.

A huge festival is being celebrated at Hairakhan and Babaji makes me dance again and again in front of the crowd, telling people that I am Mirabai, a well-known devotee of Lord Krishna from the past.

I feel light, lost in Him, only He exists for me now, an intoxicating

Presence. Babaji is considerate, gentle, caring towards me and now He doesn't make me carry out heavy work. There is a large contingent of Indian devotees here accomplishing all kinds of tasks including a number of women who have undertaken to take care of the work in the kitchen. I watch them: they are graceful, motherly, harmonious, full of spontaneous love and affection, accepting their role of housewife and mother quite happily, unlike women in the West who rebel against this role. For an Indian woman doing housework, caring for the family, their children and their husband is accepted without any complaint. To serve the husband is a sacred undertaking in India, the wife regarding him like a guru, with dedication; in the past women even threw themselves onto the funeral pyre of their husband when he died.

Almora, 6 July 1975

I am passing the long period of the monsoon in Almora, spending a short time meditating in my hut before exploring a little then staying at Tara Devi's house where I am in contact with many people. No longer a recluse any more I read books, meet people and study Indian culture, slowly understanding and merging myself in a way of life so diverse and different from Western civilization.

The rhythm of life is slow here, calm, linked to daily activity, a ritual in itself but always the same. It's as if people live their lives waiting, but for what? They watch their appropriate destiny unfold, it being determined firstly through their birth, then their caste, then marriage, which is always decided by their parents. For them the ultimate reason for their existence on this earth is not the material life, it is beyond life on earth, beyond life and death; they believe that in this world we are only temporary travellers who have come to purify some karma, it is a place to pass through, a purification.

I am slowly getting used to becoming like an Indian woman, very unlike my life in Italy when I was always extremely busy, a young activist frenetically involved in politics and in all types of social activities, searching for romance and human love. Now it is so different, it feels as if I have become a nun who has renounced the world and most particularly the idea of having a husband, or a partner. It is the furthest thing from my mind now; Babaji has become my divine, spiritual Love.

Benares - Assam

Benares, 15 October 1975

I am living under a peepul tree on the banks of the Ganges in the city of Benares, regarded as the most ancient and sacred city in India and I've just met two young Italian men. Babaji is travelling again so in the meantime I have decided to make this pilgrimage.

I am sick, with terrible diarrhoea and I feel so terribly weak, as if I could die at any moment. Every few minutes I have to go to the bathroom. Very slowly I walk along the small streets that lead to the ghats, the steps leading down to the river's edge, where they also cremate the bodies of the dead. Here death is accepted and displayed in front of all and everyone, while in the West we try to hide it, to reject it. In India death is considered part of a natural cycle and in any case people believe in reincarnation.

In the evening many sadhus come to the burning-ghats to meditate at the smouldering fires of the dead, to contemplate impermanence, the frailty of the body; some smear their bodies with the ashes from the funeral pyres. Pilgrims come to Benares from every part of India, many wanting to die here because tradition has it that if one dies in Benares one receives liberation. They sit near the river, waiting, and the narrow streets leading down to the ghats are lined with sick people.

When a body is carried down to the Ganges people sing a song: 'Only Ram's name is real'. The smell of the burning dead bodies is mixed with the odour of wood-smoke, incense, spices, cows and fried food. People take baths in the river without paying any attention at all to what is floating on the water: charred wood and debris from the funeral pyres, dead animals, rubbish, devotional offerings. Even so I am very moved by the sight of men and women standing in the Ganges with linked hands, offering the water of the river as a prayer to the Divine and to the Sun. The whole scene makes my head spin, I feel dizzy and I am reminded of Dante's Purgatory. I feel nauseous, have stomach pains and cramps and begin to think that maybe I'll also die here in Benares, I don't care about anything any more. Maybe then I'll really experience union with Babaji.

I am tired of being separated from Him, the whole situation causes me so much pain, especially on an inner level. He pushes me to succeed with the meditation but I find it too difficult at the moment, even though it is the only thing that interests me, the only thing that makes sense. I realize that this is the way I can reach God, but the path is too hard and solitary. Although I know that one has to be ready to sacrifice everything for the Truth, will I ever have the strength to do it?

Vrindavan, 10 January 1976
Babaji is taking me with Him on a long journey to Assam, on the border with China. I told Him that it would be dangerous for me to travel to a border area without any visa or passport but He answered me: 'Babaji is the supreme Governor of the whole of India,' and so everything will be fine.

Assam, 16 January 1976
It has taken three days to get here, travelling by train in a third class compartment sitting cross-legged on some wooden benches. Babaji and a few other people travelled in a more comfortable compartment. In India I am learning to become patient, learning to repeat the mantra everywhere, in every situation, observing my mind. Sometimes my legs were so painful and I looked out from the window onto the immense, dry Indian landscape passing me by. The distances are enormous, the view monotonous, always there are people walking, it is the same everywhere, like industrious ants fighting for their daily existence, for survival. This land of India resides in my heart now, it has become the rhythm of my thoughts, slow, nostalgic, contemplative.

People in Assam are very kind, oriental-looking, the women extremely graceful and they sing some particularly beautiful songs for Babaji. They invite me into their houses as if I am a special guest and ask me how it was possible that I came to meet Babaji. They are surprised that I travelled here from so far away. I answer them that I don't really know myself how it all happened, just that His Grace called me away one day from the greyness and dullness of the world I was living in.

We have been to visit an ancient Mother temple dedicated to Kamakhya Devi, near the Brahmaputra river. It's a mysterious, underground place, dark and almost frightening, smelling of old butter, oil lamps, food, dried flowers and various other offerings. I find that I don't get very excited about visiting these temples, it is only Babaji that interests me. He is a living God, who talks to me and teaches me something, but the immense faith of these people also gives life to these stones, these images.

105

Return to Hairakhan

Hairakhan, 15 February 1976

Malti, a German woman, has arrived in Hairakhan. She was only going to visit for a short time but has now decided to stay for longer and so now there are two of us Western women here. She is very spiritual and sensitive and has written a book about sacred dance; she is beautiful, reminding me of a Flemish Madonna. Babaji gives her a lot of attention and for the first time I feel jealous, because I think she is more mature than myself, more ready for Baba, closer to God. I always feel immature, childish and unworthy. Malti sits close to Babaji as if she were with her best friend, whereas to me He appears predominantly like a severe father figure.

25 February 1976

Today I came across Malti pale and shaking, because Babaji has told her to leave immediately, throwing her luggage into the riverbed. I asked her why this has happened, but she has no idea. Maybe she has become too proud of the attention that Babaji has given her, of all the importance. Maybe she has become too attached to Him. Who knows the answer? I watch her leaving with tears in her eyes.

Babaji is a severe teacher, sometimes extreme in His methods and He reminds me of a Zen Master: the sort of person who might occasionally and unexpectedly beat a disciple with a stick in order to swiftly shatter a mental block.

10 March 1976

We have had a mild winter and it has been even more relaxing because we have rooms in which to sleep and protect ourselves from the cold. Babaji has initiated a grand building programme and all the time He is busily occupied checking all the work is being carried out properly, the placing of every single stone. His body has become stronger, more male, more human.

This afternoon I watched Him from the steps leading down to the river. He sat in an open space down by the riverbed, crouching beside a German woman who has recently arrived, teaching her how to paint. Sitting like a magical child in the warm winter sun, He is able to transform the energy around Him with just a simple gesture of His hand or a single word.

Sometimes He shouts at the Indian workers and then He becomes transformed into someone powerful, full of authority. He has knowledge about every single task that is being undertaken here, not least being an extremely able and precise architect; He is a perfectionist.

Fire-ceremony near the peepul tree, Muniraji (right), Shastriji (standing)

Ranikhet, 16 April 1976
Muniraji, a long time and close devotee of Babaji has built a place for Him near Ranikhet, high up in the mountains among the foothills of the Himalayas, at an altitude of 1800 metres, and we have come here for the inauguration, guests in Muniraji's house.

Last night, in front of a large crowd, Babaji gave a public speech saying that Muniraji· is a great saint from the past, a guru and He now wants all of us to pranam to him and show him respect. Strangely enough, only his wife refused to bow down. Babaji also said that Muniraji is a greater person than Lahiri Mahasaya, who is referred to in Yogananda's book, because he has been with Baba for many lifetimes, while Lahiri accompanied Him for only a few days and He added that Muniraji was an important Tibetan Lama in his last incarnation.

From Ranikhet one can see the snow-covered peaks of the Himalayas, even as far as Tibet and Nepal and Babaji is planning to build a large temple here.

The mountain people are special in this area. They resemble Tibetans, ancient, strong, traditional people and their hospitality is beyond imagination: they will always offer a person shelter in their homes. The guest is considered sacred in India, because people believe that anyone who comes to their door could have been sent by God, or even be a manifestation of God Himself. In their houses one is received by a warm, motherly embrace and the older women are the most delightful ones, like Muniraji's mother, an old, amusing and wise mountain woman. In this part of the world women know the art of living, how to nourish their children and sustain life itself, how to make the best use of the food available and to cure with herbs, the natural medicine. They understand magic, how to work with and transform subtle energies.

I feel protected and loved by them, because to them I am Gaura Devi, the 'white goddess', the name Babaji has given me.

Almora, 3 July 1976

Once again I am spending the period of the monsoon in Tara Devi's home in Almora and my sadhana is becoming easier, daily a more peaceful routine. My aberrant mind has begun to surrender.

I am pleased to be in contact with my parents again and they are now sending me some money regularly from Italy, partly because they understand that I am not about to give up so easily on this path I have chosen.

Meditation has become easier as well and I am beginning to meet more people again. I exchange news with them, especially sharing information about Babaji, repeating again and again the effect of this incredible, divine experience upon me.

1 August 1976

Yesterday the police arrived here in order to check my documents and by doing so they discovered that I have remained here in India for four years without any visa or passport. They intend to arrest me and put me in jail unless I leave the country immediately.

I cried desperately for one hour, the idea of being separated from Babaji is utterly unbearable. I am praying to Him so earnestly in order that He might help me, to bless me, to make it possible for me to remain with Him.

Return to Italy

Delhi, 7 August 1976

I have travelled to Delhi to find Babaji and He told me not to worry but that I should only speak the truth, both to the police and to the Italian embassy and so I did. I arranged an appointment at the embassy and told them all about my situation, that I have lived here a long time without any documents and that I want to spend the rest of my life in India with my guru. I said that I was even prepared to go to jail for this, because my life no longer had any meaning without Babaji and even in jail I can repeat the mantra. They seemed visibly moved by my sincerity, gave me the necessary papers which will enable me to travel, together with a plane ticket to leave the country, which then must be reimbursed from Italy.

I returned to Babaji again full of anxiety: what will happen now? When will I be able to come back to Him? Once again He told me not to worry, that I have His blessing and assured me that when I do return to India it will be with a permanent visa. He took me to one side alone with Him and said in a very loving way that I have been with Him during many past lives and that I belong to Him. He added that I may have forgotten my past, but that He remembers it all and that in the future nothing and nobody will be able to take me away from Hairakhan. I myself will want to go away, but I'll not be able to.

I asked Him what I should do in Italy in order that I may return and He answered me very calmly that I should just wait with full faith, everything will happen by itself. He also said: 'Do everything without any selfish purpose, only for Me, and then the world will appear to be just like a game for you.'

I am leaving with much hope in my heart, knowing I have another test to overcome, but to be so far away from Him is so painful, I love Him immensely. At the time of my departure, He said: 'I am coming with you.'

Milan, October 1976

I have met up with Piero and Claudio, who I travelled to India with originally. They are in Milan and have opened a Tibetan Buddhist centre. I have left my parents home and have come to stay with them, taking refuge here and helping them out. They have both become monks and are following a similar path to myself. We are living like brothers and sister, trying to organize lots of events and making contact with old friends who have also discovered a spiritual path.

The political situation in Italy has become rather unpleasant. The upper middle class became quite scared of the students as well as the hippie movement and they have imposed a thick wall of protection around themselves for their own sense of security. There exists a real tension on the streets of Milan and one can't easily walk around wearing strange clothes. I also had a tattoo applied to me while I was in India and people look at me strangely but I don't care. The hippies and warriors have disappeared from the streets and people go to work, running, with fear, with a hard heart, interested only in money, once more dressed in grey. The streets in Brera are empty and now they are building elegant restaurants there; Milan appears sad again, a dark place, black. Of the flower children only a few deluxe boutiques remain, selling expensive, colourful clothes. Cheap restaurants don't exist any more, it's difficult to meet up with people on the streets or in the communities, the bourgeoisie have stifled it all, closed everything down.

The only new things to emerge are the spiritual groups like our own, and now the message is more obscure and occult but much more meaningful. It's an inner quest, to study spirit, in order to really change the individual human being before being able to change the world. We invite everyone to our Buddhist centre; the house is open for dinner, meditation groups and those willing to help with the work. Translation has begun on the first Buddhist texts into Italian and we are also writing articles, spreading our new message.

We are organizing the first Buddhist meditation course to be held in Italy and Lama Yeshe and Lama Zopa will come here from Nepal. I can hardly believe that I will be seeing them here, a part of the Himalayas in our Western world. I recall Lama Yeshe's last words to me when I was leaving Nepal: 'Remember that we will always be together.'

I have worked hard in helping to prepare everything: cooking, cleaning, translating, making telephone calls and I feel so happy. Claudio told me: 'I don't know who this Babaji is, but I thank Him that He has been able to transform you like this.' He's been impressed that I can work so hard now and really enjoy doing it.

Many people have booked to attend the course, more than one hundred. I don't know what it is that attracts all these people to Eastern religion, probably the frustrating nature of life in the West and the apparent impossibility of finding any answers to the many inner questions from the Catholic religion.

12 December 1976

A large place called 'il Macondo' has been rented in Milan for the occasion. It is where many religious groups now meet including a Rajneesh group, the Hare Krishna movement and followers of Shiva and the Buddha. The mixture can be confusing, but it's the beginning of a spiritual search, the start of an alchemical process, and one day, from all these many elements a new way of living will emerge. I remember Babaji saying that His movement was going to become a large, international, underground movement.

Lama Yeshe tells me that one of the biggest misunderstandings in the West is about tantra. The purpose of tantric practice in the yogic tradition is to utilize human energies and transform them. People often seem to think that we can continue to indulge in our unconventional lifestyle and call this a tantric way of living, but tantric practice is an extremely serious yoga, a way to quickly purify us from our illusions.

27 December 1976

I have been here for a few months now and have just celebrated Christmas with my parents and grandparents. While they were all involved in the festive celebrations I went and switched on the television and glimpsed a documentary showing pastoral scenes from India which made me feel acutely nostalgic. After living in India for five years, returning to live in Italy is like entering a completely different dimension. I'm no longer able to enter into it with the same passion or desire as before, in fact the game that is played out here seems particularly sad and confused, full of suffering. Only the existence of the Divine gives life any meaning. I no longer feel able to participate in anything that I did before, like chatting with friends, going to watch stupid movies at the cinema or on TV, eating in restaurants or looking for romantic adventures and because I am now vegetarian even the smell of fish and meat disturbs me. Also it no longer seems important to be dressed in elegant clothes or to take care about the way I look and I have no desire to have my own home.

It was fortunate that I met Piero and Claudio. Ours has been the generation of pioneers, discoverers, the revolutionaries and spiritual seekers. I see that some of our old friends have continued with their political activities even to the extent of being involved in terrorist groups, while others have lost themselves in drugs, some addicted to heavy drugs. Other people though, like ourselves, have followed the path to India to seek out a teacher and embark upon a search for the spiritual life. When we meet now we exchange experiences and are united again through a new and different outlook on life that has filled us with an enthusiasm for living. We have discovered an answer, a meaning for our existence, and have seen light emerging from the darkness of our minds and out of the confusion of city life.

Pomaia, 15 July 1977

I have been to London for a few months, living in Tiziana's house and doing many different jobs in order to survive: working as a waitress, in factories, in a large hotel. London is an open-minded, uninhibited city and it has been a fascinating experience for me, plus I have improved my English.

Now Piero, Claudio and Massimo have found a wonderful place in Tuscany, in the countryside, where they want to organize a Buddhist centre. It's a beautiful old house covered in greenery, with gardens and a view of the green, sunny hills of Tuscany. The house is very large, with a tower as well as small rooms for meditation. People are carrying out building work, cleaning, generally organizing the place and have developed a dynamic and enthusiastic group energy.

25 July 1977

We have organized a course in Tibetan Buddhism to be held here at Pomaia in Tuscany. Lama Yeshe and Lama Zopa are coming again from Nepal and it's going to be a great occasion. We are setting up this place as an experimental community, incorporating the principles of spiritual discipline and I sincerely hope the experiment will work.

25 September 1977

Lama Yeshe and Lama Zopa have come again from India, bringing with them a huge golden statue of the Buddha. Lama Yeshe always remembers me from the time I spent with him in Nepal and he is like my second guru. I learnt a great deal from him, in a more intellectual way than with Babaji and this was an essential preparation for my mind. He resembles Babaji inasmuch as he also emanates an incredible love, a warmth emerging from the centre of the heart, overflowing with light, wisdom and bliss.

It is easy for me to accept and integrate the philosophies of both Babaji and Buddhism because they both propose the science of Yoga, the knowledge of the mind. They teach detachment from the material world, the path of Dharma, which is the eternal religion of humanity. Since I met Babaji I am no longer interested in having a relationship with a man any more, it is as if my relationship with the guru and the Divine has become the centre of my life. Our relationship with the guru is the purest expression of love and begins when we are able to detach ourselves from our selfish human needs. The guru offers divine love, the love for God.

The meditation courses in Pomaia have been very successful, with so many people opening to the presence of the Lamas, receiving their ageless wisdom and experiencing their energy; a spiritual nectar which emanates from them, a subtle essence that is indefinable. We opened the centre with a grand inauguration ceremony. I organized a group of young women to dance in front of the golden statue of the Buddha and enjoyed cooking for more than one hundred people.

Also, quite miraculously I have managed to obtain a new visa so that I can now return to India. While I was in London I married an Englishman, which entitled me to receive a British passport and with which I can stay in India indefinitely. On the same day that I received all the necessary paperwork a letter from Babaji also arrived telling me that He is expecting me: one of His magic tricks.

Milan, 30 December 1977

I am leaving for India with three Italian men, Settimo, Paolo and Filippo together with their girlfriends. We are the first Italian group to go and see Babaji. During the period of time that I have spent in Italy I contacted many people and spoke to them about Him. It gives me immense joy to have been a link and an instrument in His work. The West has great need of the message contained in Eastern spirituality, the path of self-knowledge that is taught by the Indian and Tibetan masters. This is the change yearned for by the human soul and the only hope left to bring about real transformation in the world, a unique possibility for self-realization, to understand the meaning of life and to change society for the better.

When I was younger I always dreamt of a revolution in the West and used to think that this could come about through politics, but now I realize that a profound inner revolution needs to take place within each one of us before there can be lasting change externally. The two run in parallel and both are necessary if we are to create a positive way of living, as well as truth and happiness on our planet. I am reminded again of the slogan of the 1968 revolution in France, which stated: 'The revolution will be total, or it will not be.'

At Hairakhan Again

Hairakhan, 5 January 1978

After more than a year away in Italy I have returned to Hairakhan, to Babaji, and my joy is unbounded, immeasurable. The time spent in Italy has been very important to me, an indispensable period of growth and maturing, learning and integrating all the experiences and teachings that I have received. And while I was there in Europe I also received everything I needed, a place to stay, a job, friends, a new visa and the joy of assisting Babaji with His work by making contact with people and being able to transmit His message to the world. In Italy I met up again with a woman called Lisetta, who I had first known in Nepal where I had been the means of arranging for her to meet Babaji in India. She now wants to build a centre for Babaji in Puglia, southern Italy where she has a house. Also Farua and Faruli who I had met in Almora have a piece of land in the same area, at Cisternino and they want to construct a temple dedicated to Lord Shiva. In Milan I got to know Federica, a woman who has been searching for God for a long time and who left immediately for India to meet Babaji.

When Paolo, Settimo, Fillippo and I arrived at the hotel in Haldwani we met Leonard Orr with the first group of Americans to make the journey here to meet Babaji. We made preparations to travel to Hairakhan together by embarking on the long walk up the river valley, finally arriving here yesterday evening. It seemed that Babaji was waiting for us to arrive, sitting in front of the old cave where He was first discovered. When I saw Him and He greeted us it caused such an overwhelming emotional response in me, perhaps the most intense and unforgettable of my life, my whole body shook and my legs trembled. Babaji gave me a radiant smile, laughed and joked with my Italian friends, asking me: 'Did you bring some more hippies?' He sent Settimo and I to spend the night in a new cave that has recently been excavated in the rock-face close by to the old one.

Babaji has changed and has put on weight, there are many people here including quite a lot of Westerners and a number of new buildings have been constructed. I have brought a whole suitcase of presents for Him to distribute, because today is the evening of Epiphany and in Italy it is the time when children receive their presents. Filippo gave Him gold, incense and myrrh. Babaji received it all like a child, with amusement. I desire nothing more in my life; I was so happy I could have jumped for joy. All I want now is to be with Him.

10 January 1978

I've noticed that a great many changes have occurred during the long period of my absence. Yesterday, down by the river, Babaji took me by the arm and said: 'Now Babaji is international.' Also He is different, speaking more, making jokes, conversing in English, meeting us more on our level; I am surprised. Now He often asks people to massage His feet and is no longer the ethereal and inaccessible figure that He once was. He has become more approachable, closer to us.

I start doing my sadhana again. In Italy I had become lazy, but now I jump into the cold river in the morning and begin to meditate again.

Babaji and Gaura Devi

15 January 1978

Babaji is showing me so much love and keeps me close to Him as He never did before, as if I were the returning prodigal child. He wants me to continue studying Hindi so that I am proficient in the language and He asks me to translate for Him on behalf of the Westerners. I feel that I have probably been through a period of karmic purification so that I am now more worthy of being close to Him. These days He compliments me in front of the Indian people and tells them that I am His true devotee. Without doubt, in Italy I passed an important test, because there are so many temptations in the West, materialism, modern comforts, and I was able to resist them all. Babaji asked me if I had slept with a man, I replied that I hadn't and He told me that now I belong only to Him.

25 January 1978

Now Babaji often calls out my name with much love and an intense sweetness, almost embarrassing me: He spoils me, giving me several presents. I have become a medium between Him and the Western people who come here, I must talk to them, explain many things about Babaji, my experiences with Him and how to live here.

He had told me I should take special care of the Italians who came here with me and He became upset with them, because they became completely intoxicated after taking datura, a powerful and potent Indian plant. Yesterday I had to spend the whole night with them sitting around a fire, watching them, because they had become completely unconscious. Today Babaji told them to leave, but maybe He will forgive them.

Also today I had to speak with a young American woman, who sleeps in my room and has evidently fallen in love with Babaji. She doesn't understand that He is not an ordinary man and that there is no chance of a romance developing. I try to explain to her that my love for Him is altogether different, divine love and that I can never think of Him as just another human being, but she even seems jealous of me; my God, what a mess! The other members of the American group who are visiting here are ecstatic in Babaji's presence and Leonard Orr, the person who is leading the group told me that Babaji had appeared to him physically in his room in the USA and that is the reason why they have come here.

Babaji has commenced the construction of a temple across the river, on gufa-side and He has erected a large placard saying: 'International Temple of Hairakhan Vishwa Mahadham, the Great Centre of the Universe.'

I am afraid of becoming proud because of all the attention He is giving me, but I know that Babaji is also taking care of my ego as well; I am more happy than I have ever been in my life before, as if a gigantic dream has been fulfilled.

30 January 1978

This morning I watched Babaji taking a long walk along the riverbed under a pure azure-blue winter sky, followed by His new disciples, the yogis and pioneers who have come here from every corner of the world. He moves with tremendous agility and strength, sure of Himself, but He is also gentle, barefoot, humble, like a great saint, His body covered only with a blanket. With His long black hair and holding a staff in His hand He reminds me of a shepherd.

He comes closer to us nowadays, to help us, speaking our language, playing our games, joking and teasing us, and when He looks into our eyes with great love He transmits His light to us. If I look into His eyes I am struck by the clarity, the purity of His love, it's an experience that shakes me to the core, as if truth is penetrating every fibre of my being.

3 April 1978
We have been travelling with Babaji on a long trip through Rajasthan, accompanied by a huge crowd. It was Holi, an Indian festival with an almost

carnival atmosphere and I dared to throw a bucket of coloured water at Him, wanting to shorten the distance between Him and myself; I would like Him to be my divine friend.

When we arrived back in Hairakhan Malti was here again from Germany. She has published a book there, the first to be written about Babaji, entitled *Message from the Himalayas,* and has brought a group of Germans here with her. It has to be expected that before long there will most probably be many more groups of German people beginning to arrive.

I am still a little jealous of Malti and her close relationship to Babaji, to God. She has a spiritual beauty, solemn, detached and in His presence she can maintain a tremendous tranquillity. Recently Babaji has taken to spending time in the garden painting beautiful, simple water-colours and now He keeps Malti close at hand in order to pass Him brushes, or just watch Him. His paintings are perfect and naive, very simple: the water, the sky and the mountains are the recurrent themes, but the colours He uses are unreal, golden, fiery.

Babaji – the painter

10 April 1978

Today Babaji gave a public speech and this is an unusual event. He told us that the world is going through a great social and spiritual crisis, that there will be many wars and natural catastrophes and humanity is in danger. He advised us to undertake forms of purification, that we should pray and prepare ourselves and repeat the mantra Om Namah Shivaya: He said that this mantra, the mantra of Lord Shiva gives strength in the face of any calamity, it's the Divine Power.

He went on to say that the time has come to spread His spiritual message everywhere in the world in order to save humanity.

12 April 1978

Malti spoke to me about Findhorn, a large community in Scotland, where she has been with her father, also a teacher of sacred dance. It's a New Age community, founded in the sixties. People are encouraged there to learn to communicate with the angelic beings and nature spirits, and are growing miraculous flowers and giant vegetables in no more than the sand of the beach; they have built up the community by listening to God's voice and learning to live together. Malti told me that when she saw Babaji's photograph for the first time in London she recognized Him immediately, and took the first available flight to India.

20 April 1978

Two elegant women have arrived here from wealthy, noble Indian families, Prem and Deviji. Babaji behaves with them like an Indian Maharaja, like an accomplished movie actor and I'm almost annoyed because with us Westerners, on the other hand, He pretends to behave more like a hippie. The other day He even played at being the lover with a young Indian woman, I couldn't believe it. It seems obvious that the girl has probably fallen in love with Him and wished to be courted, but why does He play this game? To cap it all I even saw Him smiling with erotic complicity with the aging mother of the young woman. Of course I remember how He acted with me in the beginning and I also know that all His play-acting, everything He does in fact, is a teaching, but even so I still feel disturbed by it all. I talked to Malti about this and she said that from her viewpoint Babaji just gives love in the form that we need it, but I feel that His teaching is more complex, it's a lesson in detachment, encouraging us to look beyond desire.

3 May 1978

I notice that many other women are now physically attracted to Babaji, especially German women. It's upset me and I have tried to explain to them that we cannot behave with Babaji as if He were an ordinary man, but who knows if they understand! They look at me with suspicion, regarding me as if I were a frustrated nun and are unable to understand my devotion for Him. From my perspective though they fail to show Him any respect and I feel Babaji has to act out an unpleasant role now, He pretends to play the part and I don't like it.

The other day I summoned up the courage to ask Him why He plays these games with these women and He answered me: 'Ask them why they come here from so far away to see Me, what they want from Me.'

The ashram is suddenly invaded with this erotic energy, heavy and unpleasant. I wish He could send all these women away, but I know this is not possible, He has to help them. One woman told me today that Babaji had touched her body and she is proud of it, but for me this would only be humiliating. Even so Babaji is also using me to try and explain something to them, but I don't really enjoy this new drama.

15 May 1978

The Indian people talk to me about Babaji's leelas, explaining that God is always engaged in 'divine play' with His devotees in this world. They recount to me stories about Ram and also Lord Krishna who used to engage in divine play with the gopis, his female followers. It has become clear to me that, in effect, Babaji is continually teaching us through jokes and games, often in a way as if to say that our human world isn't to be taken too seriously, that ultimately it doesn't exist. But I don't like it at all, this suffering that is inherent in the life of every human being: why can't we just have a happy existence? On one occasion somebody asked Babaji why God permitted the existence of Maya - the great illusion of creation - and Babaji replied that Maya is just the Lord's play. These days He offers us daily examples of this through live demonstrations: turning Himself into a clown in a circus or acting as if He were a cat toying with a mouse, a wild cat indeed, and in this way He plays with our attachments in order to transform our desires.

25 May 1978

There are now many physical comforts in Hairakhan and Babaji has become more permissive, in order to cater to the numerous and different people coming here, to all their needs. We are now permitted to drink tea, to have a meal in the evening, mattresses are available in the rooms for people to sleep on and toilets have been installed. Babaji wants me to change as well: I can't wear my sadhu rags any more but should wear a sari, be elegant, to play the role of the hostess for the many guests who arrive. I am expected to teach the concept of karma yoga to the Westerners, telling them about the simple tasks to be done, showing them how to keep the ashram functioning. Through this interaction with other people I discover that I am often authoritarian, sometimes unpleasant or presumptuous with them, as well as proud. I find this administrative role difficult but also because of it I realize that I still have much work to do on myself and need to improve the way in which I relate and interact with people.

1 June 1978

Federica has arrived here from Italy, from my home town of Milan. We sleep in the same room and have prepared a special seat there for Babaji and He often comes to visit us. He sits with us, plays with our possessions, our human toys, our pens, bags, knick-knacks and so on, just like a naughty child, teaching us how to use these material things with greater awareness. I can also see that Malti, for example, is very much a Western person who is able to live in the Western world and not feel inclined to follow an ascetic path yet still remain close to God. Babaji is now showing me how to relate to material things not only with detachment, but with care as well, because everything is comprised of energy and shouldn't be wasted.

Federica has become a disciple of Aurobindo and the Mother and she is insistent on the following point: we shouldn't retire from the world, but we should be able to transform it instead, bringing light into darkness, creating heaven on earth. I have certain difficulties with this approach and realize that I am more removed, more rigid and Calvinist in my attitudes and this is something that Federica argues with me about.

15 June 1978

I am enchanted by Babaji's flexibility and His ability to adjust to each person and every situation. When dealing with the local village people He can be extremely down-to-earth, becoming one of them, a poor mountain person, talking about stones and potatoes, sharing their simple problems and most of all teaching them about honesty. Then when He is relating to the sophisticated people who arrive from the big cities, Delhi or Bombay, He transforms Himself into an oriental prince, beautiful and worldly. With women He plays the seductive man, with us Westerners He is the severe Master yet also full of love, with children He is youthful, tender, an ineffable mother/father figure.

His endless play and kaleidoscopic ability, His magical transformations, it all continually fascinates me; it's as if He constantly adopts many different forms in order to help us, coming down to our level of understanding in order to take our hand and lift us one step higher, towards Him. An ancient Sanskrit prayer says: 'Oh Lord, Your play in a human form is most strange and mysterious.' The bridge that exists between Him and ourselves is His continuous, infinite love.

2 July 1978

Malti has left and Surja, a young Swiss woman, has arrived. The monsoon has fully started and Babaji spends most of the day sitting on a large swing in the kirtan hall, while Surja is swinging Him. This daily show has provoked all sorts of different reactions from the people present, because Babaji smiles at her, touches her with His head as He rocks to and fro, smiles mischievously - what is He teaching us? Probably to be aware of our own projections in respect of the drama we construct around our interactions between man and woman, our greatest Maya. At first I felt jealous, but the game is too obvious to deceive me for long. During this period I have conscientiously begun to meditate again because I don't want to be unnecessarily distracted.

Yesterday Surja rushed into the room that we share and was in tears because Babaji had treated her roughly and she resents it; I explain to her that most probably Babaji is mirroring her desire and she nodded. After a little while Babaji came into the room and told her to begin a meditation retreat for an indefinite period, fasting and in absolute silence.

Shastriji, Babaji and Malti

5 July 1978

Babaji has now exempted me from manual work and allotted me other duties. Instead I have to write all His correspondence, to speak initially to all the new visitors who frequently arrive, as well as translate for Him and take a hand in other minor official duties, it's like being a secretary. I feel proud about this role, probably too much. Since Babaji keeps me so close to Him, I have to struggle with my ego, my pride and my haughtiness towards other people.

It's not easy to have to organize others, it's a difficult training and sometimes Babaji plays with all of this as well, creating situations so that our ego grows more and more, until He can catch it and destroy it, burst it like popping a balloon.

12 October 1978

The rainy season, the monsoon, has once more come to an end and as in every other year another tropical autumn follows, incredibly green, the air clear, it's almost like a second spring has begun. The gardens in Hairakhan are full of roses and the farmers are preparing the fields after the rice harvest, ready for the new crop. Like every other year at this time a fresh cycle of learning begins and small groups of Westerners begin to arrive here more frequently. I find that I am also beginning to regain my sense of harmony and equilibrium again, through the practice of meditation in the morning before undertaking my work around the ashram during the day.

2 November 1978

Two days ago a group of us climbed Mount Kailash with Babaji. We didn't set out until the afternoon and stopped at a house in a village in the evening to sleep there. We sat with Babaji around a big fire and He asked me to massage Him at length on His back, in front of everybody. I knew that this was a sacred ritual and that it could also be for the others present as well, because I thought He wanted people to see that He can be touched with a certain purity and sincerity. For me Babaji resembles a murti, a sacred but living statue, and every gesture towards Him is an expression of worship for me, a puja, an act of adoration.

After a while we all sat in silence with Him around the leaping flames of the fire. Suddenly Babaji took my hand, holding it under His blanket and my heart skipped a beat; I was intensely moved, this simple gesture touched something very deep inside me and it felt as if my heart began to melt, filled with a blissful feeling, a deeply profound sensation. Babaji went to rest in His room and for the rest of the night I remained awake sitting by the fire, not even lying down but filled with ecstasy, my mind completely silent. From time to time, I could hear the sound of Om within me, the vibration of which was also evident in the room as well. In the very early morning, at about three o'clock, before everybody else woke up, I took a cold shower outside in the dark. Again I felt the sound of Om inside me, and it also pervaded the valley and mountains round about, everything vibrating: it was as if an electrical current was passing through me, the sound of it almost deafening in my ears and yet at the same time there existed the presence of a great silence.

15 November 1978

Now every time I see Babaji, I get this intense sensation in my heart, a sudden ecstasy, which paralyzes my mind: a spontaneous void achieved without effort.

Everyday at about sunset I massage Babaji's feet after His bath, a time of deep communion and union with Him. His feet are particularly poignant for me, they represent His presence on earth for us, a sign of His sacrifice as well.

The other day He said to me: 'I am making a great effort to unite heaven and earth.'

2 December 1978

The first cold days of winter have arrived and in the morning Babaji lies on a blanket in the sun, surrounded by some of us. There is now a yogi in the ashram, a young Indian disciple, a true brother for me. Babaji often calls both of us to accompany Him and sings a poem to us from an ancient book. It's the story of Gopichand, from about one thousand years ago: this famous and wealthy King was married with two hundred wives but he gave up his kingdom to practice yoga, renouncing the world. He became the disciple of the celebrated guru Goraknath and received yogic teachings from him. Babaji often speaks to us of renunciation and austerity.

A few days ago He took us on a walk to visit Goraknath's dhuni, situated on the way to Mount Kailash. According to tradition, women must never enter the sites dedicated to this guru, because he was a brahmachari, but Babaji insists I enter and sit near Him in the dhuni, telling me that I am allowed to come inside because I am a yogini now and not a woman any more. He tells me that a true yogini is elevated above any man.

At dawn, after His bath, Babaji sits with us in the garden and every day He wants me to massage His feet with sweet-smelling oils. It becomes a daily ritual and I prepare a place for Him to sit with His shawl and blanket close at hand. I feel like a priestess and realize I am becoming greatly attached to this physical service that I can offer Him and it scares me.

In the kirtan hall yesterday somebody asked Babaji how it was possible to reach God and He replied: 'It is only possible when we reach Shunya, a state of complete emptiness in our mind and only a yogi knows how to do this through meditation. God is beyond name and form.'

15 December 1978

I am starting to read various books about Old Hairakhan Baba, a previous form of Babaji in the late 1800's. The tradition of Shaivism and Indian yoga has existed for thousands of years and even this small village and these hills are pervaded by the divine energy of Babaji. At times it feels like a miracle that I am here at all, an unmerited blessing. I can't think about my future or anything else in my life, only He exists. The one and only desire I have is to be at one with Him.

5 January 1979

This is the first time we have celebrated Christmas and remembered Jesus in a formal way. We have put together a theatrical performance and Babaji wants me to play the Madonna and He calls me Maria, in Italian.

15 January 1979

I meditate a lot, going to take my bath in the river at three o'clock in the morning before everybody else does and then afterwards I can sit in meditation for 5 hours, until 9 o'clock. I have no desire to do anything else now. It feels as if my body is constantly pervaded by an electrical current and when I leave my room it's difficult to walk, my body feels as if it is floating on air; Babaji laughs whenever He sees me. After a few hours of meditation, I have to discontinue because I become physically tired, otherwise I would never stop. When my mind reaches a point of silence it becomes infused by a white light, bright and blissful, without any distractions, just filled with awareness and the feeling of a tremendous psychic power.

My relationship with Babaji has changed again. There exists a direct, telepathic link with Him, beyond words: He can see all my thoughts and He answers them immediately, directly. I have no doubts about this, because He always gives me confirmation with a gesture or a word. This contact with Him is constantly present now even when I am not in His physical presence. I dream of Him almost every night and even in my dreams He is teaching me something.

30 January 1979

Babaji has built a small room for me and He has put a chair in it where He comes to sit every day. I also have a cupboard where I am to keep some of His things and His money, I am happy that He trusts me. Often He invites important Indian people into my room for a tea party and I have to prepare fruit juices and drinks, while He entertains the guests like a perfect host. He continually distributes to others all the presents that people give Him, ensuring that this material energy is made to circulate all the time.

The Indian devotees adore Him, contemplating the Divine in Him, touch Him, prepare special food for Him; Indian women spoil Him in a tender motherly way and He allows them to play with His body as if He were a doll, dressing it up and adorning it.

Through adoring Him, we are adoring a symbol of ourselves, something which each one of us would like to be, our own divine Self. Babaji is a skilful Master working on our projections like an accomplished psychologist. He allows us to play for a while, indulge ourselves in our attachments or desires a little, but sooner or later they are denied us, refused and He forces us back again onto ourselves, even rejecting us. It is not uncommon to see Him suddenly tell somebody to leave, sometimes quite harshly, unexpectedly, without any apparent reason. I feel He is particularly hard with the people from the West, not allowing them to remain here for a long period of time. Also the games He plays out with women is another teaching. He always mirrors the feelings we have right there in front of Him, what we really are, although we don't always recognize it immediately ourselves; and yet in a moment or two He can transform and elevate us. He gives of Himself unconditionally.

2 February 1979

Yesterday a porter stole something from a rucksack belonging to a Western woman and Babaji beat him with a stick in the kirtan hall in front of everyone until his hands were bleeding. He regards the matter of stealing very gravely and is particularly harsh with people when they are dishonest, trying to teach both the villagers as well as ourselves to act honestly and responsibly. He controls the prices charged for things, not wanting the local people to exploit Westerners or treat them like tourists to be cheated.

Sometimes He participates in the village meetings, listening to the villagers' requests, teaching them how to administer justice, encouraging self-government. One day He told them that they can make use of all the unused land around here, because it doesn't belong to anybody, and ultimately it belongs to Him anyway. A few days ago in a public speech He spoke about revolution and a great change coming to the world. He has a revolutionary spirit, pushing people towards change.

5 March 1979

Springtime has arrived and Babaji has just returned from a brief trip away. He has brought back with Him from Delhi an expert gardener: He only wants roses to be planted in the garden, which has to become, He said, as beautiful as Lord Shiva's paradise. I think He wants to teach us how to transform the planet.

Babaji has begun to be well known now and many rich Indian families arrive, generously donating towards the ongoing cost of building the ashram. Everybody works on this project, Indian and Nepalese workers together with men and women from the West, excavating the mountain, lifting one stone after another from the riverbed. It is no longer necessary for me to be involved in any of this physical work, but my inner work is becoming more and more intense and profound. The collective effort of people working together is tremendously moving to experience and Babaji says that every stone that people lift is also releasing them from a karmic burden, creating a fragment of the new world.

7 May 1979

It's extremely hot and in the evening Babaji sits under the starry vault of the sky. People sing softly about Lord Shiva's glory and even the gentle rhythm of the flowing river appears to sing the mantra incessantly. One can hear humming sounds from the jungle at night, as if the whole valley is resounding with prayer. In the dark we can often see strange lights floating along on the river or across the mountainside and Babaji says that these are the light bodies of saints who live around this area. He recounted a story saying that there are ninety secret caves hidden in this valley, where very advanced yogis reside. They are able to live without any food, taking their nutrition from the air and the water, great yogis who meditate continually, nine of them immortal. They only emerge from their shelters at night in order to bathe in the river, which is when we see these moving lights emanating from their bodies.

3 July 1979

It's constantly raining and almost impossible for people to leave their rooms.

It's the best time for developing concentration and practising meditation, because it's difficult to do any practical job outside in the ashram. I asked Babaji if He could teach me some new yoga techniques because I don't feel the mantra is working for me any more, but He doesn't respond, then becomes very angry that I have asked Him and slaps my face; I doubt whether I deserve such treatment.

27 July 1979

Yesterday Babaji came into my room early in the morning. He told me He would give me an initiation in meditation and I immediately felt extremely emotional. He brushed His hand across my forehead and the top of my head and gave me a breathing technique, transmitting to me a deep and powerful experience. Then He took me down to the river and shaved off my hair with His own hands, before inscribing circular patterns on my head. From that moment on I started to feel an incredible energy on the top of my head, almost burning my scalp. I came back to my room, my whole body shaking. He told me to fast for twenty-five days and during this period I should remain in my room and not talk to anybody.

28 August 1979

I have fasted and meditated continuously for the twenty-five days and it has been an incredible experience, quite unforgettable.

The first week I felt extremely weak and sick, but then my body started to be nourished in a different sort of way, as if by a subtle energy. Gradually I began to be able to concentrate for hours, I felt light, able to sit in meditation for long periods of time quite easily, five or six hours. During the third week I started to feel exceedingly hungry. I couldn't sleep during the night any more, instead I sat in meditation without a break. At the end of this period my body felt exceedingly weak, but I had become ethereal, ecstatic and I did not wish to start eating all this gross food again. I felt that my body had become pure energy and light, my mind separated from thought, becoming joy and consciousness. Babaji always came to visit me during this time, allowing me to touch His feet for a few minutes, occasionally giving me a morsel of food to eat, usually fruits or nuts. It was sufficient for me to retain my strength; all the time I continued to feel a tremendous current of energy on the top of my head, raising my life energy upwards into space, so that I perceived the capacity of my soul to leave my body and fly into some other dimension.

3 September 1979

Now I would like to spend all my time doing nothing but meditating, day and night: I am longing to experience this subtle bliss, this divine power pervading my whole being. I observe my mind, watching as thoughts vanish and an ocean of unknown consciousness remains. It is impossible to describe, a dimension where the mind dissolves, where only visions are left together with the energy of the heart. I feel united with an infinite, cosmic spirit, perfect, omnipresent and omniscient, always and only Him, Babaji.

Today I was sitting with Babaji, automatically repeating a mantra in my mind to release my mental tension, when Babaji placed a finger to His lips indicating silence. Now I know I can't even use the mantra any more, my mind should be empty.

29 September 1979

My link with Babaji is now extraordinarily profound and I receive an immediate response to any of my feelings or thoughts. But dear God, how long it has taken me to be able to feel really close to Him! Probably many life-times in fact. Yet now I feel an endless bond with Him that nothing can break, it is indissoluble, I know that I am a part of Him for ever and ever.

Sometimes when I look into His eyes I feel at one with Him, in unison with His heart, a sister of the same unique story.

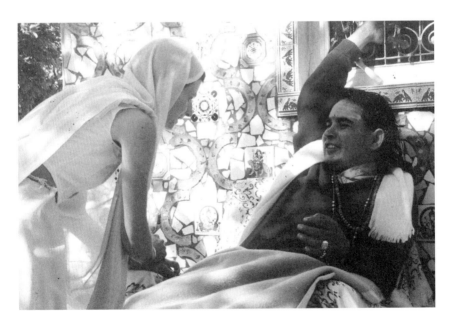

'Sometimes when I look into His eyes...'

Ranikhet, 3 October 1979

Yesterday we crossed the Gautam Ganga, still swollen with the water from the monsoon, in order to travel to Ranikhet and attend the inaugural celebration of the new temple constructed and dedicated to Babaji. The water of the river was turquoise blue, transparent, the air clear and full of nature's perfume, the valley lush and emerald green. The porters helped us to cross by linking arms in a long chain with Babaji the first in line, powerful, sure of Himself: like the king of the jungle, a tiger, eternally young.

16 October 1979

Today Baba was seated with the Himalayan mountains ranged behind Him, shining in the sun. Great yogis often meditate in the eternal snow, and due to a combination of the high altitude, the rarefied atmosphere, purity of the air, the peace, silence, cold and solitude, the mind is automatically transported to another dimension.

It's part of the practice of yoga to learn to bear cold and hunger and many other discomforts. Shiva is the ascetic Master, whose teaching is to transcend the gross, physical consciousness, to go beyond the material world of matter. He asks for tapasya from His devotees, sacrifice and austerity.

Hairakhan, 3 November 1979

Babaji has gone travelling on tour around India for three months and I remain here in Hairakhan with a few other people. I have been exempted from doing manual work now and have plenty of time for meditation in my room. Every evening I can hear the ashram guard, a very poor Indian man, singing a truly delightful song celebrating the glory of Babaji. I am still moved by the simple faith of these people; perhaps it is their contact with nature, the solitude of the valley and the silence of the mountains that makes them more pure and receptive to the presence of the Divine. Due to our pride and apparent mental sophistication, the Westerner thinks he already knows everything, yet the truly wise man, they say, is the one who knows that he doesn't know. Faith in the Divine is first of all an act of humility in the presence of the mystery of the Universe.

The West has come to Hairakhan

4 February 1980

More and more Western people are coming to Hairakhan, as if transported here by the wind: Babaji is calling people from every corner of the world.

Sometimes I don't like their presence, because into this place of peace has arrived this craziness from the West, neurotic, restless, dark and complicated minds. It's not peaceful any more. People pounce on Babaji and impose their selfish requests on Him, their egotism and frustrations and they pretend that Babaji can solve all of their problems, as if He were a psychoanalyst. During these days I am occupied most of the time translating Babaji's words from Hindi for them and I am irritated by the questions and demands that they make. People want miracles from Him, they expect Him to know about their past and predict their future, to solve all of their economic problems, to be cured of their diseases. Very few people arrive here to ask Him about the Truth or the way to reach it; usually they only want solutions to their personal problems, their human difficulties or to have their desires fulfilled. One day Babaji told me: 'I give everything, but very few people ask me for the real thing I have come to give.'

Maybe it is my pride that makes me think this way, because the guru helps people out of his compassion on whatever level they are at; perhaps I am lacking love.

5 March 1980

I don't seem to have much time left for meditation any more because I am so deeply involved in taking care of the flood of people who are arriving here every day. In addition I have to serve Babaji: write His correspondence, take care of His things, all the various presents people bring for Him. I miss the simplicity of the old times. Every day is like a kind of Christmas now, Babaji is busy keeping everything in order, distributing clothes, sweets, pens, watches, jewellery, shoes, books, bags, photographs: the bazaar of life has come to Hairakhan. Wealthy Indian people come here along with freaks, spiritual tourists, vagabonds travelling around India, mad people looking for help, frustrated women looking for a husband, people addicted to drugs and the sick.

There are some people who come here who are spiritual seekers, yogis and Babaji's disciples, but they are a minority.

Babaji plays the part of the ringmaster in a circus, directing everything, pretending to be one of us in order to help. In His grand plan I am to play the role of the austere nun, a character that many people don't like. Babaji also needs our help, not for Himself personally, but to carry out the work, to be part of the divine plan in the world.

There are four or five Westerners who have chosen to stay in Hairakhan for a longer period of time, yogis who meditate, work and carry out their sadhana, a few of His disciples who are prepared to roll up their sleeves and become deeply involved. One in particular, Har Govind, a Swiss man, has decided to stay here for ever. All of us are busily occupied every day organizing everything: managing the office, the construction of sleeping quarters, food, blankets, mattresses, washing arrangements, people's individual needs and now we also have the arrival of piped water and electricity.

Some of the people who find their way here are very beautiful, like fallen angels and they even resemble Babaji, with the same traits, both delicate and exotic, exhibiting some of His youthfulness and His light.

'Babaji plays the part of the ringmaster in a circus...'

15 March 1980

Babaji speaks in public and it is truly a novelty when this happens. He speaks in a strong, sure way with irony and vehemence in His voice. 'The whole world is going to experience a total crisis. There's going to be wars, destruction and the only people who will be saved will be those who repeat the name of God, because the mantra is more powerful than the atomic bomb.'

4 April 1980

I literally run around all day, serving Indian guests in my room, talking to the Westerners when they arrive, explaining, consoling and also caring for Babaji all the while. Babaji is often brusque, severe, unpredictable, sometimes He sends people away again on the same day that they arrive and if they ask Him why He refuses to answer, provoking everybody like a wild psychiatrist. In the evening He puts on a performance, sitting on His dais, playing a guitar that belongs to an Italian man, playing and joking with the children, the Western women and the sophisticated Indian women; He plays the mad joker, divine, impossible to fully understand, ineffable.

I read a book about Shiva's dance, Shiva as Nataraj: He dances with the world and the entire creation. He creates, preserves and destroys many universes with the rhythm of His movements. As He dances He is sometimes gentle, sometimes wild, carrying a flame in one of His hands, while beneath one foot is held the prostrate body of a demon dwarf, which symbolizes our ego. It's enough to make one frightened and alarmed.

20 April 1980

The tea parties that take place with Babaji in my small room are happening more and more often. In India the primary means of expressing love is considered to be that demonstrated by the mother and so consequently the main manifestation of that love is to give food and nourishment. One can never enter an Indian house without being offered something to eat or drink. Also Babaji gives things to people according to their status, their need, always knowing the perfect present for everyone. Recently He has also been giving me many presents of sweets and clothes. I am expected to be elegant and fully play my part in this drama. He treats me like a spiritual wife and one day He said to me: 'When will you finally come back to Me, I have been waiting for you for a long time.'

The Lord is always calling us to Him in an act of infinite love and only our darkness and our ignorance keep us separated from Him, but our souls will never find true peace until we are united with Him again. The love affair we have with the Divine is a unique relationship, the only complete and real one. Even in our endless search for human love we are only really looking for Him, longing for union with the Lord, the integration of original unity with consciousness.

3 May 1980

We have spent some languid days with Babaji in the tropical heat. Although we still work hard Babaji now gives us long breaks in the afternoon, taking some of us to the river with Him when He bathes. We put soap on His body, wash Him, perfume and massage Him, continuing our play with the divine doll. Every gesture, every action, is used by Babaji to teach us something through this drama we call life. He wants our minds to remain attentive in all circumstances, full of concentration, pure and alert, without any useless or superfluous thoughts. It's a new meditation focused in action, a new exercise in discovering equilibrium. We are to learn to perform all of life's activities every day of our lives without any selfish desire, learning simply to serve the Divine Plan, taking light into darkness, truth into ignorance, peace into conflict, love into aggression.

Babaji works on all our emotions and human conditioning, sometimes creating paradoxical situations in order to teach us that we have to face the conflicts within ourselves as well as the confrontations that build up between us. He often provokes competition, jealousy, ego-trips, pride, puffing some people up as big as balloons before amusing Himself by deflating them, as if piercing them with a needle. He creates the actors for His magical movie, making us interpret the part that is most useful for us so that we may draw closer to the truth. Community life is a perfect stage for the spectacle.

Sometimes, to look at Him from the outside Babaji seems like a madman, a teacher who lacks seriousness, a destroyer, a peculiar master who even breaks established traditions, arranging mock marriages and making fun of people all the time. At other times He becomes extremely serious, severe, deep in concentration, strict, precise and perfect with rituals. Without any doubt I am certain He only pretends all of these characteristics for our benefit, expecting maximum concentration from everyone else in their learning: everything is a leela, divine play, an enactment, but it's also a serious business, a school of learning.

4 June 1980

Now Babaji often gives speeches in public, talking about karma yoga, the yoga of action, work offered to the Divine without any expectation of the outcome. He tells us that we are now living in an era of action but also a time of revolution and destruction in the world, a time of great peril for the whole of civilization. It is no longer possible to step aside, to hold ourselves back, to remain passive, because we must now participate in the great revolution and global changes. He is most specific in saying it is not just a spiritual revolution but also a political and global revolution on our planet. He says that there will be many wars and natural catastrophes all over the world occurring in conjunction with the great spiritual revolution and it is necessary for us to become strong. He proposes an integrated yoga; even yogis and yoginis, He says, should become spiritual warriors and fight for truth. A New Age is coming, a new spiritual era, but the passage from the old to the new will not be without conflict and difficulty and we should be making preparations.

For me His words are like nectar. Ever since my childhood I have believed in world revolution and change for the benefit of humanity, in an ideal. It was exactly this kind of viewpoint which was instrumental in bringing me here to India in the first place, searching for new answers.

3 July 1980

With the rainy season beginning again, outside activity almost comes to a standstill and we spend more time in the kirtan hall. Once more we push Babaji on the large swing all day long, while He works with our minds. In His presence the mind is continually confronted with the same things. Nothing escapes Him and He plays tricks with all our thoughts, our innermost feelings.

Sometimes He takes Shastriji and myself along with Him in the afternoon when He goes to bathe in the river. During the monsoon season the water in the river becomes muddy and so we take long walks, searching for clear, underground springs, which are numerous along the riverbed. Shastriji is an extremely learned man and Babaji speaks with him in Sanskrit, reciting old poems, proverbs, telling ancient legends and myths; it's an abundance of wisdom and sometimes Babaji speaks to us about parables and poems that are from an unknown, archaic language. These moments with Him are heaven for me, it's like living in the Garden of Eden, but without any desire to pick the forbidden fruit from the tree any more, where it is not necessary to discriminate between good and evil; I am completely fulfilled. With Babaji I feel as if I am a child again, guided by His hands, the only effort required on my part is to try and be as empty as possible, innocent once more.

Today at sunset I watched Babaji swinging Himself from one of the branches of the Mother tree at the Satikund, speaking to us in a profound way, laughing from His heart, inviting us all to have greater simplicity, to be content; it seems such a simple thing but it's the most difficult thing in the world: to be happy.

9 August 1980

They have built a new, large room for Baba, very elaborate and kitsch, all made of shiny materials, an enormous mirror on one wall. Babaji has named it 'the Palace of Mirrors'. The esoteric significance is profound; it's another teaching, Him being a mirror for us. His mind is pure and empty, and so we can project on Him our needs and fantasies, see them and transform them.

He is working incessantly now, from 3 o'clock in the morning, until late at night, taking care of every single detail of our lives, from moving the stones in the river for construction projects to the nervous crisis of a young American woman who has only recently arrived. Also I feel tired, since I have to serve

Him in numerous different ways and many people envy me because of my position, which I do not find at all easy.

Nothing is ever perfect enough for Babaji. He scolds me often, He is never satisfied and tells me I should pay attention to every one of His gestures and every thought that I have. He keeps repeating that He wants heaven on earth, a mandala full of harmony and perfection, a creation of beauty.

In addition He is teaching us to perform all the Vedic rituals once again, many of which have been largely forgotten in more recent times. The Vedas are the most sacred and the most ancient scriptures and they offer a science of the universe, where everything has a place within a cosmic order. Creation itself is seen as a ritual, in which men and women can consciously participate. Through worship and developing a new relationship with nature, people can learn to purify themselves through simple contact with earth, fire, air, water and ether. Sadhana is spiritual purification and so is discipline.

3 October 1980

Many Italian people have arrived recently and sometimes they irritate me because they come here with their usual preoccupations: spaghetti, drugs, the sun and love affairs. Babaji sends many of them across the river to the gufa-side of the ashram to stay, so they are free to do what they like. One day, while accompanying Babaji to the gufa-side and climbing the steps up to the nine temples, He said to me: 'This is the path of the "black boys".' Who knows what He means by this or the significance of what He says. Many complex and difficult people are coming here, but Babaji is able to completely transform them all within a few days, it's a miracle to observe. He seems to be in a hurry and sometimes I ask myself how long will He remain here with us on earth.

I'm becoming friends with Letizia, a beautiful young woman from Milan, with a face like a Tibetan, sensitive, sweet and serene. Some of the people from the West who have chosen to reside here now help with the workload and I am developing some good friendships. The community is growing and a large office is being organized very efficiently by the Americans, managed by Radhe Shyam, an older man, along with the help of a few other people. Babaji is offering us an example of a different way of living, which demands a great deal of effort from everyone so that the community functions perfectly, but in this way He is teaching us a positive lifestyle for the future.

He encourages everyone who has come here to live together in unity, all these people from so many different countries, races and religions, and most particularly He develops union with the Indian people by harmonizing and blending our cultures. We must abolish our sense of difference. He has told us that in the future our organization will be vast and international and that Hairakhan will become a great, international pilgrimage centre, where people from different religions will be welcome to practice their beliefs. Hairakhan will become even more holy than the city of Benares, which has been spoiled nowadays by tourism. People will only be allowed to live in Hairakhan permanently when their worldly desires have come to an end, otherwise people should live in the normal world completing their karma. He told me that at some point in the future only real yogis and renunciates will stay here on a permanent basis.

30 December 1980

This year Babaji wanted all of us from the West to organize a big Christmas celebration, with a theatrical performance of the Christmas story, dance, angelic songs and many presents to distribute. He seems happy and speaks of the unity of all the world's religions. He told us that a huge world-wide crisis has begun and the forces of evil are trying to destroy the earth with atomic energy, but the Divine wishes to prevent a total catastrophe. Whoever has faith in God will be saved and after a far-reaching revolution a new era will emerge based upon spiritual and moral values. All the old world leaders will be replaced, changes will occur and the Dharma of India together with the wisdom of the Vedas will guide humanity towards a brighter future. He said that most of us, His Western disciples, have been yogis or saints in India in the past and in this life we have been reincarnated in the West in order to fulfil our desires for material well-being, but now our task is to bring to the West the wisdom of Indian culture and spirituality. The world will undergo a great crisis and many wars, but the Om Namah Shivaya mantra, He said, is more powerful than the atomic bomb because it is the Divine Power itself.

5 January 1981

Babaji is so beautiful when He speaks in public. To me He seems like a mixture of the Archangel Gabriel and Che Guevara as He transmits to us the message proclaimed to humanity by all of the ancient prophets: in order to be true human beings we should become warriors of light, spirit and truth.

20 January 1981

Baba is organizing different work groups. The American people take care of the office and the administration, the Germans organize discipline, the Italians undertake practical work down by the river and construction projects, while the Indians take care of the kitchen and the temples.

I am busily occupied serving His physical body and I am so happy. Sometimes I feel like a mother towards Him and in this way I fool myself into thinking that I am being useful.

These days He is always surrounded by people, every moment of the day, even when He goes to bathe. Everybody wants to follow Him when He is walking, they want to touch, or massage Him. Just one look from Him can change a person's heart in an instant, His touch can heal many things and He gives of Himself unconditionally. Sometimes I become so very tired that I don't have any time left for meditation. On those occasions I can only concentrate when I sit at His feet, sitting in the garden or on His terrace in those moments of blessed communion, in silence and peace.

3 February 1981

A few days ago Babaji became angry with me, because I answered Him back in a stubborn way and He told me to leave, to go back to my home country, He even slapped me across the face in front of other people. I couldn't believe it and I cried all night. The next morning once again He insisted that I should leave and so taking a blanket and torch with me I started to run barefoot to the top of Mount Kailash.

It was raining and I reached the summit feeling exhausted, cold and wet. I became scared, because there isn't any shelter there, but suddenly the sun came out and dried everything up. I spent the night sitting with my back against a wall to protect myself from the cold wind and even managed to sleep for short periods. I had a dream, where I saw Babaji and suddenly understood why He was angry with me, because of some deep psychological resistance of mine. Even so, for two more days I didn't have the courage to leave the mountain and return to Hairakhan and so I rested in a small hut, which I discovered half way down the mountain. I lit a small fire, drank the rainwater, but had nothing to eat and hardly slept at all.

On the third day I returned because I had no strength left in my body and I could hardly walk. Babaji was sitting near the riverbed as I approached, looking at the work being undertaken there and I went towards Him, my body trembling with so much fear of being rejected, of being sent away again. Babaji called me to Him in a very loving way telling me that now I have understood and done a great penance on Kailash; He called a man over to massage me and to give me a glass of milk. He said that it had even been necessary for Him to send the sun to appear on top of the mountain in order to save me.

Even just the idea of being far away from Him is terribly painful for me to contemplate. My days are now full of His presence only and my biggest joy is to be able to serve Him. Sometimes I am afraid of this intense attachment to Him and I think that some day I'll also have to give that up. Let's hope that day is very far away.

4 April 1981

Every afternoon I wake up Babaji with a fruit juice and sit alone with Him for a while, under the big peepul tree. I look at the valley, the river flowing in numerous channels, the green hills of Kailash. I sit still with Him, immobile, my eyes open, in silence. I watch my mind: a few thoughts pass by, like clouds, but they are insignificant and don't disturb my equilibrium any more. I only hear the sound of the river, it's rhythm and melody, while everything is enveloped by a bright, white light, dazzling. Babaji's form dissolves in it and I disappear with Him. The contours of our physical bodies disappear and at times the light is so strong that my eyes are burning.

Yesterday Muniraji came from Haldwani. He is an ancient master and sat near Babaji. In a very similar way he also dissolved in the same vastness full of light, in the sound of silence, while the river sang a last song.

Babaji and the peepul tree

30 April 1981

The summer nights pulse with the life and sounds of the tropical jungle; voices of the local people, dogs barking and wild animals somewhere in the distance; cows, the beasts restless and complaining when they sense the leopard about or if they are unsettled by the noise of the wind. The tropical stars seem very close. Yesterday there was a huge snake in the garden and an Indian man seized it and killed it in an instant using a perfect technique. Babaji sits outside on the new terrace and His body emanates a distinct perfume in the dark. He is always pervaded by this strong fragrance, left also on all His clothes; often we realize when He is nearby because of this perfume. I massage Him softly, in an act of communion, accomplished so often, giving thanks for the sense of peace, the joy of reliving this every day, for the miracle of His presence on earth.

3 May 1981

Babaji makes everybody work a great deal in the summer, sometimes until 8 o' clock in the evening, personally checking everything is done properly. On a few occasions people had to work all night with the help of kerosene lamps in order to finish the roof of one of the new buildings: there are many rooms, a hospital, a school and nine temples dedicated to the many Indian gods and goddesses. He told us that one day thousands of people will come to worship in the valley of the Gautam Ganga.

He is still playing with the women, acting the part of the divine lover, like the ancient god Krishna with the gopis, the milkmaids who were in love with him. The Indian tradition says that all the mind of a human being really wants is the eternal love of the Lord and to be in union with him. This union is purely spiritual but in order that we might move towards that state Babaji has first to break through our coarse, outer shell. The other day He told me there are two main things that attach us to the material life: food and sex.

7 June 1981

It's so hot and humid again and many Western people become ill. When individuals first come here they go through an intense purification process which is often painful. Babaji asks everybody that they should shave off their hair and dress in traditional Indian clothes. Women should give up their vanity, the hippies their pride and long hair, and everybody the image they have of themselves. Our egos are under constant pressure with Baba, we have to obey Him unconditionally and do the most humble jobs. When we enter into competition with each other or there is jealousy, Babaji deliberately humiliates us in public, in front of everyone, without mercy.

8 July 1981

Rain and rain again, time passes slowly and quietly. Every day the villagers bring fruits and vegetables to Babaji: mangoes, cucumbers and maize which He distributes with generosity to all.

Sometimes He takes my little stove out onto the terrace and cooks some delicious rice, mixing it with all the vegetables that the villagers have brought Him in the morning, adding butter and spices and serving it up on large banana leaves. He teaches us about abundance and prosperity, to enjoy God's gifts. In the past He taught us lessons about austerity and now He is showing us a new situation, where many material things are being brought here and we should enjoy them with gratefulness, but also help to make the energy circulate, redistributing things, giving to others. Baba re-uses everything and doesn't keep anything for Himself.

25 August 1981

Sometimes it's very difficult for me to be in close proximity to Babaji because how is it possible to be like Him, remaining perfectly still and absolutely aware, silent, empty, with eyes open, completely present, emitting nothing but a radiant light, all at the same time!

Babaji told me the other day that it's not the time any more to close one's eyes, He wants warriors, yogis immersed in action. I think of the Japanese, their martial arts, where to succeed is to remain still, centred, the victor being the one who is able not to move, who is empty, knowing how to make use of his adversary's strength. Here in Hairakhan we are involved in a spiritual battle, fighting first of all what's false and negative inside each one of us, but Babaji has told us that we will have to fight in the outside world as well. We will not always be here, many of us will have to go back to the West where the political and the spiritual revolutions will be forged together in order to create global change. When Babaji speaks in public these days His words are more determined and more revolutionary. He even told us that He is against non-violence, because it is necessary to be brave and courageous.

My only wish now is to remain with Him for ever, but the other night I had a strange dream: I came to Babaji's room but He was no longer there, He had left us and I cried desperately outside the door to His room. Who can tell how long Babaji will remain on this earth.

3 September 1981

The valley is pervaded by a strong yogic energy: many people meditate, sometimes all night, some fast or take a vow of silence, others pray. Babaji's disciples have come here from all over the world, from America, Italy, Switzerland, Germany, Sweden, Holland, Canada and Australia. Each person has a story to tell of how Babaji called them, magically, from so far away. Now it's a time of integration on the planet, an integration of the values of the West and the East. India can offer to the world the science of Yoga, the eternal, ageless knowledge of the Vedas, the Dharma, the spiritual path, so that men and women may be elevated to a divine state of being.

Babaji now speaks English fluently, while before He pretended He couldn't do it. I have also discovered that He speaks Nepalese, Tibetan, Bengali and the language of Assam as well. Nobody knows where He learnt all this, how He came by His physical body or where He came from and He doesn't speak to anybody about it. Prior to His sudden appearance here nobody had ever seen Him in the area before. His presence here remains shrouded in mystery.

The only thing for certain is that His body is not like ours: He seldom sleeps and He never gets tired, the amount of food He eats is negligible and He seems completely unaffected by cold or heat. When we walk with Him in the mountains we can see that His body possesses incredible energy, He climbs like a young deer and flies over the rocks on His descent. He doesn't have any personal needs, doesn't ask for anything for His own comfort. All the things that people give Him He treats as if they were toys and distributes them to others. He offers us love, but without any attachment to anybody or anything in particular; He doesn't get really angry even if He shouts sometimes, because there is no emotion connected with it. He doesn't seem to have normal human emotions.

His energy is infinite and He gives to all in an open-hearted way. To come near Him is like approaching a powerful wave of peace and positivity; His physical form is a magnetic field of an incredibly high potency that attracts all and is irresistible. When I'm in His presence I have the impression that we are all flying around Him like insects buzzing crazily around a lamp, prepared to be burnt by it, attracted by the light, ready to die for love.

The ashram functions perfectly, guided by Him, because He can unite the various energies to a common purpose, as well as the different races from all over the world, yogis, families, children, the rich and the poor. Each person has a duty to carry out and a function to perform, and in its harmony the ashram resembles a model village, a beautiful experimental utopia realized on earth. I know that this is only possible due to the exercise of His constant authority and who knows what will happen if one day He is not here any more.

Babaji is becoming more and more a teacher for our daily, human life, offering an example, showing us the actions necessary so that Truth and Love can be put into practice. Once somebody asked Him what was the meaning of Dharma and He answered: 'Truth, Simplicity and Love.' So easy to say, but very difficult for people to realize and put into action.

6 November 1981

Today there is a huge crowd of people around and Babaji looks tired, irritated and He tells many of them that they should leave. I feel a heavy presence in the atmosphere, a chaos of energies which have to be ordered, cleaned, purified. When people arrive here they think that Babaji can solve all of the problems they have in their lives; I sense their intolerable level of suffering, it is apparent to me and the situation seems inextricable.

However, within two or three hours Babaji has changed the dynamics, making everybody work a lot at various tasks, not allowing anybody time to meditate or think about their personal problems. People have to move quickly, adapt their minds to the task in hand.

In the evening all the people are so tired that they can hardly move and Babaji smiles with amusement, because now people's minds are in a state of surrender and He can begin His work. He works with the energy of the heart, directly, straight and powerful, cutting through everything. We have to come to terms with all our feelings, confront the darkest and most painful aspects of ourselves, which can be distressing, and become fully aware of who we really are. He promises us tremendous joy at the end of the journey, a joy emerging from His eyes, in all of His gestures and movements. He is sure of Himself, perfect, impeccable, strong, gentle and flexible, ever changing, totally free and spontaneous, the all.

15 November 1981

A young, black woman has arrived and Babaji looks so beautiful near her. He possesses within Him the features and traits of every civilization, the essence of every race. This evening He gave a fiery speech on the equality of all races. I was very moved by what He said and began to cry. He told us that

143

humanitarianism is the only true religion and that we should be ready to fight for truth and justice. Once somebody asked Him why He was talking about fighting instead of peace and He said: 'Peace will come only after revolution, after great change.'

Now every morning at 5 o'clock I go to His room after the fire ceremony, bringing with me a cup of weak coffee and I sit alone with Him for a while in complete solitude and silence. I still get scared at times like this, because it's so difficult to be alone with Him. I feel that my mind is never pure enough and I still continue to have negative, useless thoughts. Babaji tries to help me relax and eases the situation by asking me to read Him a letter, tidy up and fold some clothes, clean something. It's difficult to face divine truth without tension, without desires, being open, receptive, as He would like me to be.

25 November 1981

I spend some wonderful time at His feet at dawn each day, sitting with Him outside His small room, observing the rhythm of my heart merging with the sound of the wind, merging with Baba's immensity. I breathe with Him, while He is quietly watching each moment, absorbed in His visions. I would like so much to be at one with His mind, to be able to see and know everything as He does. Babaji remains an unfathomable mystery of which He can only reveal to us a fragment, only that which we are able to receive. I am exceedingly grateful to Him for this precious time spent with Him in the morning, for this sacred communion. I feel a part of His play now, taking care of His things, each object a piece of our world, a symbol of our human condition. The moment when silence becomes my reality I am transfigured into a glow of unreal light, I feel a part of Him, forever a spark of the divine consciousness.

I don't even look at Him now when I am with Him, His body is just the symbol of an infinite Presence, omnipresent, omnipervasive, all knowing.

He gives me so much love, often calling my name with such tenderness that it touches me deeply, and said in such a way as if He needs me, requires my service. Now I feel fully accepted and I see that it has taken me several years to reach this point, to be able to receive His energy. It's a vibration of immense peace and power.

3 December 1981

I often have to translate for Babaji and He is using me as a kind of filter between Himself and other people at times when His direct presence would be too intense for them to bear. I am very grateful for this role, it is a precious gift, because I am able to hear what He is teaching people, what He is trying to transmit to them, what is seeking to be resolved through the innumerable human stories.

Between Him and myself, He often uses Shastriji as a filter, the old sage who always accompanies Him, sleeping and eating with Him. Babaji tells us many stories, sings old poems and relates legends from the ancient Indian tradition, sharing the wisdom of thousands of years. He recounts stories about the great yogis of the past; each of them having to complete some enormous sacrifice, giving up every attachment, in order to reach Truth. The path of divine realization, Babaji tells me, is the most difficult task in this world, an arduous path to follow, similar to trying to walk on a razor's edge. He told me that in the Kali Yuga all yogis trip up on some obstacle or another and even sadhus fail to carry out their practices, some because of an attachment to food, or sex, some due to an attachment to power or wanting to be gurus before they have even become disciples. I look at Baba and feel perplexed. Who knows what will happen to me if one day He leaves me, I have doubts whether I could manage alone, it's only His Grace that allows me to continue tentatively on my path.

The other day, while I was massaging His feet in the garden, He told me: 'I am tired, I am going to the Himalayas.' I asked Him if He would take me with Him but He replied smiling that it would be too cold for me there.

27 December 1981

This year there were hundreds of people who came here for Christmas and Babaji had a large marquee erected over on the gufa-side in order to accommodate everybody. He told us that this was an historic celebration, because it's the first time that the birth of Christ is being celebrated internationally in the foothills of the Himalayas.

We can host large numbers of people, all sleeping squeezed onto mattresses or rush matting on the floor. There is space for everybody, as well as an abundance of food available, tons of sweets and fruits, all offered by those who attend. They have brought so many presents for Baba that I don't know where to put them any more.

We also celebrated with a huge yagna, with offerings made to the fire of incense, flowers, grains, milk, perfume, all accompanied by the recitation of many, many mantras and according to the ancient Vedic tradition. It's collective prayer, where fire represents the Cosmic Energy, the subtle essence, which burns and consumes matter to purify and transform it into light.

Babaji's love keeps us all together, packed next to each other on the floor with our sleeping bags, sitting cross-legged and eating from large banana leaves in the garden, crowded together in the evening to sit in the large kirtan hall. In order to be able to pranam to Him, one has to queue in line for more than an hour. Everybody works with enthusiasm organizing and preparing everything, Indian women sing while cooking around the fire all night, then during the day men serve the food for hours on end carrying it around in buckets.

Hundreds of people and their children come from the villages around and we have prepared a huge Christmas tree and a present for virtually everybody. Babaji made us open a chai-shop and a small Italian restaurant on the bank of the river, where for three days everything is to be distributed free of charge: we are to offer this feast to the Indian people, who themselves are always hospitable, to this land which welcomes us with so much love, to mother India who embraces us and permits us to have this unforgettable experience.

Yesterday, I felt like crying when I saw a long line of Western pilgrims walking up the river valley. They finally arrived here after such a long journey, carrying their luggage on their shoulders, looking for the answers that we cannot find in our own countries, searching for the guide that we didn't have and for a light that we couldn't find in the dark streets of our sad cities. The Divine is calling us to India, one of the poorest lands on the planet, to a Master who looks like an ancient Christ in His humility, His simplicity.

I am quite overcome. On Christmas evening Babaji had us sing *Alleluia* and our traditional Christmas carols, while people dressed in white, depicting angels, danced with candles and Babaji invited us to pass the light around to all those who were present. I saw the eyes of the Indian children shining with amazement and wonder, all their faces lit up, ecstatic, while Babaji played with a group of Western children on His dais, laughing merrily.

4 January 1982

Babaji has said that from now on all the Italian devotees should wear black. He has given them a leader, a man who He has called Kali Shani - Kali is the name of the goddess warrior and Shani the name of the planet Saturn, considered in India to be the planet of destruction. I am shocked by this new leela of Babaji's and fortunately He didn't tell me to wear black. On the contrary, He asked an Indian woman to bring me some white saris from Bombay.

I have an uneasy feeling about this development, all these blotches of black moving around the ashram represent a strange symbolism to me; Shani walks about holding a large, iron trident all the time with a plastic snake wrapped around it. Babaji conferred on him a special initiation while in Bombay, during which He said in public that this young man had already been the personification of the planet Saturn in a previous life. He added that it was necessary for him to incarnate at this time in order to witness the great revolution and destruction that will affect the future of the world. Babaji speaks more frequently now of a future world crisis and I have begun to be really concerned, automatically collecting certain items together in my cupboard. Babaji specifically speaks of the nineties as the years of huge change on this planet.

10 January 1982

The 'black' story is developing into a spectacular theatrical performance. There are numerous Italian people in the ashram at the moment, more than fifty and they all go around, both men and women, dressed up like Mother Kali's followers. The women especially look very solemn and when they are around

Babaji it makes me feel quite anxious. Babaji tells us laughingly that this is the 'Black Army', because now the time has come for war: the devotees who are yogis and yoginis should become soldiers of Bheru Baba, the head of Shiva's army, who defeats all the demons. According to Indian mythology Shiva is the god of destruction, the one who at times of crisis all the gods call upon when they need protection. It is Shiva who eliminates the forces of negativity and restores the harmony that has been lost. He fights accompanied by his Shakti, his female counterpart, sometimes personified as the warrior goddesses, Durga or Kali, one represented by the colour red and the other black. They have the power to defeat in combat any demon.

I'm amazed at this development; Babaji's play in this whole matter is too much for me. When everyone assembles in the evening in the kirtan hall to be with Him the entire performance resembles a Fellini movie: young men with shaved heads, dressed in black and with an air of ferocity, stand around like bodyguards, Shani stands nearby with his trident looking like Rasputin and the Italian women covered in a dark veil of black resemble witches or black widows and evoke in me a sense of danger.

In addition there has also been an increase in the work rate, as if Babaji is in a hurry. The new soldier devotees have to carry stones all day, lifting large rocks from the riverbed under the instructions of an ex-Major from the Indian army. Even the women have to undertake some of the heavy work. Babaji continues with the construction programme, promising us many comforts for the future. The other day He told Har Govind that He wants Swiss gardens at Hairakhan.

Besides those dressed in black some people wear orange; the yogis and yoginis who attend to the dhuni dress in this colour. Babaji Himself dresses up in all sorts of different colours, wearing any of the clothing that people give Him. He moves around amongst us like a magical joker, building His living theatre, His school. These days I really do see Him as the dancing Shiva, Nataraj, the great god who destroys ignorance through His cosmic dance, breaking through all our illusions, our attachments and states of mind, everything that is impeding us from being divine, at one with Him.

A few days ago He called the tailor from the village and told him to make a joker's costume for a boy, to be made with strips of material of every colour: the boy wears it in the evening and dances in public. Nearby, the women dressed in black dance and weave around him, their movements a mixture of the mystical and of Western sensuality, the Indian men too have their own intense rhythm, while the Indian women also dance in their oriental style; now the show is complete. Prem, an elegant and sophisticated Indian woman, stood there horrified and said to me: 'But this is a circus!' and it's so true.

15 January 1982
I tried to ask Babaji why He created the 'black story' and He looked at me

threateningly, asking me in return if I also wanted to wear black. I gave up my questioning. The other night I had a dream in which I saw Bheru Baba, who told me that He is dark because only black has the power to destroy darkness and evil, being of the same power as the negative forces. Only black used by the Divine can do this.

I have begun to look at the Italian man Kali Shani differently, from an altered perspective, because now I see strength and courage in him. He is literally able to stand for hours close to Babaji, perfectly still, fully concentrated, without any sign of tiredness.

Even so a part of me is becoming anxious and I ask myself how long is it possible for Babaji to remain among us, because He is giving Himself so completely to everybody, playing our human games with infinite patience, coming down more and more to our human level. He has put on weight, His body swollen, He often looks tired, sometimes there seems to be a coarseness about Him similar to our own, because He is absorbing our negativity and our problems. Often He tells me His health is not good, asking me for medicine. Inevitably I compare Him to the Babaji of the early years in the seventies, pure, a form of perfect beauty, like an angel appearing to have come from another dimension; we couldn't reach Him on His level and so we want to bring Him down to ours, making Him share our human condition. This is His task on earth, I know, but it's painful to watch. Yesterday He called Shastriji and me to Him and sang a sorrowful song: 'Your Beloved is on the cross, don't you see, and how will you be able to reach Him?' I was totally and utterly shocked.

20 January 1982

Sometimes He plays the part of a child with me, a Divine Child who needs care and assistance. He calls me to put His things in order, comb His hair, give Him a glass of water, or prepare something to eat. I feel useful, and to serve Him is for me a way of being in communion with Him, feeling accepted by God, part of His work. It's also a way in which I can express my gratitude to Him, my immense appreciation for all that He is giving us on this earth with His presence, His teachings, His work of transformation on every aspect of ourselves, on every cell of our being. He is preparing us to be the living organisms for a different sort of experiment on earth, to bring light into the denseness and obtuseness of our bodies, to purify our hearts, and He is giving us an example of a love for humanity that is lived out in every moment, in every gesture and action in our lives.

His teachings can be applied to every single situation we meet in our daily existence, so that every day can become a sacred puja, an act of adoration for that energy which sustains us, which is our life's purpose. Babaji is always teaching us precision and perfection in all that we undertake. He wants extreme cleanliness from us and goes around the ashram with His stick, checking every dark, neglected corner; when He comes to my room, He checks if there is any dust around, ensuring my sari is perfect. We can't leave dirty pots in the kitchen, dead leaves in the garden, rubbish lying around anywhere, clothes left unwashed; spiritual purification begins not only with our physical bodies but also in our relationship with Mother Earth on which we stand.

Babaji's own room is incredibly orderly. He gives great attention to each and every little thing, taking care not to waste anything. In this way He offers us an example of how to conserve things, like showing us how to save a needle, or an elastic band, to re-use a piece of paper or an envelope; behind every material object there is human energy, labour and work. He scrupulously counts and administers money, distributes second-hand clothes, folds coloured wrapping paper, re-utilizing anything that may be useful, all with great care. He often gives away money to the Indian workers, but with shrewdness not ostentation, always giving the right gift to the right person. What is demonstrated is a model of a different universe, a place of the future, where we can utilize human effort and the energy of the earth in an appropriate manner, respecting nature and not abusing it any more. He told us that the new world will begin from Hairakhan and that He is preparing us for our role.

Everywhere in the garden He is planting seeds, as well as mango trees, papaya, pomegranate and cherries. He had us remove stone after stone from an area close to the riverbed creating a beautiful field where we are to grow rice, grain and vegetables. He also wants us to keep cows and horses.

He wants beauty and divinity for humanity. In the past yogis were looking for the Divine only within themselves, meditating in solitude, but in this epoch of transformation Babaji wants to change nothing less than the whole planet, because the Aquarian age is about to come.

Many of us have arrived here due to an inner calling and we have travelled the roads of the East in search of an ancient wisdom that we were unable to find in our own countries. We were seeking knowledge which would help us make sense of our human existence, looking for a spiritual answer which neither communism nor capitalism has yet been able to offer.

3 February 1982
The rhythm of the work has become hectic, Babaji makes people work until 2 o'clock in the afternoon, shouting that He has little time. Sometimes He becomes angry, especially if people are lazy, indolent and then He sends them away, even using His stick on them. He asks people to make the maximum effort, because through all this physical work He is making us perform a spiritual practice. Yesterday I was shocked, because He caught hold of a young woman and beat her on the back with His stick, breaking it on her shoulders. Then He gave the broken stick to me in order to glue it back together again. In a moment of courage I dared to ask Him why He didn't teach with love and He answered me that love has gone to the Himalayas and that when people cannot understand with love He has to employ force. Then He also slapped my face

two or three times, in a manner that He has never done before, because of my obstinacy; sometimes I rebel when I have to face a task which I find too unpleasant or onerous.

I also work non-stop because there are so many people here and I have to take care of so many things: my tiny room has become full of stuff and Babaji's room now resembles a small palace. It is my duty to always be near Babaji, ready to translate His correspondence, but also I should not cling to Him like a leach and know when to disappear and leave Him alone. Many people are jealous of me, because these days Babaji keeps me so close to Him and I have to face a lot of jealousy and envy, especially from women. Sometimes I get caught up in the game, in the competitiveness and I feel bad. I know that Babaji wants me to remain neutral and indifferent in these sort of situations but it's not always easy.

I feel that we jump on Him like hunting dogs as if He were our prey, everybody wanting to be as physically close to Him as possible, looking at Him, touching Him, wanting to receive one of His smiles, a sweet, a present, seeking to serve and massage Him. Today He was sitting in my room, on a chair, with His arms and legs flung wide apart, while some young Western women were massaging Him, when He suddenly turned to me and said: 'Eat, eat, take as much as you want, finish me up.' I was the only one who could understand, because He spoke in Hindi and I remained stunned by His words. I also feel guilty at times, because of all the time and attention He has given me in order to help me to change.

The situation in the ashram has become difficult, with so many people packed in the small rooms, a really heterogeneous group, Indian families, children, well respected people as well as the poor, and a whole mixture of Westerners all with their individual problems. There are young people addicted to drugs, those who are lost, other people who are mentally disturbed, going through a crisis or who are gravely ill. They all hope that Babaji can magically solve everything, perform miracles, remedy incurable diseases of the mind, solve business difficulties, their poverty or marital problems, even sort out marriage arrangements; we want Him to console and protect us, to solve complex psychological problems, reassure us or predict the future, we want love, attention. This is representative of the range of miracles that are requested of Him. Our human suffering is immense, never-ending and sometimes I ask myself what Babaji can really do for us and why God can't alleviate all this pain immediately and remedy the situation.

Once I put this question to Babaji: why doesn't God always intervene and help us with His Grace. He responded saying that Divine Grace is always present, but the law of karma has been created and is even superior to God and so the Grace can only act according to certain karmic conditions. Karma is the law of cause and effect, by which we have to reap all the fruits of our actions. Babaji said once that karma comes into play with the first movement in the mind, with the very first desire. One way to purify the mind is to incessantly repeat the Lord's name.

The Indian mystical tradition contains many stories of saints who spent years in seclusion, only repeating a mantra, trying to realize the Ultimate Truth. In this age Babaji wants us to meditate while in action, working in the world; maybe it's a little easier or perhaps it's a more difficult challenge. I am trying to do this here in the middle of all this activity, in this Babylon, and I often lose my sense of equilibrium: if I meditate, I don't feel like speaking with many people, if I am in constant contact with people and involved in their problems then I lose the concentration I need to meditate. Probably Babaji wants me to be able to do everything with an empty mind, like a child, open, just allowing energy to pass through me.

15 February 1982

I have become friends with a beautiful young woman, Afro-Italian, who Babaji has also told to wear black and He calls her by the name of mother Kali. She is exceedingly happy about this, laughing, and I suddenly feel that black can be a powerful energy, promoting courage. We are Lord Shiva's yogis and we should have courage, be able to face the world, even absorb poison and transform it, as in a tantric process.

Once more Babaji is playing a cat and mouse game with the women and I have to confront the sexual energy and purify it, transmuting it into psychic energy in a subtle way, as if it were an alchemical process transforming base metal into gold, in the same way that all the physical energies need to be refined and turned back into light.

Sometimes Babaji embraces me ever so tightly, almost hurting me, but without any romantic illusion. It's a contact of energy, of love too in a certain sense, but nothing to do with physical human love; my body functions now solely for meditation, to channel all the vital and psychic energy towards the highest ideal and the highest knowledge. Also I know that my life is dedicated only to Him and to the spiritual work.

Even so there are times when I still feel disturbed by watching Babaji playing with the women, touching them and provoking them. Sometimes the entire ashram seems pervaded by this vibration. Yet I am also conscious of the fact that this sexual energy is what largely predominates in the world today and that sex is one of our greatest attachments on the physical and material level.

Babaji reflects and purifies, He elevates and transforms constantly with a degree of sacrifice that is extremely great for Him, in a similar way to that in which every guru has always done. Every prophet and master who has come to the world of human beings has had to carry the burden of this cross.

A couple of days ago Babaji told us in the kirtan hall that while on the cross Jesus received his fourth and ultimate initiation and through that initiation he became one with God, having overcome the ultimate test. Sometimes I am scared that this sort of constant sacrifice is what He is asking of me and I'm afraid I'll not be able to see it through; I want to run away, escape. Babaji asks for huge sacrifices from all of us here and sometimes I don't feel up to it; I feel too cold in winter, too hot in the tropical heat of summer and the monsoon, there are too many discomforts and there is not enough good food. Also one is always surrounded by people, in constant contact with them, it is difficult to have any privacy, never possible to take a holiday, and there are even times when I feel so closed up in this valley, separated from the outside world, that it is as if I am in purgatory.

Today I was looking out on to the valley, full of people, pilgrims from all over the world: a group of Italians all dressed in black lifting and carrying stones, some other yogis and yoginis dressed in pink and orange going down to the river to clean and prepare all the implements and utensils used in their ceremony, the Indian people working in the fields, women sitting in colourful circles busily cooking chapatis on a fire, children playing in the water, an old Indian sadhu sitting in meditation like an ancient sage and a Western woman just dancing ecstatically. It's a complex community, fascinating, finding its unity in its diversity, a common goal achieved through the love for the guru and a devotion to seeking truth. In the evening in the kirtan hall I observe all the people looking at Babaji, they are so happy, blissful, their faces lit up by His light, like stars rotating around the sun. They are like angels singing about the glory of the Lord and Babaji is happy too, transmitting to us the pure joy of His blissful consciousness, His love, His immense peace. At night I only sleep for brief periods, but extraordinarily deeply. At His feet I feel completely fulfilled and lack for nothing.

3 April 1982

Summer has begun and it's already very warm. It is the time of year for the Navaratri festival; nine days of celebration dedicated to the Divine Mother. Hundreds of people have arrived in Hairakhan and there is little enough room for them all. People are camping everywhere, sleeping wherever possible, in the kirtan hall, under the trees, crowding in. The Indian people especially seem to be able to fit in anywhere, their bodies take up such little space, they have so few requirements only needing a few pieces of clothing to change into, a blanket to lie down on and some bread to eat. If the wars occur that Babaji has foretold then they will be the people who will be able to survive because they can easily live without electricity, petrol and gas. They are vegetarian, know how to work the fields with no more than their hands, can build a small hut in a few minutes, or construct a simple bridge with rocks and they can live around a fire in the open as if it were their home.

Babaji is teaching us about all these things and especially to be patient with each other and be supportive. If two people don't like each other, He will put them to sleep together in the same room. If somebody is attached to the idea of

152

having private accommodation, then Babaji will certainly put that person in a large uncomfortable dormitory room. Sometimes there are empty rooms, but people have to live together in order to break down selfishness and egotism, our sense of superiority, in order that He might shape us to His will.

This time the festival is glorious, large amounts of money flow in through donations and Babaji performs huge yagnas. There are prayers, singing continues all through the night and there are bhandaras, celebratory meals for thousands of people. We cook without respite beginning at dawn and from Haldwani come trucks and horses laden with provisions, it's a realm of abundance in this country where there is so much poverty. Everything is offered free of charge, but money is donated spontaneously and so we automatically realize a utopian ideal: those who are rich give most and the poor give in some other way. Everybody is eager to serve, to help in whatever way they can and this spirit of service is one of Babaji's main teachings. I think that if humanity could learn to live in this way we would solve all of the world's problems.

Yesterday Shastriji gave a public speech and said that Babaji, in the Kali Yuga, the age of darkness, is giving us a taste of the Satya Yuga, the age of Truth.

10 April 1982

The celebration is over. Today is my birthday, but I don't dare to say anything. Babaji told me one day that I cannot celebrate my birthday any more, because I have started a new life which began on the first day I met Him and so I should think of myself as being only ten years old. I am extremely tired, but happy. Babaji keeps me near Him continually and every day my small room is transformed into a party room for receiving guests; Babaji endlessly distributes food, presents, smiles, words of wisdom, playing with us as if we were eternal children. I accompany Him like the priestess of the ritual, in fact He told me that He is the king and I am the queen and that everything which is His belongs to me too. He has put all His money in my cupboard and told me I can take and use whatever I want. I know I should be careful not to become proud with all this attention.

15 April 1982

An older Italian woman has just arrived, an old friend who first met Babaji many years ago and we sleep together in the same room. She is quite wealthy and has decided to build a temple for Babaji in Italy, but I also realize that she is quite anxious about money, rather attached to it in fact. Every day Baba asks for her purse from her bag and distributes her money to the poor Indian people. She is so upset and confides in me that she doesn't want to carry her purse around with her during the day any more in case Babaji gives away more of her money, but she doesn't dare do that. Babaji is amused and ironically observes the game, continuing the training. Last month in Vrindavan He ordered her to offer food to a couple of hundred sadhus in the city.

The other day, another leela took place involving a homoeopath who was enormously proud of his profession: Babaji took all the bottles of homoeopathic remedies from the hands of the man and mixed all the little pills up together before distributing them to those people present. I think He is teaching us not to be superior, to overcome our pride and not to be presumptuous with our limited, human knowledge.

17 April 1982

Babaji has played out another bizarre leela, one of His cosmic jokes. He married Har Govind, the Swiss doctor, to Kamalata a young German woman, in a real ceremony organized by Himself around His sacred fire-pit, telling Har Govind that he will find peace now, but I immediately felt that He was preparing some sort of a trap as well. Har Govind and his wife love each other very much and are of course, also attached to each other. The day after the marriage ceremony I saw Babaji calling Kamalata to be near Him all the time and taking her with Him for long walks. It was as if He was courting her.

Har Govind feels desolate about this separation and tells me that he is crazy with jealousy, but Babaji gives him no respite. He knows everything and has not finished yet. After about ten days of this Babaji announces in front of everyone in the kirtan hall that Har Govind is a very great yogi and because of that he is permitted to marry more than one wife and that this will not adversely affect him in any way. So Baba's intention is to marry him to a young American woman as well and now of course, it's Kamalata's turn to undergo a training in being jealous, as if this situation were not already bad enough. We are all quite surprised and horrified by this turn of events. Babaji really married Har Govind again but in an informal ceremony, then put them to sleep together in the same room for ten days. Then He suddenly called them out in public, scolding them and telling them to leave the ashram, accusing them of doing something impure, of making a bad mistake. Har Govind complained to Babaji that it was He who had married them and who had involved them in this set of circumstances, to which Baba replied that being placed in this situation had been a test, in order for him to prove himself and that Har Govind had been unable to pass it. Babaji added that when He comes to this world He always comes to give us amrita, divine nectar, but that we always choose poison. He reminded us that there are two primary attachments in life: 'Food and sex.'

I remember that I became upset once, because He was mischievously smiling at a blonde woman. He said to me: 'I have given you the highest path, the path of yoga, don't look back, don't look around, don't look to see what a man and a woman do together, it's the path which leads to hell.'

2 May 1982

Today I translated a speech for Babaji in public and I felt as if I was attending a political meeting: Babaji speaks now like a warrior, telling us that the plight of the world should now become our main concern. He told us that what is necessary is that we should simply become humanitarian, act kindly towards each other.

Wisdom is sometimes so simple that it seems too obvious, and because our minds are complicated we cannot grasp it.

10 May 1982

Sometimes there is terrible jealousy amongst us all particularly in respect of Babaji, most especially among the women. We are more emotional, more inclined to be attached to Him, wanting to receive His attention or expressions of love and Baba plays incessantly with all these emotions so that we may overcome them. We take notice immediately of the smallest, pettiest things, like to whom Babaji is giving a sweet, or a piece of fruit.

I remember, long ago, during a tour, in the midst of a huge crowd of people, Babaji said that whoever wanted a sweet could stand up and come to Him. So everyone stood up, hundreds of people, like little children desiring attention, just to receive this insignificant gift from Him.

Prem and Deviji, two lovely Indian women who come from wealthy families, frequently compete together for Babaji's attention. He sometimes treats them as if they were queens and then in the next minute He screams at them to pack their bags and go away for ever. On one particular evening He made fun of them in public, in front of everybody, by gesturing to give one of them a gift then giving it to the other, repeating the scene a few times.

He is also exceedingly strict with me if I fall into the trap of being competitive. There is one particular German woman who always aggressively snatches out of my hands whatever I am about to pass to Babaji, so as to give herself status by carrying out this service. When I become upset or angry about this He tells her to do it more and more. I am to remain neutral, indifferent, so that my ego does not become involved in the predicament.

On other occasions He protects me, when for example if someone is jealous of me, but He only does this if I have remained innocent in the situation. One day He forced a woman who was envious of me, to clean all the toilets in view of Baba and myself while we were seated romantically together on His terrace. Little scenes like this are repeated frequently. It's like being in constant psychotherapy, to force us to look beyond our pettiness, our selfishness, the limitations of our ego. I often watch all these scenes and feel disheartened, because people are fighting with each other; just to be one centimetre closer to Him they walk on His heels, women want to massage Him all the time, men want to stand near Him, to feel a sense of importance like some sort of general in an army.

It all resembles a movie of which He is the creator, assigning us the various parts of the characters involved like an expert director. Once He said to me: 'I have made all of you ministers, officials, kings, princesses, but I am nothing.' At times like this I feel ashamed to see my own needs so readily recognized and accepted. It's a theatre, reproducing our human condition and we act like eternal children, always greedy, demanding gratification and never satisfied, while, as all the teachers say, it is desire and our own limitations which must be overcome in order to bring our consciousness to a state of peace and in union with the Divine.

The bodhi tree

1 June 1982
Today I felt so hot that I almost cried. When I walked I tottered unsteadily and could hardly remain standing up. I sat exhausted by Babaji's feet, outside His room and He caressed my head, pointing to the large bodhi tree under which we were sitting, telling me I should love this tree, water it and put perfume on it, because it's a living entity and will always protect me, not just from the heat. It's like a natural air conditioner, He said and in fact it's true that sitting there under its branches one feels comforted. I watched Babaji, dressed in pink, hardly sweating, while His skin emanates a subtle fragrance. The wind blows

through the parched valley, the river seems to be made of light and I can sit near Him, thoughtful, a faithful servant, made happy just by His presence. I am reminded of an Indian song: 'My Lord, just allow me to sit outside Your door and wait for You, and it doesn't matter if You will come or not, I'll always sit here, waiting for You, for eternity.'

Time passes quickly when you are near Babaji. At each dawn and dusk in His company when I can just stay in communion with His light, His silence, it brings me to another dimension, where eternally there is Shiva's tree, His river and His mountains and eternally the Master holds the disciple's hand on the path. The way is eternal as well, already at one with the destination, the eternal infinite present.

I am so happy that I am afraid of losing all this, because I know that beautiful things never last for long enough on this earth. Sometimes, if Babaji just so much as reproaches me or I make a mistake I cry desperately for a long time because I feel fragile, so far from perfection, not worthy of Him. I am so afraid to break the magic of His presence with my stupidity, my inadequacy. Babaji often consoles me if I become too depressed, calling me to Him with a remarkably gentle voice, endeavouring to help me overcome the pain of separation that I feel, until that day when I'll be complete, at one with Him. In no way is He trying to deceive us: the path is long and difficult and perhaps the most important virtue is patience.

1 July 1982

Today Shastriji and I bathed Babaji in the river, already flooded from the monsoon. Babaji parades around now with a large belly, strutting like a proud peacock, His stomach having grown immensely this year and making Him resemble a Chinese Buddha. His body is swelling up and I have seen this occur with some other yogis. Perhaps it has something to do with some particular breathing practices; He tells us, smiling, that He has two babies inside. We put soap on Him, shampoo His hair; His skin is like silk, like that of a baby and yet at the same time His body feels strong like iron. His body is delicate, smooth, unreal, emanating a strong, natural perfume. He took my head and Shastriji's head, knocking one against the other telling us that we have been together over many lifetimes, the old Indian sage and the young Western woman.

It's sunset, the sky is full of red clouds, surrounded by a huge rainbow. It's like a dream, an ancient fairy tale.

15 July 1982

Babaji walks around all the time in the rain with a woman holding an enormous umbrella over His head and I am suddenly jealous again, feeling so stupid, ungrateful for all that He is giving me. During the monsoon He requests that I should spend most of my time inside my room in meditation, but it's difficult, I find it hard work, I'm still restless. At one time all I wanted to do was meditate but now I find it so laborious to curb my mind, even after so many years.

I watch Babaji walking far away down the river valley and I feel melancholic, strange. I would like nothing more than to be close to Him, but when I am with Him it's not enough, because I would like to be at one with His mind, to see and know the Divine completely. I feel that Babaji is making this pain of separation even greater and deeper on purpose so that I am forced to practice my sadhana and make even greater effort towards purification, looking for Him within myself more and more.

The river valley and the temples on gufa-side

159

It's so difficult to erase all useless thoughts. The mind is faster than the wind, Baba said, and it's so true. After so many years of practice I feel continually bored repeating the same mantra, I am losing faith in it, no longer having the enthusiasm I had for it at first when I savoured the divine energy. Now it is as if nothing special is happening, and I feel dejected.

25 August 1982

We have celebrated Lord Krishna's birthday with a grand theatrical performance and the village children were spellbound, enchanted by Babaji and by all of the people from all over the world, it is magical for them. The rain is torrential this year, the jungle green, luxuriant, full of fresh growth. Babaji takes us with Him for long walks to the villages and enters all the poor people's houses, talking at length with them, trying to help them with their problems. He told us the other day that we should do something for these people, for the development of the valley of the Gautam Ganga and we should learn to serve humanity, especially the needy.

The ashram is well organized now by a group of Americans, who write letters and have published books. Babaji wants publicity now, He told us that the time has come to spread His spiritual message to the world. He has foretold that the spiritual movement will now spread all over our planet, leaders of countries all over the world will be replaced during a period of great change and the future age will be religious with an awareness of the Divine, a new positive era for humanity. All spiritual leaders, He said, will come to Hairakhan. Our work now is to change our hearts and Hairakhan is our spiritual university.

3 October 1982

Another autumn and as always at this time of the year a fresh period of spiritual training begins at Hairakhan; there are already many people here and the ashram is overcrowded. Every morning at five o'clock I sit alone with Babaji after His short fire-ceremony because now it's the only time I can spend with Him quietly. I wait for Him in the small dressing room adjoining His bathroom with a thermos of weak coffee and I read Him the mail. He looks at the sealed envelopes and tells me what to answer without my opening them, telling me if that person can come or not, and what he or she needs.

The ashram now has many rooms and can host more than two hundred people. The place is not as charming or romantic as it was in the early years when it was a wild, isolated place in the jungle, but Babaji is well known now and His teachings are for the many.

A lot of children are also being brought here and Babaji has said that they are the future of the world and that the married devotees should have babies and bring them to Hairakhan. He is very affectionate towards them, caressing and kissing them, playing with them, even though they are under His training as well. Occasionally He is strict with them which makes them cry and just like the adults they are sometimes afraid of Him and when this occurs He has to dissolve their tension.

It's difficult not to be scared in the presence of Babaji, I am still afraid of Him too, even after so many years. To be in the presence of an energy so intense, penetrating the very depth of my soul, it feels as if I'm standing in front of divine judgement. Although it's an opportunity where I can learn to be absolutely transparent, I also remain afraid of not being loved, accepted, or not being worthy of Him.

Babaji continuously works with this fear, to allow love to flow, so that we can surrender and just express ourselves simply and naturally around Him without hiding anything. The only quality He doesn't allow is our pride, but He is gentle with our weakness if we acknowledge it to Him. The first impulse of our ego when we are with Him is to want to appear superior and important; women want to look beautiful, just as they do in the ordinary world, in the game played out in conventional society. Babaji asks all of us to shave off our hair, dress the same way, pranam at His feet in order to learn humility, and to recognize our ignorance; only by recognizing it are we able to undertake the long task of integration and healing.

5 November 1982

The energy in the ashram is a grand composite representing many different kinds of people. Babaji moves around like a wild cat, like a crazy psychotherapist, magically catching hold of our minds, forcing us to confront our own identity and then to surrender. He cannot give us any spiritual food before first having us solve the psychological blocks within the depths of our psyche.

The Western mind is particularly polluted but also highly sophisticated in deceiving itself in numerous ways, adept at auto-illusion. It's a mind dependent on television, accustomed to continually changing channels, dreaming up numerous fantasies and illusions, clinging to that kaleidoscope of subtle and perverse images that it creates. Babaji wants us to switch off the television screen of our minds, creating circumstances where we can say no to our self-deception and choose truth instead of fantasies, reality instead of a dream state. His choice of therapy is a constant alternative theatre, where He highlights our attitudes and beliefs, amplifying them in a visible way both clearly and grotesquely, so that we see the stupidity and absurdity of our problems.

He is like a consummate movie director requiring us to be the actors in this drama, just asking us to play our part well, with detachment, with a sense of humour, aware of the process. He is reproducing in microcosm the complete drama of life.

'A lot of children are also being brought here...'

Some time ago He told a young American man that he should always stand close to Him carrying an unsheathed sword like a minister of justice. Shani is already positioned there holding a trident, like the king of the Italian people and I think that they will both have to remain standing there in this manner until they understand what this leela means and are then able to move beyond the play. He is always improvising situations, treating some women like queens as if they were Cleopatra, giving them beautiful silk saris, or seating them in a special place near Him with a parasol and fan. Then, suddenly, He may tell them to leave immediately, shouting at them when they don't understand and take the game too seriously. Often He shouts angrily holding His stick threateningly, in a theatrical gesture, giving us shock therapy like a rash Zen master, attempting to break through our mental rigidity, to make us jump up immediately, shaking us out of our conditioning. Often one can meet people in tears down by the river, sometimes collapsed over their rucksacks, preparing to leave because Babaji has sent them away and they don't know when they can return. It may be that they reach Haldwani or even Delhi before coming back, having realized, digested and understood their teaching and only then will Babaji consider allowing them to stay here.

He is psychologically torturing Prem, a rich Indian woman, telling her first to come to Him and then to leave immediately, only a few seconds afterwards. It's a hard training for her, because she is from a very good Indian family and her pride is obviously hurt, but it seems that she has to go through all this.

29 December 1982

This year I became extremely tired during Christmas, with a multitude of people here all expecting a present. A large marquee was organized but it poured with rain incessantly and the marquee became flooded and then collapsed so that everywhere we sat or ate food there were streams of mud. Perhaps this is one of Babaji's jokes. Water dripped everywhere and the outdoor kitchen was drenched but despite all of that somehow we managed. Although the weather has become very cold, we all squeeze together in the kirtan hall and keep singing, sometimes eating under the portico. Babaji is showing us that we should never get dejected, but face every obstacle with courage, overcoming it all like warriors. In fact, people are laughing, thinking this is one of Baba's leelas, His divine play. It would be nice to be able to face all of life's difficulties in this way, without making everything into a drama, considering every happening as part of a teaching, a test in the great theatre of Truth.

Babaji had me wrap numerous presents with coloured wrapping paper for some important Indian people, valuable things, which He gives away without any hesitation. Although He gives great attention to the needs of the poor, I notice that He also treats the wealthy with particular regard and respect, although He's not concerned about giving certain people greater privileges. He knows how to treat everybody according to their particular needs and their expectations, teaching us to fully respect our differences and diversity, because we are not all equal, each of us having a specific karma to go through.

He told us that this is a special Christmas, which will not occur easily again, because so many races and cultures, religions and different types of people have united in peace, working together in a collective effort, searching for God.

Now we even have electricity at Hairakhan and I observe the valley from the top of the temple steps: the cave and the nine temples, the fire in the dhuni in the garden continually burning, the small local village opposite, Babaji's special peepul tree and our rooms, now comfortable. Babaji has built so much in just a few years, a small, experimental, model village, a university for the spirit, a workshop for the mind, where we can learn to become truly humane, moving towards our highest potential.

5 January 1983

It's an extremely cold winter, but Babaji has now given us many facilities: there are bathrooms, warm water for people who want it and don't go down to the river to bathe, we can go to various chai-shops for breakfast, there are mattresses to sleep on, in fact so many amenities which we did not have before. Even so I am not happy, I miss the magic of the old times, when I didn't have any material things to care for and I could just sit quietly with Babaji around the fire in the dhuni.

Babaji's school of learning carries on and the stones to be lifted and carried from the riverbed are never ending. He has given yogic initiation to many men and women and is teaching us all how to be in the world, preparing us for future action through renouncing and overcoming our attachments and desires, working towards a higher, divine reality and consciousness. He told us that we should adopt a new slogan: 'Jai Maha Maya ki jai!' which means, victory to the great Maya, the Mother as Manifest Creation as well as Cosmic Illusion. She is not and cannot be differentiated from God, being His manifestation; we should learn to merge in the great Energy, using it, transforming it, according to the plan of Truth and Love.

Babaji is showing us this ability, moving amongst us with the agility of a dancer, transforming everything with a gesture, a look, destroying every atom of darkness and negativity, changing everything with His light. I see that He has so little time left for Himself now, He is always with us, without a break.

I become afraid that He will exhaust Himself and that some day He may leave us, because He is really carrying out an enormous task.

25 February 1983

Now I wake up at three o'clock in the morning in order to be able to do everything in time and often I don't eat anything until the evening in order that I don't become listless or sleepy, because I don't want to miss a second of Babaji's presence. I'm surprised that I don't get hungry or feel weak and Babaji jokes with me: 'Are you eating, my daughter?' When I walk I feel very light, as if my feet are not touching the earth and when I close my eyes, I could be anywhere. I fall into a trance-like state quite spontaneously and automatically, not conscious of my surroundings, lost in a subtle state of bliss. I am longing to be at one with Babaji with all my heart, I would like so much to be able to see, feel, know and to move like Him. At times this sensation occurs for a few seconds, especially when I am serving Him and I feel myself in tune with Him, with His gestures, as if my hands and feet have become part of Him.

In the morning He sits on His terrace to receive people and He puts His feet on my lap, but I have even lost the desire to massage Him, I just like this contact, this sense of belonging. In the evening, when I pranam to Him in the kirtan hall, He puts His hand on my head and I often stagger back to my seat feeling a shaking in my being and an intense energy on my head, transporting me to another dimension.

4 March 1983

I am serving Him twenty hours a day and it has become just as He told me it would be once before; that one day I wouldn't even have time to eat or sleep any more. It's necessary for me to pay attention to all His gestures and actions and be ready to pick up what He forgets, to prepare a seat for Him wherever He goes and to translate all His words with the utmost concentration. I know He doesn't really need all this care and attention, this obsession with caring for Him, and that maybe it's even a burden for Him.

I think He allows all of this to happen just for my sake, to give me the opportunity to feel myself near Him concentrated on God, because I don't like rituals but can relate to this living statue, that speaks to me, looks at me, teaches me something continually.

5 April 1983

On these summer afternoons Babaji receives many people, especially Indian guests, all crammed on His terrace, waiting. He has instituted a guard to stand outside His door, who announces to Him the names of the people who want to see Him, and then gives permission for them to enter, but I can always enter together with Shastriji in order to help take care of everything.

We sit in the shade of His beautiful tree and Babaji prepares fresh fruit juices, generously offering them to everyone and distributes nuts, sweets or dried fruit. People appear to be so happy in His presence. He emanates a continual aura of peace, joy and fullness. Often we sit in silence with Him for a long time, a silence so full and vibrating with energy, with the occasional sounds of the jungle round about and a subtle ecstasy pervading the valley; at His feet our minds find rest at last.

He is often strict with me, severe, wanting to teach me a perfection that I find difficult to maintain and sometimes He gives me a slap or scolds me. Then afterwards He calls me back with much love, telling me not to be troubled or concerned, because, He says jokingly, in India wives are accustomed to being beaten just as they are in Italy, but He adds that this is something that I will not have to worry about any more.

He would like me to be precise, full of concentration in all things, not too slow and not too fast, observing my mind. I am able to achieve this way of functioning if I can clear my mind of thoughts, think of nothing and allow myself to act automatically, guided by a higher power.

At every moment we receive Shakti from Him, pure energy, then we can become empty, inspired. It's by no means straightforward, especially for a person from the West, to accept that from now on we have to give up our individual will and carry out the Will of God, and that this is divine law. I remember an old saying from the Buddha: 'When you are able to forget yourself, you will meet Me.'

The other day while bathing Baba in the afternoon He spoke to us about these things. Deviji was crying, because she had to leave Him and return to her home and Babaji said to her: 'Why are you crying? This body is nothing, it comes and goes. The only important thing that exists in the universe is the Will of the Lord.'

10 May 1983

The routine has changed again and now at sunset five or six of us give Him a bath in His new bathroom that has been constructed, and He sits for a long time talking to us, giving many teachings. Shastriji is always there, the elderly sage who knows by heart all the legends and ancient stories from the Vedas and from the Indian epics and he often recounts these tales.

Today Babaji spoke to us about the Divine Power, telling us that on the day that this energy enters us our actions, everything that we do in fact, will be inspired and guided by a superior consciousness, able to manifest miracles. I asked Him how it would be possible for me to reach this stage of development and He replied that I should never forget the name of the Lord because He will guide me.

10 June 1983

A few days ago I was restless and sitting pretending to meditate, when Babaji arrived and said to me: 'You left the name of Ram, but you didn't leave your attachments.'

Yesterday He sang me a sad song, 'The boat of my life is old and decrepit. It is sinking and I beg you guru of compassion to guide me across the river, help me to cross the river.'

15 June 1983

Prem, my Indian friend is very desperate. Babaji is torturing her psychologically all the time. He calls her to Him and then tells her to go away in front of everyone. She is a woman from a wealthy and noble Indian family and for her it is terribly humiliating to submit to this kind of treatment but she has a lot of pride and a great deal of attachment to the physical body of Babaji and He plays with those feelings. Sometimes when she meets Him in the garden He amuses Himself by hiding behind bushes.

Sometimes Babaji's love play with women still confuses me, even if I know that He is only and always teaching something. I have completely detached myself from the physical need for men while as a young woman in Italy my love relationships were always at the centre of my life.

I recently read a book about the tantric path: sometimes gurus use the sexual energy and even certain drugs as a technique to achieve a certain state of ecstasy, in part using it to purify and destroy attachment itself, and in part to reach a certain stage of transcendent awareness. They say that Shiva uses the poison of desire as a means to transform attachment and finally destroy it. On one side we have the ascetic path of renunciation and on the other side, the tantric way of transformation. Sexual desire is the strongest and most potent desire in human beings, because from the sexual act new life comes. Yet if we can conquer and master this desire we can then make use of this pure spiritual energy, known in yoga as the energy of the kundalini, the subtle psychic current, residing in our bodies at the base of the spine. Through celibacy, the practice of being a brahmachari, we can awaken the kundalini itself and reverse the energy's vital course, from its downwards tendency to an upwards one. In this way all our subtle centres, our chakras, will open and allow us to receive mystical knowledge.

25 June 1983

Today I watched Babaji walking hand in hand with a young Indian woman, it looked so romantic, something serious, but it is just another show, I know it now for what it is. Babaji called me to Him immediately afterwards and asked me: 'Have you ever watched a love drama?' He said it with one of His ironic smiles, far beyond our human limitations and even beyond any sense of seriousness.

When Lord Krishna used to play his flute on the banks of the Jamuna river, all the gopis, the milkmaids who were devoted to him, used to run away from their houses in the evening to be with him. On the night of the full moon the sound of Krishna playing his music would attract all the souls to him, they would dance happily and so be enchanted by God.

The legend states that at a certain point Krishna abandoned the gopis in order to teach them about real devotion, the devotion for the invisible Spirit. They cried desperately for a long time, but this suffering of separation was necessary in order to bring them closer to the Divine.

10 July 1983

Last night, at about one o'clock in the night, Babaji called me to His room together with Swamiji, because He was feeling very sick. He had so much pain in his chest and great difficulty in breathing; I became extremely scared. Today

He felt better and decided to travel to Ranikhet, because the Governor of the state of Uttar Pradesh is coming here in person to take Him there by helicopter. He wants us to take great care in preparing to welcome these important officials, including all the officers and the army personnel who will be accompanying the Governor. There is a great deal we have to organize and sometimes I get really fed up with all these official procedures, but Babaji wants us to give them a perfect welcome, to observe all the necessary formalities and respect the recognized protocol properly. When I was younger I rebelled against all the rules, especially those of the middle classes but now Babaji is showing us something different, teaching us to adjust to every situation because it exists for a particular reason and to participate in any type of performance, like impeccable actors. The psychodrama always has a didactic and therapeutic function, for at the end of the event we are able to understand more about the ultimate sense of reality.

'...Krishna playing his music would attract all the souls to him...'

25 July 1983
Babaji has returned from His trip to Vrindavan, and while He was away I stayed here in Hairakhan meditating a lot during the beginning part of the rainy season.

I don't have much time left for myself any more, being busy all the time around Babaji. When I meditate now, even for few minutes, the concentration

168

comes easily, immediately and I can quickly detach myself from the outside world and feel a peaceful silence within me, a deep stillness, an expansion of consciousness. Even when I have my eyes open and I simply look in to an empty space in front of me, I can easily see it flooded with bright, white light, pervading everything around, transforming my reality.

In the long, rainy afternoons I sit alone with Babaji under a canopy outside His room, lost in His light. The outline of His physical body begins to disappear and I am just left with a Presence, a mysterious power, vibrating with intensity and luminosity. I feel at one with Him for a few moments, not even guru and disciple any more, just belonging to the same Spirit. He jokes with me, telling me I am His wife, and now I understand what He means, the significance of the union of which He has often spoken.

2 August 1983

Babaji has built a new dhuni down near the river, in the midst of the garden and overhung by some enchanting rocky outcrops; telling us that thousands of years ago there was an ancient, sacred fire-pit here. He had already designed and built the fire-pit with His own hands, an octagonal shape, signifying He said, the eight arms of Jagadamba, the universal Mother, and now the building is complete and it is to be inaugurated. This dhuni will be the home of the Goddess, of Maha Shakti, the great cosmic Energy and the fire will be kept alive day and night, with havan performed and offerings made to the fire, morning and evening.

He has told Har Govind, the Swiss doctor, that it is his duty to care for the dhuni, that he should always remain here as a yogi, keep the fire burning and also offer yogic training to other people. Babaji Himself has now given special initiation to several people who want to remain in Hairakhan and become yogis and yoginis, giving them orange coloured clothes to wear and instructing them to renounce the world and dedicate their lives to God. They have been given a code of living, to worship the fire, meditate around it morning and evening, they can marry but must only live in ashrams or spiritual communities, never working for money, only for the Divine. They are the Hairakhandi yogis, protectors of the sacred fire and it's light.

Sometimes people stay up all night long, chanting mantras and praying around the fire; it has become an important place of meditation. Babaji told us its importance in one sentence: 'Without a guru there isn't any knowledge and without a dhuni there isn't any meditation.'

Like everything Babaji has built, the dhuni is a place of great simplicity and beauty with the sweet sound of running water nearby, situated among banana and mango trees and with a extensive garden now being created.

Today Babaji also initiated Lok Nath, an American man, and gave him the rules for a yogic sadhana, telling him that there are three main enemies of a yogi: 'greed, lust and anger.'

15 August 1983

Babaji has immediately started to play tricks with the new yogis, the young men and women dressed in orange to whom He has given initiation. He arranges situations to confront them about their pride, their insecurity in their renunciation of the world or with various other temptations: a beautiful young woman, money, sex, power. For instance He gave numerous duties to an American man to perform, a position of importance involving a great many responsibilities in the administration of the ashram, but a few days later He shouted in public that the man was a spy from the CIA and told him to leave the ashram immediately.

On another occasion He called a young Indian man to Him, a yogi, very proud of his knowledge in meditation, telling him to initiate others into meditation, which he did. After a few days, He called all the people together who had received the initiation, insulting them, because they accepted to undertake it, telling them that it was a test and that people with strong faith should only follow Him.

Another time He beat Sitarami, an American woman, because she had made an offer of money to a young Indian woman and had followed her around for a while because some considered her a kind of goddess. Babaji shouted that even if we see gods and goddesses flying in the sky, until He tells us what they are we shouldn't believe in them. He is demanding an inflexible faith from us, people who are unequivocally prepared to embrace an attitude of total trust and complete surrender in Him, to let nothing else remain.

17 August 1983

I am learning to eat very little, sometimes nothing all day long, but I feel constantly nourished by a subtle energy. I work hard, but I am not tired and when Babaji calls me, I run instead of walk. Only rarely do I feel hungry, just occasionally in the evening and I feel strong even though I have become quite thin. A small gift of prasad from Babaji, just a morsel of food from His hands, is enough for me to feel regenerated and through that small amount I feel I am receiving the entire essence of food, of the earth, the sun, from which it all comes.

Today in the afternoon when it was extremely hot, He called me to give Him a shower, alone with Him on His terrace. I felt moved by this, because I could soap him, massage Him, comb His hair and although I know that these aren't important things, for me it's also a test, a proof of purity. The more He plays with the women the more He tests me, giving me an extensive training in detachment and perhaps preparing me for future work.

The other day He showed Himself completely naked in front of an Indian woman, with impassiveness, ironic, wild, with me standing near Him, like a nurse with a doctor. The woman became pale; I know she has to accept the nudity of the physical body as if it were a natural occurrence. Babaji is a revolutionary teacher, direct and without compromise, ready and determined to confront any darkness that may exist in our soul and only by facing the truth can we then work to achieve resolution.

25 August 1983
In the evening I become extremely tired sometimes and I fall asleep in the kirtan hall, right on the window sill where I am sitting near Babaji. When this happens He throws a banana or an apple at my head to wake me up. At other times I make such an effort not to think, that I then forget everything I have to do; it's difficult to carry out practical things, to remain with my feet on the earth, but maybe Babaji wants to take me to the sky.

Now that I don't have to participate in all the rituals any more I can make use of that time in the morning and evening to meditate instead. Babaji told me that I can carry out my worship alone in my room in just five minutes using only a stick of incense and I am happy about this, because I feel closer to God when I am alone. I can concentrate more fully in solitude, feeling the divine energy within me. God is not external to me any more but is an experience lived by each one of the cells of my body, in every movement of my mind, in each of my breaths. One day Babaji sang me a song, telling me that God is beyond every name and every form. I remember another occasion when I was sitting near Him in my room and my mind was automatically repeating a mantra so as to overcome my tension, when Babaji placed a finger on His lips and He made a sign indicating to me to maintain a silence that is beyond the mantra as well.

27 August 1983
Today somebody asked Babaji what He thought of Christ and He said that Jesus lived in India and Tibet when He was very young, receiving many yogic initiations. He added that Jesus had also been in Benares becoming a disciple of Babaji in that city, receiving teachings there and shaving the hair from his head for the first time. He said that the cross was the fourth and last initiation for Jesus and in that moment he became one with God. Christ, Babaji said, is always present among us, assisting us in his astral body.

Today was Lord Krishna's birthday and Baba kept me near Him all day long expressing so much tenderness. I had to sit with Him, eat with Him, massage Him; sometimes I feel overwhelmed by all this attention and what is more, I even find it difficult just to remain in His presence for such a long period of time.

29 August 1983
Today Babaji embraced me lightly, placing His face close to mine; the touch of His skin like that of a child, soft like velvet, the gesture made with a childlike innocence, angelic, transmitting His energy to me. I also remember when I was

a young girl that these wonderful innocent moments were among the most precious times spent with my friends, when I could share an embrace, a simple contact, brothers and sisters with no sense of sexuality. Babaji is a divine friend, someone perfect and His love is a subtle union of spiritual energy. I am touched by a deep tenderness, almost frightening because I have to give up everything of myself, let go of every last resistant remnant of my mind and have total faith. Sometimes love comes close to feeling like death, and divine love is, in a way, the acceptance of this ultimate state.

3 September 1983

Yesterday Babaji became angry with me, because of some mistake I had made and He told me to leave, to go from Hairakhan. At night-time I couldn't sleep and about midnight I crept outside the door of His room, feeling desperate. I sat in the dark, without making any sound and I started to pray to Him mentally to forgive me, to give me a sign. After half an hour the door suddenly opened: Babaji had heard my prayer, He told me off gruffly but stroked my head, forgiving me and sending me off to sleep.

Now I know that He can hear me at any time; whenever He tells me to leave my heart breaks, I can't think of living far away from Him. Every day spent near Him is so incredibly precious, His constant teachings fill up every moment of my days and now I often feel I am thinking, moving and acting in accordance only with Him.

5 September 1983

I greatly admire Deviji, a beautiful Indian woman; she is kind and gentle. She has an intense relationship with Babaji but strangely enough I never feel jealous of her, because she shares her experiences with me and I can learn a lot from her. Above all we never enter into competition with one another but co-operate and collaborate, even to the extent of complicity in respect of Babaji, trying to get His love and His attention, trying to catch Him for ourselves. He often keeps us together with Him as if we were two sisters and in my room we organize small parties for Him, where we prepare food, some presents, massage His feet, fan the air around Him. He allows us to play this game, playing the king in His palace, talking and joking with us as if we were His queens or courtesans.

I feel that Deviji approaches Babaji in a very different way to many of the other women. She has tremendous respect for Him, to her He is God not just a man, a divine statue to serve, adore, pray to and worship. In the evening she performs a beautiful and elaborate puja to Him in the kirtan hall, making her offerings to Him in a sincere and meticulous manner. Babaji often talks with her spontaneously and at length but I am not envious, admiring her for those qualities that many Indian women have: beauty, virtue, grace and strength while at the same time joyfulness and kindness.

I note that Babaji has a special relationship with the Indian people, a particular respect and consideration for them. Religious people in this country follow a dharma, that is to say a path of morality and spirituality. In this context family life and marriage are extremely important for them, as is the responsibility of bringing up children, their sense of duty in the world and honesty in their work, which they perform with a sense of service and self-sacrifice. To this is added an awareness of the possibility of God's existence in their life, a sense of surrender that does not amount to resignation but is an acceptance of karma, of destiny and of a Divine Plan which guides their lives.

They have a simple but special relationship with Baba. For them it is quite normal for God to take a human form, quite natural to obey and surrender to Him with total devotion. They adore Him with full spontaneity, like children; I notice that we Westerners have complicated minds in comparison and we always want something from Him while Indian people ask for so little, just giving Him their love, satisfied just to be near Him, contemplating His beautiful form, to be in communion with Him. Babaji often behaves and communicates with them as if with a close friend, not so much in His role as guru, but laughing, joking and talking, making them feel united with Him through their service.

He has built a kind of royal court around Himself, where everybody has a role, a particular function with a symbolic meaning. On the esoteric level these roles closely represent different types of divine consciousness and the performance of these roles is, in the main, a precise training, having the power to gradually develop in each individual a sense of union.

At times I feel Hairakhan is a grand alchemical laboratory, where Babaji, the expert magician, mixes and transmutes all the elements, so as to manifest the final product. Once, when He slapped me, He told me with great affection that He was beating me in the same way that gold is beaten by the goldsmith, in order to make it into pure gold.

7 September 1983

Today somebody asked Babaji, why He wasn't teaching Kriya Yoga, the breathing technique, spoken about by Paramahansa Yogananda in his book, *Autobiography of a Yogi*. Babaji answered in a loud voice that to speak of Kriya Yoga in this way makes no sense, it is a distortion, that is to say everything, all action, working, walking, even eating, it is all Kriya Yoga and we should learn to dedicate all our actions to God without any expectation of the outcome.

In the ashram we are now organizing many activities and Babaji is playing with people's egos when they start to become superior or are eager to make decisions or give orders to others. It's the 'boss syndrome', as we call it jokingly, present in each of us. I notice that Babaji chooses on purpose people who want to be important or wish to order other people about and He tells them to organize everything, giving them positions of responsibility. As soon as their egos pump up, He continues to encourage them to give orders while at the same time telling the rest of the people not to obey them, creating a huge drama and paradoxical situation. It's Babaji 's way of slowly forcing negativity to rise to the surface, so that the person concerned can then face these traits and overcome them because these habits are outmoded.

I watch one robust American woman in particular, who runs around in the manner of a general of an army, getting completely worked up giving complicated instructions to people, while they are hardly listening to her. Babaji appears amused and laughs at the entire show.

12 September 1983

Many Italian people smoke hashish continually, they are lazy and have no discipline. Today Babaji shouted at me that it's all my fault, because I started to bring all these people to Him, but a few minutes later He called me over to Him again and said: 'Yes, Italians are really undisciplined but they are My greatest devotees.' Italians are not unlike the Indian people, they open their hearts to Babaji with love. On the other hand, there is an Italian subculture and some of them roam around like vagabonds and layabouts, using drugs like a ritual for collective unity. I did it myself when I was a young woman but now it is different. The spiritual path requires discipline and control over one's mind; now it is necessary to learn to become strong, able to practise concentration. The use of drugs is a means of running away from the effort required by this way of life and from any sense of responsibility. Babaji told me I should teach Italian people not to smoke hashish, but it's a daunting duty, because they have no intention at all of listening to me.

He places most of them to live on the far side of the river, the gufa-side of the ashram, where He allows them a certain freedom to experiment and go through their experiences until they come to a greater understanding, because knowledge has to come from self-experience. It is also true though that Italians can be very warm-hearted, spontaneous and generous but these days I often feel a stranger amongst them, because even if I was a hippie myself for a long time, Babaji has now changed my life completely and I have come to feel more Indian than Italian.

In the Shaivite yogic tradition all these various elements and energies are utilized and transformed and so Indian sadhus often smoke, because hashish can help to calm the mind, to block many useless thoughts, change coarse habits and help a person to reach a transcendent state of consciousness. In tantric practice the physical body is of great importance, because it's the manifestation of the Shakti, the creative energy and it can be utilized for yoga; Hatha yoga, fasting, and various other ascetic practices help to awaken the subtle energy, the occult power. The science of the subtle body is the great treasure that Indian yoga can give to the West. The goddess Kundalini, symbolically represented by a golden snake, is the Energy of Light, guiding us to experience directly, within ourselves, the existence of another reality. Yogis of the Shaivite tradition have no fixed rules and they don't necessarily even conform to the Vedic tradition, even if they do respect it. For their practice they have to achieve a certain discipline, but that may be different for each yogi, so instruction is only conferred directly from guru to disciple thereby meeting the requirements of each individual person. There is only one rule, valid for all: to totally immerse and sacrifice oneself in the fire of the yoga practice.

25 September 1983

Babaji is leading me through a deep, inner revolution. I can see that my life is now completely ruled by my spiritual practice and I should not be deflected from my purpose. From the very first moment that I wake up in the morning until the last moment when I go to sleep at night, my mind is focused only on Him, on Babaji, on God, the Truth, whatever name we want to give to that consciousness which we wish to develop in ourselves. All my work, every gesture that I make every day, has become like a practice for me, an instrument to understand something, a means to further purification. My life's aim has become just one thing: the realization of Truth and nothing else. Babaji has taken a human form to give us a constant example of what a human being can achieve, the potential divinity within each person.

On a few occasions I have tried to perform a puja to Him in the kirtan hall, holding a lighted lamp in front of Him. He took the flame from my hands and started to wave it in front of my face, teaching me that He only resides inside myself. Once again I was doing pranam to Him today when Baba asked me: 'To whom are you doing pranam? I am your own Self.' On another occasion I was walking in the jungle with Him and I stumbled on a stone because I was intent on looking at His feet. He turned towards me and said: 'Look inside; outside there are many difficulties.'

5 October 1983

I don't know what's going on but Babaji now wants me close to Him all the time, I am under His constant supervision. At times I run away, to talk with some friends, in order to feel human again. A few Western yogis always remain close to Him now, like bodyguards. They serve Him, but they also create an impenetrable circle around Him, sticking close to Him, fighting with each other to obtain His attention, to be one centimetre closer to His body, in competition to hand something to Him or receive a gift from Him. Babaji works with all these emotions, provoking jealousy so that it can be faced and overcome, inflating our pride and conceit until people are so full of themselves they become puffed up like a balloon ready to be punctured just at the right moment. Being in the presence of Baba a person can never feel really safe. If you feel a sense of pride about a certain position of responsibility it will soon catch you out, it is by no means uncommon for Him to suddenly take it all away again. At every step He is teaching us humility, because our desire to assert our individuality, our ego, is the cause of every one of our illusions and the source of our suffering. We have become separated from the Divine, from our divine home, resembling fallen angels who ultimately only cause ourselves pain by trying to affirm a separate sense of identity.

13 October 1983
Today I asked Babaji in what sense Maya, the cosmic illusion, exists and He

answered that what is existing is the projection we make on reality; our dream exists but it is just our imagination. He added a song: 'God and Maya are One together.' Nothing of what's existing can be different from its creator.

Shastriji explained to me that things in themselves are not good or bad, because everything that exists comes from the Divine, even that which is apparently negative; it is an illusion to think otherwise, the result of ignorance, born out of our attachment.

Desire is the beginning of separation and suffering. In the Christian religion the concept of separation is symbolized by original sin and whatever meaning or significance we wish to give to the famous apple, it's the symbol of a personal desire and a lack of surrender to Divine Will.

14 October 1983

The Governor of the state of Uttar Pradesh is here again accompanied by about a hundred people, army and police personnel, various important officials. Babaji moves like a great king amongst them, organizing a royal welcome. When I compare Babaji now with the person I knew a few years back, thin, ascetic, silent and extremely serious, He is so very different.

Today He has become the perfect host, and I help Him choose elegant clothes to wear. He told the Governor that a great political crisis is about to engulf the entire world, we will witness war and destruction on many levels, enormous changes and natural disasters. Speaking in this way has been a constant theme with Him recently. He says the changes are necessary and that He has to prepare us for future events. The Governor is more than eighty years old and has been the disciple of many great masters. He is famous and well known in India, but in the presence of Babaji he becomes like a child in front of a distinguished young father. Babaji is always sure of Himself, a master of every situation, perfect, powerful.

10 November 1983

Once more autumn comes and the air is fresh and clear again. Early in the morning, on Babaji's terrace, I feel as if I am in paradise. The first rays of sunlight turn the valley a wonderful pink colour, the flowing river shines brightly and the running water is repeating a constant mantra; nature praises the beauty of creation. Last night there was a full moon and the valley was magical with angelic spirits, the mountains resounding with the songs people were singing, people from all over the world coming to visit the great Master in the midst of the Indian jungle. Sometimes I become afraid of losing Babaji, because His presence amongst us is like a beautiful dream and dreams never last for ever. Every morning, when He emerges from His room, I look at His feet with gratitude, thanking Him for the daily miracle of His human form on earth.

25 November 1983

Long mornings with Baba, meditating near Him with my eyes open, concentrating on the empty space in full awareness. These days the white light I usually see is being transformed into a golden colour that is quite intense and I hear a subtle sound within me, a constant companion, an all-pervading melody; if sometimes Babaji speaks He almost breaks the enchantment.

Yesterday He told me He was tired and He lay down with me on the carpet of His dressing room. I became scared, but Babaji just embraced me softly, putting one hand on my heart and the other one on the top of my head. I remained there with Him, motionless, for something like half an hour, sensing only the sound of my breath attuned with His in a regular, quiet rhythm, and a remarkable silence and peace pervaded everything. All I experienced was the subtle union of two souls, two energies and two lights. It felt as if Babaji were like an angel, near me, soft and warm, protecting me. When He stood up I touched His feet with deep reverence for a long time, moved by the experience of this sacred communion, of this grace. Babaji looked into my eyes like a child, with such innocent shining eyes and immense sincerity that I cried, sensing the intense purity that He was communicating to me, and then He dried my tears with His blanket.

'…with such innocent shining eyes and immense sincerity…'

23 December 1983

We are making preparations for the celebration of Christmas and today Babaji

178

became angry with a group of Americans, telling them that they had spent too much money and have exaggerated the care required in making arrangements. He added that Christmas is not about material things and that this is the last Christmas He is going to celebrate. In an angry mood He took three jackets which different people had given Him recently and wore all three of them together, one on top of the other. As I have done so often before I watched Him play out this human drama for us.

I've noticed that many people ask Him for big personal favours and treat Him like a magician with a magic wand who can solve all of their problems. Very few come in search of the truth and fewer still are prepared to sacrifice something for it. I feel irritated and get upset when I have to translate people's demands: requests for money, wealth, good health, good fortune in love, success, and only rarely do I hear people desiring God. Just a small minority of people are His disciples and carry out their sadhana, able to accept making the effort and sacrifice required for spiritual practice.

Occasionally Babaji gets really mad, especially with the Italians, He screams at them, complaining that they are always sleeping, are lazy, take too many drugs, are always after sex; and yet the other day He took my arm and told me that the Italians are also His greatest devotees.

4 January 1984

The Christmas celebrations went on all night with songs and dances from all over the world. Then on the first of January Babaji called us down to the riverbed and gave a long speech about the new world that is about to come, but told us we will have to work hard for it, karma yoga, the yoga of action, the supreme practice for these times.

He invited us to unite, to organize our groups and spread the divine message everywhere in the world.

10 January 1984

When Muniraji comes to Hairakhan from Haldwani Babaji wants us to welcome him with particular respect, as a guru and a saint. We should go down to the riverbed in order to receive him, pranam to him, prepare somewhere for him to sit and perform puja to him in the kirtan hall. Every time he comes here it is my duty especially to prepare a puja and serve him, as well as arrange a small party for him in my room.

Babaji is trying to establish a special relationship between Muniraji and myself, as if he is also to become my teacher and maybe, I think, he has been one in some previous life. Certainly he is a special man, with a beautiful, oriental face, gentle, very quiet; his presence emanating a feeling of great peace and tranquillity. He rarely speaks, as if his mind is empty, he is remarkably humble, never making a show of himself, always attentive to serving Babaji and everybody else; a great example to others.

Sometimes, if Babaji has been hard with me, Muniraji comes to my room to console me with exceptional kindness; his house in Haldwani is always open and he arranges for me to eat and sleep there whenever it is necessary, acting towards me like a father. He lives and works in the world, as a businessman, has a family, many children, and yet he seems detached from it all even though he is involved in all these worldly activities. Babaji told us that he incarnated as a householder in order to teach people that one can be a person working in this world and be a saint at the same time. Certainly he is an example of impeccability and completely dedicated to Babaji; he serves the ashram, sending to us all the necessary provisions that we need in trucks from Haldwani and whenever we visit him at his home we are welcomed with a smile.

Once Babaji told us that there will come a day when Muniraji will have a great duty to perform on His behalf and it crossed my mind that perhaps at some point in the future Babaji will disappear again, as mysteriously as He arrived, back to the cosmic consciousness. The other day Babaji and Muniraji looked into each others eyes with the same smile on both their faces: radiant, delightful, languid, ironic, the same infinite awareness.

13 January 1984

Sometimes I am worried about whether Babaji will be able to continue to deal with all these diverse energies present in the ashram, people coming and going all the time, ever-changing situations and difficulties. He engages Himself personally with all of the problems that each person has, even the most insignificant. I understand the great suffering of each of these people, all their tremendous needs and requests for help, because this is all part of the human condition. I am also aware that Babaji is working with everybody's energy, taking their problems on Himself and absorbing it all to such an extent that it makes His physical body swell up, even to the point where He becomes ill.

I feel His infinite compassion, trying to help us on every level, showing us a way out of our human difficulties, because this human existence can be like purgatory, and we have come to this place to purify ourselves, to learn about sacrifice, to liberate ourselves from some of our ignorance and the darkness accumulated from previous lives. Babaji is able to show us the way in which we can gain liberation from this state, but then it is up to us to actually take the necessary steps, because He can't do everything for us even if He is there to hold our hand.

I often find myself asking how long He will remain with us; the situation is intense and with so many people continually coming here it all often seems too much and perhaps there is little time left. I feel exhausted myself from all this work but also feel I have to remain close to Him. Yesterday He said to me: 'My queen, come back home, I have been waiting for you for a long time.' I asked Him what He meant and He replied: 'You are my queen, but not the queen of this world, the queen of paradise.'

The human journey is a search for perfection in its entirety. All the religions have commented on this question but human beings have usually rejected what has been offered because it has too often been presented in the form of churches, power and dogma, separated from the reality of daily human life. The path of Indian yoga is more difficult to refute because it offers us the opportunity of inner realization, something each individual can experience for themselves in every cell of their body. Yoga is the greatest science of the mind, a challenge to be undertaken in the search for transcendental knowledge. Even scientists, faced with the mystery of the stars, know that in this universe which is continuously in motion, the speed and energy of light is the only constant existing reality.

14 January 1984

Babaji wants me to feel a sense of union with Him, a state beyond my ignorance, my limitations and inadequacies because I know really that my higher self is already at one with Him and that His form is only the external projection, symbolic of my own divinity. Yet even He alone cannot give us everything and it is presumptuous of us to think otherwise. While I realize that I should be able to maintain being humble it remains a difficult balance because I know there are still areas of darkness within me which obscure the totality of light.

Now Babaji insists that I always sit close beside Him, dresses in clothes the same colour as mine and has me walk side by side with Him like a good friend and talks with me intimately and in confidence. Maintaining my equilibrium is not easy and I know I should not become too proud or want to boast to others about what He is giving me, otherwise He will take it away again. Only when I am able to feel I am nobody and nothing, completely empty, not existing any more, almost like a separate entity, does He fill me up with His love, as if I am a part of a lost unity, a fragment of the All.

He resembles the divine bridegroom in an ancient tale, because all of us want to unite with Him alone, with the Lord, it is what we are missing in our lives. It's Him and Him only, yet it is also Her, the great Mother as described in scripture, it is the Source and the Origin of creation, the primordial Energy, the ancient Wisdom, the Power, God and His Shakti united forever, Masculine and Feminine, Ying and Yang, Void and Fullness, Stasis and Creation. The Divine is duality in unity, nothing and everything, my existence or yours, our own consciousness.

Today Babaji asked me: 'For how long have you been with Me?' Spontaneously I answered: 'Since the beginning of time,' and He seemed very happy with this answer. He calls me to Him constantly, with a continuous, silent act of love, so powerful that I become afraid, afraid of the suffering I will experience if one day I should lose Him. Often He looks so intensely into my eyes that I become embarrassed, because I would like to merge in Him, but I

181

am afraid I might die. I withdraw when He embraces me because I am fearful of my attachment. I wish to be as pure as light, merging in the light, totally immersed in it beyond every form and every limitation.

'He told me that He will always protect His devotees...'

15 January 1984

It is no longer possible to rest during the day, I continue without a pause. Even at lunchtime Babaji takes me to eat with Him and Shastriji across the river to the gufa-side of the ashram. I am flattered and happy, but I am feeling so tired.

Gaurhari, a young Indian man, is delighted to cook some light, delicious food for Him. We sit in a small room above the cave and while Babaji is eating Gaurhari massages His feet with motherly love. Babaji offers me food to eat from His own plate and scolds me if I refuse to eat enough, but when I am in His presence I feel as if I am able to live off nothing more than the air. After lunch we return together to the other side of the ashram across the river and He takes my arm while walking. I feel the touch of His hand, soft, scented and warm. At times I become embarrassed, but He always makes a joke to make me laugh or engages me in pleasant conversation in order that I may feel relaxed. I still do not find it easy to remain in His presence, it is only His love that forms a bridge between us.

25 January 1984

Early in the morning I take a stove to Babaji's dressing room in order to heat some water for Him to wash His hands and I choose His clothes. Occasionally He listens to the world news on the radio, sometimes to some devotional songs. The other day He told me that there will be a third world war and that He will save Russia and India. Then He added that after He has departed there will also be a large organization devoted to Him, a big, international movement, working towards global change for the planet. He told me that He will always protect His devotees, even during times of war and destruction. It's so long since I have read a newspaper or heard any world news, none of it has occupied my mind because I have only involved myself with His presence, with His demanding training. Somebody asked Him: 'What sort of revolution will you make?' and He answered: 'A green revolution.'

30 January 1984

During these cold winter mornings we often sit with Babaji on His terrace for up to half the morning, gradually warming ourselves up in the sun, two or three of us sitting on a rug quietly at His feet, together with some of the people from the village. Baba shares with us an ancient, forgotten wisdom, talking profoundly in an old, deep voice, such a contrast to His young-looking body. He tells us parables, fascinating stories from the past, with a great sense of humour, skilfully ridiculing the conventions of the world. I feel that something is changing in me, an old knot is melting in my heart and I allow myself to relax in the sun, feeling safe in His presence. Thoughts come and go, but don't disturb me any more, they blend with the natural sounds around, with the energy of life, with the harmony of an inner song. I feel a deep peace, because I know that I am walking on a path with no return, without any uncertainty, a difficult one, exhausting, but it's the great Way and it has completely taken hold of me forever.

183

Mahasamadhi

2 February 1984

Babaji has been acting strangely for a few days; He looks tired and He has cancelled his spring tour to Bombay. He is spending a great deal of time lying on His blanket in the sun. He is not well and often in the morning in His bathroom He is sick, vomiting in front of me and I am deeply worried. I ask Him what is wrong, is He not well, but He refuses to answer me, elusive. He is so tender with me, keeping me near Him, almost like a shadow, but something is shaking in my heart. I am aware that He gives all of Himself in order to help people, without any break, so much so that He doesn't even have time to sleep any more, if He ever did sleep at all.

This morning He kept me sitting in silence with Him, for literally one hour and I experienced a state of profound ecstasy, engulfed and transfixed by a golden light at His feet. I hadn't even noticed that an hour had passed, merged as I was in a silence full of sound, absorbed in an inner music. I feel I have nothing to search for any more, God will Himself give me what I need and everything will come at the right moment, I only need to be empty.

10 February 1984

Babaji is very sick. He has a fever, the whole of His body is bloated, swelling up; it has happened to Him a few times in the last few months. He sits either in His room or in the garden and showed me a map of the world, rolling it out slowly in His hands and told me that there is only pain and suffering on this earth. Then He said to me: 'That is why you came to Me, you came here because you were suffering, you were not happy,' and He thoughtfully opened a book which somebody had recently given to Him, about the catastrophe of the atomic bombs that had been dropped on Hiroshima.

11 February 1984

Babaji isn't getting well and I am preoccupied with His state of health. He has the same symptoms He had a few months ago, when He called me into His room with Swamiji in the middle of the night: complaining of severe pain in His chest and difficulty in breathing. A doctor came this morning from Haldwani and diagnosed His condition as bronchitis which is why He has problems with His breathing. Even so He still continues to receive people, moving slowly and with weariness.

12 February 1984

Babaji remains ill and this afternoon He called some of us to give Him a bath, Shastriji, some of the yogis and myself. He sang us a song, telling us that He only has one heart, but that there are thousands of wounds and knives in His heart. He looked at me at one point and said softly: 'I have consumed all of your diseases, now it is my turn.'

He wanted to listen to a cassette of Mirabai's songs that He had received as a gift, because He said jokingly that I am like her. He repeated to us some of her words, both the most beautiful and the most sad, which she had spoken to Lord Krishna: 'My Lord, why can't I see You any more, nor can I speak to You; my eyes are red from crying and I have almost become blind from my tears; why don't You tell me something, just a few words, at least in my dreams.' And then, 'My Lord, the other night You visited me in a dream and You embraced me, you were so beautiful, adorned with peacock feathers, holding a flute in Your hands. You just touched me for a moment and that has been enough for me.' He asked me to translate these words from Hindi to all those present and I looked at Him, afraid of losing Him, of being, one day, separated from Him.

13 February 1984

I am beginning to be deeply concerned and worried about Babaji, He spent part of the afternoon with Gaurhari, the young Indian pujari and myself in His room, asking us to massage His feet. He still has a fever and considerable pain in His chest and the expression in His eyes has changed, they have become tired-looking, languid. We sat in silence with Him for a long time and I felt like crying at seeing Him suffering. We just don't understand what is wrong with Him.

In the evening, when we were gathered around Him as usual in His bathroom, He asked me to press a yantra, a symbol of the divine Mother, onto His heart. I pressed it there with my hand, but I don't understand what it all means. Afterwards I sat alone with Him for a while and wanted to pray for Him, but to whom, if not to Him? Strangely enough, as if by instinct, I started to repeat the Ave Maria and He slightly nodded His head in my direction. I don't want to disturb Him with my presence and I try to maintain a silence in my mind, but it's difficult. All of a sudden, He called my name with so much tenderness and love, it was as if He needed me; I brought Him an aspirin, but I felt useless.

15 February 1984

Yesterday morning Babaji left His physical body and there are no words to

185

describe the pain and suffering that I feel. Yesterday at five o'clock in the morning when I entered His room only Muniraji was sitting there alone with Him and he told me to sit down as well. I wanted to escape, to run outside because Babaji appeared motionless and I really felt He was suffering. I even allowed myself to imagine for a moment that He could die. I couldn't stand this thought, even for a second and took refuge in His bathroom to cry.

After a while, Har Govind called me back inside the room and told me that Babaji had left His body and that His heart wasn't functioning any more. I couldn't believe it and I started screaming that it wasn't true, that it wasn't possible. Even Muniraji suggested that maybe He had just stopped His heartbeat, as great yogis sometimes do and that we should wait and not say anything to the other people in the ashram. We sat for two or three hours in the room, four or five of us, taking it in turns to sit next to Him, but His body was becoming cold. I called out to Him again and again, touching His face, but deep down I had known from the beginning that He had left His body.

Babaji is now lying outside under the peepul tree and hundreds of people have begun to arrive here from every corner of India to receive a final glimpse of Him. In the room His face had a particularly serious expression, but the moment we brought His body outside it acquired a mysterious smile, sweet, blissful, ironic, His last darshan and teaching to us. I can't stop crying. I just want to die, to go with Him wherever He has gone; life on earth without Him is meaningless to me.

16 February 1984

We buried Babaji in the garden at about noon. While people were carrying His body all I could see was just His black hair, shaking in the air. I was reminded of Shiva's dance, when He is dancing the Tandava dance, the dance of destruction when the entirety of creation trembles. That was the last vision I had of Him.

Today, after the burial, an incredible storm erupted with thunder and lightening, the river turbulent and muddy the way it is during a monsoon, the wind blowing wildly, it's extremely cold and doesn't stop raining, it even hails. I thought of Babaji's predictions for the future of the world, of a possible crisis on the earth, of destruction and perhaps He has left for a little while in order to prepare us. I also remembered about the storm which blew for three days after Christ was crucified.

I am obsessed by one thought, that maybe Babaji has left because of us, because He had to absorb all our negative karma, all our desires, all our suffering. Without Him, for sure, I don't want to live any more.

17 February 1984

I have been completely unable to eat or sleep for three days and have never experienced such pain in my life before. I have lost everything, my father and mother, my husband, my son, my friend, my guru. I have lost the only perfect being I have ever seen on this earth and now the world is like it was before I knew of Him, dark, full of suffering and ignorance. This morning I was taken by surprise to see the village people leading their cattle to the fields, because for me life has come to a halt without Him, it is useless, empty. People here are in a state of shock and keep embracing each other, feeling alone once again on this difficult earthly journey. Last night I watched people in the kirtan hall and they seemed so grey to me, without light again, lost.

Muniraji drew me to his heart and caressed my head, but I also saw him crying. I climbed the steps up from the river to the temple with him and looked across towards the top of Siddeshvar, the highest mountain in the area, suddenly seeing a bright light, His Presence again. I know that Babaji is always there, but the human part of me cannot bear His loss. Again Muniraji pressed me to sit close to him and once again the light appeared, strong and white, ever present and I felt Babaji everywhere, in every atom, in the air, and yet my heart cannot find peace. I would like to hear His voice calling my name tenderly. I would like to be able to look into His sparkling eyes, caress His beautiful feet and talk to Him.

Once more I have to relate to an invisible God, one which is difficult to perceive. I went to the temple but I couldn't pray, couldn't relate to mute statues made of stone; I feel as if I am visiting an empty church again, in a museum of dead things. Babaji was the life divine, the Essence of all.

20 February 1984

I have locked myself in my room for three days and I cannot be reconciled about this loss, or accept Babaji's departure. I can't bear to talk to anybody, to hear their consolatory words, and above all I especially can't tolerate people telling me that Babaji is now inside me, because who will give me His energy and His love? I miss Him in every moment of every day and without Him the whole valley seems to have lost its beauty. Often I go to His small room and cry desperately, even His perfume has gone. What remains is an ambiguous, unknown Presence, difficult to grasp. The depth of my sorrow makes me feel like I'm made of stone, unable to think, utterly empty, so intense that it transports me to another dimension, maybe closer to some sort of truth. I certainly don't care about anything to do with this earth anymore, nothing matters; I would just like to sit outside His door, close my eyes and wait until He comes to take me with Him. Instead people insist on asking me about all sorts of practical things concerning the organization of the ashram, the local authorities and other people who seem lost. I find it so difficult even to answer them.

Muniraji gave a public speech and said that not even for a moment should we think that Babaji is no longer here with us. He added that it is even possible that He may return in a physical body again, perhaps soon. 'How soon?' I asked him and he said: 'Maybe within ten years.' But dear God that just cannot be, ten years without Him is impossible for me even to conceive.

Now we stick to Muniraji as if he is the new guru, but I don't like this, it bothers me. For myself, even if I love and respect Muniraji it is not possible for me to accept any form that is different from Babaji. If only I could see Him at least in a dream, to receive some message, but my nights are empty too.

22 February 1984

Yesterday Luisa came from Italy. She is an astrologer from Milan and she told me that Babaji had sent her to me, to tell me that He will come back within a few years and that I should wait for Him here. Who knows if that is true. I sat on His tomb in the garden during a break in the storm, looking at the wet earth that covers His body and I thought that His death is His greatest teaching for us, about the impermanence of every physical thing. His body was a relative thing too, transitory, but so precious to me. This ultimate lesson is so difficult to swallow, because God's physical body is the guru and the relationship with Him is so important. I feel pathetic, I don't want to become a lonely, sad saint. Har Govind passed by while I was sitting there and tried to console me, telling me that forms come and go but Babaji's work in the world continues. But at this point in time I don't care about anything or anybody.

188

Babaji Invisible

28 February 1984

A peculiar power game has commenced among the people in the ashram which disturbs me, Indians and Westerners alike: it seems that the main concerns among people involve status and leadership, who is in command, who is going to decide what to do, give instructions, or even give orders to others. The Westerners even ended up quarrelling with the Indian devotees about Babaji's tomb, about how it should be constructed; the whole thing makes me feel nauseous. What is more, some of the Westerners walk around as if they are gurus and think that they have been endowed with some divine authority; I don't want to be involved in all of this. I just feel so sad without Baba and nothing seems to have any purpose any more; it seems futile to organize anything since the ashram serves no one without the presence of Babaji. The other day Muniraji came and scolded me because of my attitude, telling me again that Babaji could return again in a few years, even with the same physical body, but I suspect he is just trying to console me. He said to me: 'Those who were less attached to Babaji's physical form, suffer less, and those who were more attached, suffer more.' I replied, that through His body Babaji gave us tremendous spiritual energy, Shakti, and Muniraji answered me saying that Babaji is giving all of this to an even greater extent now, but it's true, he added, that there are only a few who are now able to receive it. He looked at me with such gentleness and said again: 'Whoever comes, whoever goes, God is always here. Where do you think He could go?'

4 March 1984

Many Italians are here, a close-knit group mainly dressed in black and I think I understand now why Babaji gave them this colour to wear because it is also the colour of mourning. There is a peculiar air of excitement around them and now that they are left to their own devices they smoke, organize parties at night, almost appear to be happy with this freedom which allows them to do what they want; I am disgusted. I reject everybody, spending most of the time in my room alone. I don't feel able to participate in any of the ceremonies in the kirtan hall and even find it impossible to pray there any more; without Babaji's presence the temple makes me feel so depressed and every time I do go there I start crying. The yogis and yoginis at the dhuni seem equally deranged to me, they are also puffed up with pride by the new circumstances, imagining themselves to be the new gurus now.

What I would like to do is enter a meditation retreat for an indefinite period, but it is impossible for me to concentrate at the moment, because I have lost any sense of peace in my heart. Sometimes I make plans to stop eating completely so that I will die and go to Babaji. I certainly have an immense spiritual challenge to face now, a cruel way of proving my devotion lies ahead of me, because I have no choice but to relate to an invisible, silent God, and it is by no means an easy thing to do. I know that I have to be strong and take a huge leap in faith if I am truly to surmount duality and attain self-realization but something in me is rebelling, because I still think it's impossible for me to be able to walk alone without the help of the Master, without feeling His love and tangible support.

25 March 1984

Today I sat all day long outside Baba's room, under His tree, to watch the empty space filled by a subtle Presence, which I almost wish to reject. I just cried again and again, because I want to talk to Him, see Him, even if I do know that He has entered every cell of my being, almost breathing with me. I am unable to use a mantra anymore, nothing at all, I can only try to attain a state of emptiness and let Him fill me up if He so wishes. I know I have to remain here in this place, even if I'm not sure why, because this place has become representative of His being, as if He has become this valley, the mountains and the stars. I should wait here I know, but for how long?

The other day Shastriji took my hand and pressing it into his own he sang me a sad song: 'I look at the many lines on my hand and I count the years which are still separating me from You, my Lord; who knows for how long I'll have to wait to see You.' It is an enormous challenge, who knows if I'll be able to pass this cruel test, the ultimate and most difficult one; the one thing that I am certain about is that I feel like an orphan.

15 April 1984

Last night Babaji finally appeared to me in a dream. He was tall, beautiful, with a shaved head and He looked intensely into my eyes. I asked Him how it had been possible for Him to abandon us, how He could leave us in the way He did, causing us so much pain. He answered that it had been necessary for everybody to undergo this experience. I asked Him if it was possible that He would come back again and He replied that He could return but it was dependent on our merit, whether we deserved it. Then He embraced me very tightly, telling me that He would always appear to me in this way whenever I needed Him. I woke up feeling comforted and uplifted.

I know that Babaji is nothing less than Shiva Himself and that He can manifest a physical body whenever and wherever He so wishes, that He can perform any miracle that is necessary and that this period of time without Him is probably a necessary training for me.

6 May 1984

The ashram is almost empty, it's extremely hot and just like the migratory birds the crowds of Westerners have returned to the West again, but there are a few yogis who have decided to remain here continuing with the experiment of the ashram. In the absence of Babaji's physical presence and the effortless way in which He managed everything we are being compelled to become more mature, confronting things deep inside ourselves, things that were easily overlooked or discounted before, even suppressed in front of Him. Without His presence a lot of negative aspects have come to the surface in some of the people here, which had previously not fully come to light or been completely eliminated, and now it's important to recognize them if we want to face these difficulties and overcome them.

Ego and seeking power are the two main traits which are most evident and which we have to confront. In the past Babaji was the sole authority, but now if there is an organizational problem or difficulty in the community we have to make decisions on our own. Old patterns begin to emerge again; the Indian people think they have more rights than the rest of us, because this is their home; Westerners have a superiority complex, because of their culture; older people want to give orders, men want to suppress women, black yogis are in conflict with the orange ones and those who spent a long time with Baba think they know best about everything.

I see that I am also totally involved in the game now. I become terribly angry at times, although this kind of conduct never happened in front of Baba, and I discover that I am awfully authoritarian, a little dictator in fact. It is said in all the scriptures that the ego and the importance we place on ourselves and our opinions is the principle cause of all our illusions, and now I am certainly confronted by that in myself as well as in others. I remember Babaji saying just a few days before leaving His body, that nowadays nobody wants to be inconspicuous, everybody wants to be noticed and be important; because of this nobody is able to serve and therefore there will be war.

I also recall when Babaji told us that Hairakhan will be an example of a New World, a diverse human society beginning a new era and that we should be the pioneers of change. In this valley we should be able to change our hearts, truly live and work together in sisterhood and brotherhood, allowing a new humanity to emerge and the Divine Plan to unfold on earth.

7 June 1984

I am trying hard to practise my sadhana again, there is no alternative but to learn to surrender to the new situation: Babaji is not here any more, but in another sense He is always present. Unfortunately it is here in Hairakhan that I feel His absence the most, because it is in this place that I became so used to moving and breathing with Him. Some people feel the effect less than myself, but at times Hairakhan seems so deserted, neglected, a royal valley without a king.

The other day Muniraji arrived on a visit, now he has become guruji to many and he reminded me again that: 'The ones who are most attached on the physical level of reality suffer the loss of Babaji most, but His Shakti, His essence, is always there, in fact more than ever, although very few are able to receive it.' I looked at him feeling desolate because I know that he is one of the few but I do not know about myself.

Shri Muniraji

10 August 1984

We have all become terribly sick during this monsoon, contracting a virus and fever; there are only a few people remaining and we are weak, consumed with tiredness, haggard. Muniraji has gone to America and Europe to visit the various centres dedicated to Babaji in those countries and to spread His message there; I very much admire his strength and his faith.

Many people have become deeply depressed and our old enemy laziness is coming to the surface again. The ashram is neglected, disorderly, people don't carry out the cleaning carefully enough any more, they work very little, nobody runs around with enthusiasm, the rhythm of work has changed and people only do what is essential. A tendency has developed for everyone to retire into their own private, selfish space, no longer working for the common good. I find all this extremely depressing and feel as if I have been sent back to earth again, after having tasted an earthly paradise, but it's impossible for me to escape, something holds me here.

Muniraji asked me to accompany him when he travelled abroad but I refused because I didn't feel able to participate in the collective enthusiasm for the trip at the present time, I feel too sad to leave here.

Ranikhet, 10 October 1984

We are in Ranikhet to attend a large festival celebrating and honouring the Divine Mother, with songs, prayers and fire-ceremonies. Very many people have arrived here from every corner of the world. Life begins again. Every day the Himalayan mountains shine in the bright sky and people dance and enjoy the divine energy everywhere around, Baba's Presence is in everybody's heart.

Hairakhan, 20 October 1984

Once again I am getting involved in many of the duties in the ashram, mainly administration in the office. Hairakhan is coming back to life even though there continues to be many problems and contradictions. The Italians dressed in black seem confused, there are difficulties and misunderstandings, sometimes fights, mostly because of jealousy and competitiveness, sometimes with the Indian people, sometimes amongst us Westerners. Some people don't want to accept Muniraji as a new spiritual guide, while others come here expecting to experience a pleasant holiday and don't do anything, and there are a few who want to order everyone else around. We have to face the problems that human beings always have, the typical dilemmas found in every mixed social group living in community. In spite of all this, for me it's as if my earlier life is returning again along with my old passion for group living. Babaji is involving me again in all of this new work and I know I can't escape.

A few days ago I was planning to leave, to run away, and Muniraji blocked my departure, telling me that I cannot leave Hairakhan until Babaji comes back, because Babaji will return and my duty is to wait for Him.

10 November 1984

These days I often dream of Babaji. Whenever I feel that I need His help and His guidance, He talks to me, teaches me in this way.

In the morning I sit to meditate in His room, to absorb the sound of His silence, the peace of His valley and the beauty of this place which He loved.

I often wander along by the river and sit by the pure, transparent water. It is the purest water in the world, luminous, a water one can drink, clear, shining in the sun. I am reminded of a book I read long ago, *Siddhartha* by Hermann Hesse. In the story, a pilgrim, after having met the Buddha and having many adventures during his life searching for Truth, eventually becomes a ferryman on a river. Becoming an old man he lives very simply and humbly without the need to look for anything any more. What remains for him is the sound of the flowing water, symbolic of the harmony and energy of life, the sound of creation, the cosmic Om.

Who can tell who created the wind, the fire, the water, the sun and the stars, who can tell us when it all began? Nature is simply perfect in its mystery, and life itself can be like that as well if we adjust ourselves to her rhythm. It is possible for human beings to attain perfection, to be as perfect as Babaji who is an immortal example of the divinity within each one of us.

New Beginnings

15 January 1985

Once again many people are coming here to Hairakhan, some of the old disciples and many new devotees as well who have just seen a photograph of Babaji. I remain deeply moved by the devotion of people and am reminded of an occasion when Babaji left Hairakhan for a few days and on His return He told us that His real devotees carry on in the same way whether He is present or not, in fact, the real devotee does even more when He is not there.

The community is managing to be more harmonious again, organizing many things: painting, working in the gardens and in the fields, building walls and bridges. We are able to grow much of our own food and have horses and cows; Babaji has left us a precious heritage, a beautiful house for us in which to live and the opportunity to embrace change together. Babaji's presence is felt by everyone; it's in the wind, in the fire, in the water, in the prayers echoing in the valley. The new people who come here receive from Him the same signs and messages we used to get. We all live here with Babaji's spirit continually with us and probably this new situation is a training to enable us all to learn about living in this Great Presence all of the time. If it's true what is said, that everything has to be found within, even the attachment to the physical presence of the guru is an obstacle, but that is a hard test for me. A few days ago I had a dream in which Babaji told me that He had come back with His spirit, but that we killed Him again.

Milan, June 1986

I have returned to Italy for the first time in eight years. To see my ageing parents again was greatly moving, as well as the city of Milan, the place I grew up in and had so many important experiences.

These days there are many of Babaji's devotees living in Italy and in Cisternino in Puglia, there is a small, beautiful ashram. I see many friends, but something has changed deep within me and now I am only able to see people connected to a spiritual path. Here too, I find myself working only for Him and He is magically guiding me to meet certain people or situations. The mantra no longer leaves me, it's like an enchanting formula walking with me and acting for me, resounding automatically within me, until I feel that I am becoming the mantra myself, a pure energy of consciousness.

There are numerous people following a spiritual path now, prophets of a New World. They often leave the cities and go to live in the countryside, building alternative communities where they learn to grow natural food and medicinal herbs, making many other products as well.

In Cisternino the ashram has been built in a perfect Indian style, white in colour and simple, the valley resounding with the sound of ancient Sanskrit prayers. Some of Babaji's devotees have bought houses in the vicinity and they live here with their families and children, an emerging Bhole Baba City and a home for the new children of Babaji. We talk only and always about Him, almost an obsession; the way of living He showed us is instilled in us forever, together with the memory of our encounter with the Divine on earth.

I feel an old magic is at work again, but subtle and mysterious now, because the revolution is spiritual and not political any more; it's an esoteric movement, not always for everyone. I lead a regular life now, dressing normally without needing to express anything about myself on the outside; I realize that Babaji has given me a detachment from everything. I feel I am in this world, work in it, but I don't belong to it any more, I only belong to Him. He works through me, whenever I can make myself empty enough to be used as His instrument and allow His energy to pass through me.

Hairakhan, January 1987

It is mainly Western people who come to the ashram now, people who have never seen Babaji physically, but who have been guided by Him in so many different ways to come and work here; I admire them for their faith.

I often see Babaji in my dreams, I keep an old notebook that He gave me where I write them all down. When I dream of Him, I wake up comforted, almost embraced by His energy, His perfume. A few times I have woken up with tears in my eyes, feeling His absence and His presence at the same time, longing for the manifestation of the Invisible One, or the form of the Formless One. Hairakhan is still an enchanted place, with the pure light of dawn in the morning illuminating the mountains and on those incredible nights when there is a full moon the river looks like a silver ribbon and Shiva's tree offers it's branches like an eternal prayer. I observe Babaji's invisible work, silently changing people's hearts, transforming their lives.

Milan, June 1987

I am on a European tour with Muniraji, visiting Babaji centres in various countries and praying for world peace. It's beautiful to be here experiencing a new integration of Eastern and Western culture. Muniraji's method is gentle, non-authoritarian, he prefers to be considered weak rather than impose himself, while we, the disciples, often fall again and again into the 'ego-boss' trap, pretending to give orders to each other. One day Muniraji told us that only Babaji could give orders, because He was God, and we can only try to teach by offering an example.

When I am with Muniraji I am filled with divine energy again, an intense vibration; he is able to call Babaji's presence through the rituals and most especially through the great silence he inherited from Him, emanating peace through a pure, empty mind filled with the Divine. He is a Master of life, showing us that one can live and work in the normal world and have a family, while also incorporating spiritual practice as well, dedicating one's actions to God. Babaji warned us that in this age it is very difficult to retire from action, because the mind is too restless and agitated; from the first day of our birth the only thing we can do is to slowly learn detachment while in the midst of activity. It is this spiritual revolution that can change a person's heart, and thereby change the world.

Hairakhan, January 1988
Hairakhan is growing in size and so is Babaji's ashram at Chilianaula, which is situated at an altitude of 1,800 metres among the foothills of the Himalayas. It sits in a majestic valley overlooked by the far away snowy peaks. The air is crystal clear and early in the morning, in the midst of pink clouds, one feels on the top of the world. The garden is full of gigantic roses of every colour, together with all of the other Himalayan flowers and the mountain people are healthy and strong, kind, warmed by the sun, with a simple heart.

Anand Puri Ashram, Chilianaula

In Chilianaula one can hear the sound of silence pervading the valley, vibrating in the air like an electrical current, mixing with the murmur of the wind among the pine trees. In the high mountains one is nourished by the air, and the snow-capped peaks viewed from here emit a vibration of purity and eternity, very close to that of light. Hairakhan is different, it's almost surrounded by jungle, filled with the varied sounds of life; the river, the birds, the horses, the dogs and even the tigers.

I still miss Babaji's form tremendously at times and I still cry and cry, even if I know that His consciousness is here forever. I miss His direct guidance, His physical presence, His vibrant energy and especially His love. Also community life is not easy without Him and old habits rear their head again and again: ego, selfishness, power, lack of love and co-operation, jealousy and competitiveness - all of humanity's problems. We often fight and I also become incredibly angry. It is so hard. The group is the guru now, because by confronting each other we act like a mirror and then we have to face everything that is in us; it's a new training.

Babaji told us that He wanted to bring heaven on earth to Hairakhan, creating an example of a New World and I can see that many people are coming now whose hearts are beating with the rhythm of a New Age. We work a lot, keep building, growing rice, grain, vegetables, beautiful flowers, and our souls grow as well. It's not easy and sometimes I feel as if I am in a prison. I want to run away, but I know that the only thing I really want to run away from is myself.

Cisternino, August 1988
We are on a world tour with Muniraji again and have been to the USA, where people have built a temple at Baca, in the high mountains of Colorado, a land that belonged in the past to the Native Americans. It's a place where many spiritual groups live: Carmelite Christians, disciples of Aurobindo, Tibetan Buddhists, Zen Buddhists and so on. Now Babaji's temple is also there, with a life-size murti of Hairakhandeshwari Ma - the Divine Mother of Hairakhan - beautiful, like an oriental Madonna.

While in Britain we visited Findhorn in Scotland, one of the first New Age communities to be set up in the West, now with more than four hundred residents. In a similar way to that in which Babaji developed Hairakhan, in the early stages of the Findhorn Community Peter Caddy and others created the community through people's hard work and a slogan of theirs is: 'Work is love in action.' To compliment this approach Eileen, Peter's wife, channelled God's voice, the 'small voice within', and gave the community the necessary guidance for its growth. They have worked a lot with issues of authority, evolving to a point nowadays where they believe that decisions have to be made by the group and not just by one individual any more. There isn't a single, dominant leader, but leadership is assumed by the consciousness of the group, working for its continual evolution. Every day people meet together for silent meditation, learning to be inspired by a higher consciousness and by the heart.

Findhorn is based on having great faith in the Divine and listening to its constant guidance, if one can just learn to listen to the voice within. Similar to that demonstrated by Babaji, the belief of the Caddys was to aim for perfection in their work in combination with an ability to transform matter through spirit, bringing light into darkness, linking heaven with earth.

Hairakhan, November 1988

Autumn is so beautiful, the land green after the rainy season, the sky clear blue and the water of the Gautam Ganga roars over the polished stones of the river. I think I am so lucky to live here, in an international community, where spiritual seekers come from every corner of the world.

Now I work continually again, especially in the office. Sometimes I struggle with people and with problems, because I haven't entirely lost my old revolutionary spirit, but Babaji said that the New World will start from here and so I won't allow myself to give up. He also told us that a great crisis will occur world-wide by the end of this century, and that we should be prepared for this. Babaji may even come back again in another physical body soon, but for now He is giving us a training of the spirit, a fiery one.

Often we meet to speak in the dhuni, people sharing their experiences and their inspirations around the fire. The Essence of Babaji comes strongly alive in these moments, through the light of the flames, the odour of incense, people's songs and their hearts opening. Babaji has left His energy here, almost His breath. It's magical, omnipervasive, and now our work is to maintain Babaji's spirit alive here, manifested through all of us.

Milan, September 1989

I have spent five months in Italy, partly in Milan, partly in Cisternino, working, translating and organizing. In Europe and especially in Italy, the political, economical and social situation is deteriorating and our analysis in the sixties wasn't wrong: communism has failed, having become a materialistic dictatorship, but capitalism hasn't been able to offer us a solution to humanity's problems either. Power, money and materialism doesn't make people happy. Pollution, AIDS and other presently incurable diseases are the frightening symptoms of a society which cannot remain in harmony with nature, spoiling it indiscriminately and for selfish purposes. Added to this are the problems of mental pollution through alcohol, drugs, television, advertising and the stressful life of the city. The mind is never allowed to find rest, have peace, can never know and observe itself. People are afraid of solitude and silence, because they can't face themselves and their lack of love. The mind is becoming cold like a machine, a computer. A spiritual revolution is needed that is able to propose a new way of living for people, where they can find real meaning for their existence. Yoga is the most ancient science of the mind, because everything comes from and is created by the mind, and our happiness depends on the mind only. The Aquarian age is about to come and is the hope for a different world, where human beings can expand their awareness and develop psychic powers enabling them to link the individual to a higher, spiritual reality, to the Divine. It's the return to the Satya Yuga, the Age of Truth, where a person can realize his or her destiny and consciously participate in the Cosmic Plan.

Hairakhan, April 1990
Every springtime in Hairakhan we celebrate Navaratri, to honour the Goddess, the symbol of the Divine Energy, the cosmic Shakti. It's the beginning of the warm season, when the earth's fertility and abundance is also celebrated through its beauty, the great Mother adorned with fruits and flowers.

In Hairakhan the garden is overflowing with roses of every colour and the peepul tree is shining with a thousand new leaves. On these occasions, through everybody's effort, we are able to create an atmosphere of great intensity, aware of the power of being together and working in harmonious unity. Many people now arrive here from Russia and other eastern European countries, thirsty for the spiritual life. They have never seen Babaji, but it's incredible to listen to their stories about how He called them here, through dreams, visions and through meditation. Only Truth and Love can save the world, because although we can fly through space, build atomic bombs, have the most beautiful houses and clothes, we are still like spoiled children, never satisfied by all our many new toys. We will never be happy until we find peace in our hearts.

Our communities are themselves workshops for a renewal of humanity, centres of spiritual power, refuges for the seekers of Truth, points of love and light on the planet connecting with each other in order to bring new hope to the earth. We are the spiritual warriors for a New World project, developed with the awareness of the Divine. Often people will fight against us, because whoever is in darkness will hate the light, since they know that even a tiny spark of light has the power to destroy darkness.

If humanity wants to survive then the planet has to be purified of physical and mental pollution; if we believe in human values then we should fight for them because the Spiritual Age is now very close at hand.

GLOSSARY

aarati ceremonial worship including prayers and a lighted lamp performed to *guru*, *murti* or other form twice daily in morning and evening (lit. 'waving or offering of the light')

amrita divine nectar

asan seat; also yoga posture

ashram place of religious retreat for the purpose of spiritual practice

avatar a divine incarnation, great spiritual teacher

Babaji revered father (lit. 'Baba - father & ji - prefix denoting respect')

Bhagwan the Lord

bhakti devotional surrender to the Divine

bhakti yoga the path of union through devotion

bhandara feast

Bheru Baba head of Shiva's army, guardian of the fire-pit

bodhi tree see *peepul*

brahmachari a person who has chosen celibacy, follows religious disciplines and studies the scriptures

chai tea

chakra centre of psychic energy, the primary ones located at different points along the spinal column from base to crown of the head (lit. 'wheel')

chandan sandalwood paste applied to the forehead

chapati Indian flat bread

darshan sight of or meeting with holy person; also a saint, temple or something considered sacred

Devi divine mother, often referring to the consort of Shiva

dharma the manner in which creation is ordered; Truth or Sacred Law; duty

dhuni place containing a fire-pit, considered sacred and often with a continually burning fire

Divali (Deepawali) festival held all over India in the autumn symbolically celebrating the victory of good over evil, light over darkness, by the lighting of numerous candles (lit. 'the festival of lights')

Gautam Ganga the river that flows through the Hairakhan valley separating the two parts of the ashram; called after a *rishi* of the same name

ghat steps leading down to section of the river used for bathing and sometimes for cremations (burning-ghat)

gopi milkmaid in the Krishna legends

Goraknath an avatar of Shiva around the period 3100 BC

gufa-side (lit. 'cave-side') referring to the cave in which Babaji was first discovered at the foot of Mount Kailash

guru spiritual teacher or guide, the remover of darkness

Hairakhan small hill village in the Kumaon region of the state of Uttar Pradesh, northern India

Hairakhandeshwari Ma the Divine Mother of Hairakhan

halva Indian sweetmeat

hatha yoga the practice of particular physical postures, *asanas* and movements

havan ritual fire-ceremony including prayers and offerings made to the fire

henna tropical shrub whose leaves are used as a red dye

Hindi one of the major contemporary languages of India

Hindu the name given by Alexander the Great to those people living beyond the Indus river; the people living according to the Vedic tradition

Holi Hindu festival celebrated in the spring dedicated to Krishna and the *gopis*, usually involves the throwing of coloured water

jaggury large lumps or balls of unrefined sugar

jai praise or victory

Jamuna sacred river

Kali black female deity, the Goddess often depicted in a destructive form as a warrioress with a necklace of skulls, also having the capacity to transform and transmute

Kali Yuga the era of time named after Kali, one of the four great yugas or epochs that make up an aeon; the period of darkness and disintegration, of conflict and growth in materialism

karma law of cause and effect; action; destiny

karma yoga action offered to God, actions carried out without expectation of reward or outcome (lit. 'action in union')

kirtan the singing of devotional songs repeating any of the various names of God (lit. 'singing the praises of God')

kirtan hall place for *kirtan* or other devotional practice

Krishna an incarnation of Vishnu

kriya yoga the yoga of bringing about the practical experience of transformation and deeper understanding (lit. 'to move', 'the activity of the indwelling soul')

kumkum red powder symbolic of the goddess, applied separately or in conjunction with *chandan* on the forehead, female energy

kundalini energy that remains dormant coiled like a serpent at the base of the spine until awakened, usually through yogic practices; divine energy, sometimes personified as the Goddess

lama religious teacher or master from Tibet

leela the play of the Lord (lit. 'divine play')

lota container for water

maha (lit. 'great')

Mahasamadhi conscious leaving of the human body by a great saint, also the resting place of a great soul

Mahashakti great divine female energy or power, name of the Great Goddess and Mother of the universe

Mahavatar great divine incarnation, God in form, in the *Shaivite* tradition a divine being not born from a woman but able to manifest a body at will

mala a string of prayer beads, usually wooden and 108 in number, similar to a rosary

mandala a circular religious design or symbol of the universe, often used for meditation

mantra a word or phrase used as a prayer or chant; a powerful or significant sound

maya the whole of existence, subject to continual change; also illusion, endowed with the power of concealment and projection

Mount Kailash mountain sacred to Lord Shiva situated near the ashram at Hairakhan; a second Mount Kailash is in Tibet, also a sacred place of pilgrimage

murti statue or form used in worship (lit. 'image')

Nataraj the dancing form of Shiva, His tandava dance represents His five powers of creation, preservation, destruction, veiling grace and revealing grace (lit. 'King of Dance')

navaratri a festival lasting nine days in celebration of the Divine Mother including a daily *yagna*, occurring twice each year in spring and autumn

Om Namah Shivaya the maha mantra, the mantra of mantras, (lit. 'I bow before Lord Shiva') numerous translations including: 'I take refuge in God', 'I surrender to God', 'Lord, thy will be done'

peepul tree otherwise known by Buddhists as the *bodhi* tree, the tree under which the Buddha attained liberation

pranam to kneel or prostrate, a gesture of humility

prasad blessed food

puja ritual worship including chants and offerings (lit. 'adoration')

pujari, pujarini male, female person who carries out *puja*

rishi saint or sage

rudraksha (lit. 'eye of Shiva') tree sacred to Lord Shiva, seeds of which can have varying number of facets symbolizing different qualities and used for *mala;* Rudra - the 'Lord of tears' - is Shiva in His aspect as absorber or destroyer

sadhana spiritual discipline or practice

sadhu Hindu holy man/woman, a renunciate

samadhi a merging into universal consciousness, the absorption of individual awareness

samsara the cycle of birth, death and rebirth

204

Sanskrit ancient religious language of India, regarded as the root of all Indo-European languages

Satikund the tree dedicated to the Mother growing in the middle of the Gautam Ganga river a little downstream from Hairakhan, traditionally the place at which Shiva and His consort Parvati bathed together

Satya Yuga the Age of Truth, one of the four great epochs, follows the *Kali Yuga*

Shakti divine energy or power; personification of the Great Goddess; consort of Shiva

Shaivite the tradition or person devoted to Lord Shiva, regarded as the supreme form of God

Shankar a form of Shiva, 'bringer of peace'

Shiva Indian deity, the 'auspicious one', part of the trinity Brahma the creator, Vishnu the preserver and Shiva the destroyer who also brings about change and purification; to a *Shaivite* recognized as 'the pure one', the Absolute God, the supreme being who combines all three aspects

swami a renunciate teacher, usually wearing orange robes

tapasya austerities, self-denial

Vedas (lit. 'knowledge') oldest known written texts in India, circa 4,000 BCE

vipassana a particular form of meditation where attention is focused on the breath

Vrindavan Indian city sacred to Lord Krishna

yagna large ritual fire-ceremony

yantra symbolic geometric and alphabetical design usually pertaining to a particular deity

yoga the spiritual practice of realizing consciousness (lit. 'union')

yogi, yogini man, woman who practises *yoga*

Babaji's signature – *Om Namah Shivaya* in Sanskrit script

Further Information:

Babaji's main ashrams in **India**

Hairakhan Vishwa Mahadham
Via Kathgodam, P.O. Haidakhan
PIN-263126
District Nainital, Uttar Pradesh

Anand Puri Ashram
Chilianaula
PIN- 263647
District Almora, Uttar Pradesh
Tel: 00 91 5966 2560

There are a large number of other ashrams dedicated to Babaji throughout India, details of which can be obtained from Hairakhan Vishwa Mahadam or from the websites given below.
A network of ashrams, centres, groups and organizations also exist in more than forty countries around the world, including more than a dozen countries in Europe. Some of the main ashrams/centres are listed below but for further information as well as an up to date list of contacts and addresses worldwide look at: **www.babaji.org.uk** or **www.babaji.net**

Australia Shri Haidakhan Babaji Foundation, Australia/Vaikunth Light Centre for Universal Peace, P.O. Box 356, Bellingen, NSW
tel/fax: 00 61 2 6655 0840 e-mail: vaikunth@turboweb.net.au
Shri Haidakhan Babaji Temple, 489 Trees Road, Tallebudgera, Gold Coast 4288 email: garufi@winshop.com.au

Austria Zentrum des Dienens, Riesstrasse 238, A-8047, Graz
tel: 00 43 316 301960 e-mail: ilse.falk@orf.at

Belgium Siddha Shiva Center, Haagwindestraat 2, Mariakerke 9030, Gent
tel: 00 32 91 264521

Bulgaria Mimi Koleva, J.K. Krasno Selo Bl, 198 Ap. 4, 1618 Sofia
email: mkoleva@aster.net

Canada Canadian Haidakhan Samaj, 48 Hill Drive, Aurora, Ontario 24G 3A6

France 'Le Samaj', 70 rue de l'Assomption, 75016 Paris
tel: 00 33 1 4230 7087 email: f.huguies@hol.fr

Germany Bhole Baba Ashram, Kalkstuck 11, 51570 Windeck-Rieferath
tel: 00 49 22 43 6603 email: lal.baba@t-online.de

Ireland Haidakhan Bhole Baba Centre, Milmorane Basketry, Ballingeary, Macroom, County Cork tel: 00 353 26 47230

Italy Fondazione Bhole Baba, Casella Postale 138, 1-72014 Cisternino (BR)
tel/fax: 00 39 80 718 735

Centro Spirituale di Pace Haidakhandi, Localita Monte Gaudio,
1-4020 Villa San Secondo (AT) tel: 00 39 141 905393

Korea Korea Babaji Center, 105-1305 Sinmyong APT, Changhyunli
Hwadoub Namyangjusi Kyonggido
email: omnamaha@provin.kyonggi.kr

Latvia Badadzi Biedriba Latvija, Valnu 21-14, LV 1050, Riga
tel: 00 371 7 216829

Netherlands Sada Shiva Dham, Vrijenbergweg 60-62, 7371 AB Loenen
tel: 00 31 55 505 2871 email: ssdloenennl@freemail.nl

New Zealand Hairakhan Samaj, 31 Hakanoa Street, Grey Lynn, Auckland

Poland Sri Herakhandi Seva Dham, Ul. Francuska 25, 54-405 Wroclaw
tel: 00 48 71 57 5554 e-mail: amba@compuserve.com

Russia Omkar Shiva Dham, Okunjewo, Muromceva, 644099 Omsk Raj

South Africa Laina Lesicnik, PO Box 438, Mooi River 3300
tel/fax: 00 27 33 263 2275 e-mail: laina@futurenet.co.za

Sweden Haidakhan Baba Center, Nytorget 6, 11640 Stockholm
tel: 00 46 8640 6179

Switzerland Schweibenalp, Centre of Unity, CH – 3855 Brienz
tel: 00 41 33 951 2001 email: info@schweibenalp.ch

UK Haidakhandi Samaj (UK), Blaengors, Dihewyd, Lampeter, Ceredigion,
Wales www.babaji.org.uk

USA Haidakhandi Karma Yoga & Peace Center, 2353 County Road, Malmo,
Nebraska 68040 tel: 00 1 (402) 642 9238 email: peace2u@tvsonline.net
Haidakhandi Universal Ashram, PO Box 9, Crestone, Colorado 81131
tel: 00 1 (719) 256 4108 email: hua@amigo.net

Contents

Dedication

*This book is dedicated to
Ann Ridgway*

.

Testimonials

"Moira scooped Colour Mirrors up with huge determination and vision and brought us into the 21st century. I have watched Moira go through the most intense initiations in the last 15 years and I do not know anyone who could have walked the path she did and survived it with such strength and determination and the ability to take it all on board and process it until we now have the beautiful solid shiny end product. Moira is a success story that takes my breath away. She has come out of it all as a powerful healer and teacher who can hold a space for anyone who is dealing with their 'stuff', because she took the most intense initiation herself. She can love a thing right no matter how dark it looks. Moira you are a star."

Extract from Newsletter
Written by Colour Mirrors founder, Melissie Jolly
Stanford, South Africa
www.colourmirrors.com

Moira Bush

"Moira is an exceptional teacher and guide. Moira's no-nonsense approach is refreshing because it's honest and real and it prevents so much time wasting and procrastination. She draws on her life experiences and extensive knowledge and if you're lucky enough to work with her, she will guide you back to yourself. But be warned, if you want to procrastinate, deny your issues, distract yourself, waste time and avoid taking action then don't waste her time. Moira will not carry or rescue you but if you step up and draw on your courage, she will help you access all the strength, determination, and clarity to fulfil your potential – you will be so glad you did!"

Jackie Tweedie
Clarity Coach and Yoga Teacher
Coventry, England
www.jackietweedie.com

"Moira, I have never been so impressed with a teacher. Your materials were impeccable, your stories are fascinating and your ability to allow such deep personal healing of your students is astounding. You then augmented it by showing me how to turn that teaching into a business, providing years of tips and your tools. You are generous, sensitive, caring and practical. I have never seen a teacher be truly empowering to students to take what they have learned and fly with it. But you did! Thank you."

Lise Clark
Personal & Relationship Guide
Graduate of Colour Mirrors and Love & Money programs
Ontario, Canada
www.liseclark.com

"I have been fortunate to study the Love & Money course with Moira Bush. This course has changed my understanding of money and abundance. My greatest learning on this course was discovering HOW I have created the majority of my debt unnecessarily by needing to control and fix things financially with yet more credit. I now know that I need to let go and allow for the universe to work its magic. I live "just say yes and show up" and I have found that when I am in doubt, meditation is my answer to set me straight."

Susan McKenzie
Graduate of Colour Mirrors and Love & Money programs
Burlington, Canada
www.dharmadynamics.com

"Understanding the relationship between love and money and their need for joy was an eye opener. However, my aha moment occurred when the topic of 'shadows' allowed me to see how I really operate in life – as a victim of fear coming from a place of 'no one loves me and I am not enough'. Moira's coaching has helped me to see pure love in the mirror. Thank you Moira."

Nadira Dyalsingh
Neonatal Nurse
Toronto, Canada

"I had a real ah-hah moment as a result of Moira teaching me how to balance my wheel of fortune with love, joy and money. I decided to focus on joy in the everyday simple things in life. At the same time I focussed on love, especially self-love and seeing love in other people. I didn't even have to focus on the money, the wheel began to turn and the money took care of itself! My husband and I paid off our mortgage December 31st 2016, a goal we had set for two years down the road. We found that opportunities just presented themselves. Moira's teachings had a huge impact on my life and on my family."

Katharine Bork
Graduate of Colour Mirrors and Love & Money programs
Ballinafad, Canada

You can view more written and video testimonials on
www.moirabush.com

Acknowledgements

For awakening my inner entrepreneur, I want to thank **Beverley Moodie**, my first business partner and dear friend who still lives at the top of a mountain and continues to write beautiful books and inspire.

For showing me how to be a colour entrepreneur, a heartfelt thank you to **Melissie Jolly**, the alchemist who makes the colour bottles. You inspired me to love dragons and seek out a meaningful life. And, you taught me how to be an authentic beacon of light for others. I am blessed to work alongside the most generous and spiritually powerful woman in the world.

I deeply express my gratitude to each one of you, the brave **clients, students, friends** and **family** who allowed me to experiment and offer the concept of colour analysis as a tool of financial and personal empowerment. I love you!

Thank you to the darlings in my life, my son **Michael Kapp** and husband **Paul Valade** for your unconditional support and love. You make the work possible.

To **Raymond Aaron** and his team, **Rosa Greco, Chinmai Swamy** and **Naval Kumar**, I am deeply grateful that the universe bought you to my attention and that I turned up and said 'Yes' to your empowering book program and business mentoring.

Foreword

I am very excited to introduce you to Moira Bush, author of the book, *8 Colours of Prosperity*. In my workshops, I emphasize the importance of eradicating poverty thinking and using clear communication to ensure financial success. Moira's message on how colour analysis can speed up and amplify that process of change for you makes this message possibly the most important new discovery for laying down permanent prosperity foundations.

There are several 'wow' moments in this book which you will recognize yourself in the clear examples Moria shares with you. You will be able to pinpoint exactly where you sabotage yourself when you seek financial freedom. This book gives you an alternative route to get out of debt, by teaching you to work with universal principles instead of telling you to work harder.

8 Colours of Prosperity deserves to become a bestseller. I highly recommend you read and implement the new colour philosophy and strategies that Moira teaches you in this book.

Raymond Aaron
New York Times Bestselling Author

Introduction

The Millennial Business Revolution

The Self-Help industry is just one of many that is undergoing a revolution. Mentors, teachers, authors and leaders of commerce are rewriting their business plans to serve a generation of millennial adults who expect instant gratification, authenticity and a universal approach to changing all their woes with one book, one program, one tweet!

Leaders in enterprise are beginning to see the benefits of consulting, with a combination of marketing experts and metaphysical advisors, on how to evolve their businesses to appeal to the millennial adults. The millennial adults are those born in the 1980's until around 2002, the new generation with spending power – and they are not spending according to the same trends as their parents. They choose very carefully where they invest their time and money. They will favour a company who has environmentally friendly policies and who re-invest some of their profits back into their communities. They would rather work doing something they love or believe in for far less income than take a job just for the highest salary.

This generation as new entrepreneurs value life experience and knowledge more than a formal background of education and seek out role models whose teachings are based on how they personally transformed their own lives. They are also far more self-aware and strive for a life balance that is teaching us, the older generations, the value of incorporating a universal business strategy into our chosen fields of work.

Blazing a New Path

I admire the millennial generation for not compromising their personal ethics. They do not conform easily and tend to challenge existing systems of education, government and enterprise. They inspired me to try new methods of teaching business and life skills.

In the past, I have taught business and financial empowerment programs working with corporations and projects funded by governments. I have also taught colour analysis and spiritual principles to those in the alternative healing markets. The millennial entrepreneur client requires me to mentor them in one process; combining business strategies, personal development and metaphysical skills.

I have become part of a new group of entrepreneurial teachers and mentors who, through our work, are establishing universal systems of teaching that contribute towards building bridges between our material world, where survival is the ruling force and our spiritual world, where our heart is the ruling force. This book is based on my international flagship program called 'Love & Money'. It consists of the following two courses:

1) Identifying the Devils running your Finances
2) The Wheel of Fortune, followed by 12 months of group mentoring meetings.

It is a program that is quite bold in structure as it teaches business skills, personal poverty eradication, how to raise self-awareness, how to use colour analysis as a transformational and recovery tool, and is based on spiritual principles that include compassion, forgiveness, letting go of judgements and how to be in authentic power.

This program was developed over many years working in different countries. It is my heartfelt wish, that you may experience a breakthrough within these pages; whether it is clearing your debt, increasing your cash flow, healing your grief, reconnecting with your family or perhaps finding a purposeful legacy. Now is the time for you to blaze a new life path!

The Missing Link between Business and Metaphysics

I taught aspiring entrepreneurs in South Africa and England how to start their own businesses. In South Africa the success rate was high, 98% of the students I mentored showed 1 year later that they were still in business and starting to generate an income. In England the rate was lower, 49%. The 2% and the 51% that did not succeed bothered me a great deal. I also observed in seminars how participants are motivated to grow in business given new strategies and goals to follow. What they tend to not be shown is how to overcome the fear of change, or fear of failure, which causes resistance and as a result the seminar notes are never looked at again and no action is taken.

During 2002 in England I came across a system that uses colour analysis for personal and spiritual development called Colour Mirrors. At the time I was working for the government funded charity organization called the Women's Business Development Agency helping women to get off the welfare system and into self-employment. I realized that the women who did not succeed in starting up their business would be able to conquer their fears if they only knew about the colour analysis system. I resigned my job at WBDA and started to work with the South African Colour Mirrors founder Melissie Jolly and together we set up international centres of colour training and product distribution.

The Universal Approach for Learning

After 15 years experience of teaching and mentoring students using a combination of colour analysis for personal growth and entrepreneurial business training, I have witnessed the speed and effortlessness my clients benefited from when applying universal tactics to getting out of debt and poor relationships with themselves and others.

This book will show you how to master universal strategies for yourself and encourage you to follow the 3 steps towards self-awareness, how to use the 8 colour tools to support you in ending your debt and poverty habits and lay foundations for future wealth and happiness where you will never repeat your old patterns again.

Resistance from your Debt Devils

The nature of this book and the personal evolutionary training I represent is designed to dig deep into your unconscious body habits and mental beliefs, and encourage you to self-examine your hidden motivations for previous failures where your debt devils played a part. Your debt devils do not like to be discovered and exhumed! And the way they let you know they are uncomfortable with change is to resist by using your addictive habits to draw you away from this book and its lessons. Do not be surprised if at this early stage of reading you already feel the need to switch on the TV and add this book to the pile of many books you never read.

Identifying your Devils using Colour Analysis

In my own life I discovered an army of debt devils unwilling to allow me to follow my inner desire to be happy, financially free and in love. And it was colour analysis that helped me identify each single one of them and adapt their self-destruct behaviour into supportive purposeful positive action.

Case Study of a Business Man choosing Colours

In 2016 at a women's empowerment event in Toronto, I displayed rows of coloured bottles from the Colour Mirrors system. You can view this wall of colour on my website www.moirabush.com. The bottles are made up of essential oils and purified water, the oil floating on top is coloured and the water at the bottom also has its own colouring.

Dwayne, who is a self-employed businessman in finance, attended the event and asked me to explain how colour works as a transformational system for businesses. I asked him to think of one particular issue he had been unable to resolve for a long time and, without telling me what it is, pick the coloured bottle he was drawn to. He picked bottle number 14, pale turquoise oil sitting on top of pale turquoise water. I said that his choice of a solid colour bottle, turquoise top and bottom, showed a difficult time in accessing his creativity, especially for writing a book.

He was astounded as that was exactly the issue on his mind. He explained that it had been a three-year struggle and he did not know why he could not sit down and write. I asked him to pick another bottle. He chose number 16; the oil is coloured pale olive and the water lilac. I explained that in my 'Love & Money Boot Camp' for business clients, this bottle is often selected and indicates a little devil called the Saboteur. We discussed how and why his Saboteur has taken over the project to prevent him from publishing his book. He asked me what he could do to conquer his inner Saboteur. I instructed him to buy the number 16 bottle and rub the oil wherever it felt good while showering or to pour some into a bath and finish the bottle over a period of 3 weeks as a self-help transformational tool.

Dwayne phoned me 3 days later to report that over the weekend he had begun writing, feeling creative again and as a bonus he had received a surprise request to talk about his book at an event. Around 2 months later he phoned again and shared how he was investing his time following new ideas and growing his business. Another month later Dwayne sent a Facebook message that he has been asked to co-author a new book! His creativity was finally unblocked.

Why can rubbing colour on your body get beyond the devilish resistances?

Business coaches encourage a schedule to follow on a daily basis to help you overcome procrastination and increase discipline to achieve your goals. Nutritionists may advise you to eat certain foods and avoid others for better health or weight loss. All these changes depend on your positive willpower and how deeply you desire the change. However, that positive feeling is also matched by your devils' will to keep your life in the same rut. It is crucial to dig them up from wherever they are hiding in your mind and body and become aware of their existence and hidden agenda. You may be surprised to discover a debt devil lodged in your big toe whose sole agenda is to trip you up and ensure you are always late for appointments!

Immersing your body in the coloured oil and water reaches all parts of your body, the aroma essences in each of the coloured bottles works on your senses as well, releasing tension and softening the tight grip your little devils have on various aspects of your life. They cannot put up a resistance to both your intention to change and the frequencies of colour entering your body.

Colour Frequencies

It does not surprise me that clients ask for proof that a system of coloured oil and water can help them, they often ask whether they need to have blind faith to achieve results by simply bathing in them. I was the biggest doubting Thomas when I first came across colour as a transformational tool for my relationships and finances.

The First Colour Case Study was personal

The first Colour Mirrors bottle I saw in action was a turquoise bottle, numbered 30. It was recommended by Melissie to give to my son Michael to use on his acne. Michael was 20 years old and already had deep scarring on his face and neck and nothing the medical profession prescribed over the years was working for him. Melissie instructed him to rub the oil on his skin every night before he went to bed – I had to replace his pillow and insisted he sleep on a towel over his new pillow. Six weeks later his red welts had disappeared and when the bottle was completed most of his scarring had disappeared as well. At that point everything began to change for Michael, he fell in love and found his path towards his University studies. Mostly I was grateful for how this turquoise bottle, the colour of trust and heartfelt communication, opened up a deeper level of connectedness between us.

The Second Colour Case Study was not human!

Colour analysis goes beyond humans and proved to me that there was no need to have blind faith to make colour work. I sold my very first Colour Mirrors bottle numbered C2, an orange and gold combination, to a woman in Plymouth, England. Her plan was to use it on her severely spooked beloved horse called Sam. Sam had thrown her and she was told she would never walk again. She chose to ignore the diagnosis and at the time I met her, she was already walking with the help of crutches. She also chose to ignore the advice to put Sam down as he never recovered from the trauma and was wasting away in a field and would not let anyone touch him. She was instructed to rub the orange oil on his body to clear the shock. Since no one could get near him that was a problem. However, when she rubbed it on her hands, the smell was so interesting that Sam came over to investigate and he allowed the oil massage. Within 24 hours he was eating, allowed grooming and eventually made a full recovery.

The Science of Colour

Sir Isaac Newton was one of the first modern day scientists to experiment with colour frequencies. He positioned a prism so that sunlight would pass through it and display on a white background the colours of the rainbow. We also know that each colour frequency has a specific speed, red has the lowest and violet the highest speed.

East Indians practice healing on their chakras; what they say are spinning wheels of colour located at various points of the body. The red lowest frequency of colour we get from the sun is said to go into the lowest chakra, the base area of the spine. The highest frequency goes to the highest chakra, the crown area.

In essence, our bodies are colour coded. When I work with clients it is completely 100% the same results, the colour bottle they select matches the chakra colour area of the body to indicate their issues. A client with relationship issues will pick greens, the colour of the heart area. Sleep issues are indicated by the head colour violet. Money issues always come up as red and interestingly that client may also report lower back pain, the red area of the body.

Scientific studies have been made where a man is put into a blue room and finds that his blood pressure drops and heart rate slows, put the same man into a red room and the blood pressure and heart rate goes up. We have a body response to the colours we see and touch.

You also use colour as a universal language. You say, green with envy or yellow belly to indicate fear or lack of power. Anywhere in the world you travel, you know that the red dot on the faucet is going to give you hot water and the blue dot will be the cold water.

Do the Colours in Your Office Cause You a Drop in Income?

At a recent Love & Money mentoring group meeting, I had organized a field trip for the students to visit an investment company and learn about opportunities to invest in the stock market. Two of the students who were undergoing significant changes in their careers had to leave the boardroom within the first half hour and go home, one reported back that she had suffered a severe panic attack.

Clients who want to change their career tend to select green bottles. Panic attacks are also indicated by green. The lungs are in the green area of the body. The boardroom we were in was painted in a dark bottle green colour that made the room feel claustrophobic and would have contributed to triggering the feelings of being overwhelmed for the two students.

I advise anyone who asks what colour to paint their offices to consider neutral shades or pastel colours, otherwise you could literally see your clients with their money leave the room and have no awareness why you did not close the deal.

Self-Awareness is Key to Opening all the Doors of Wealth

Have you noticed people who win the lottery or inherited a fortune so often cannot seem to keep it? Having more money does not mean you have solved your poverty habits, or become more enlightened or got rid of your debt devils. The patterns and beliefs that lie underneath the concrete foundations, no matter how many hours of work and money you put on the surface, are still subject to 'something' buried under the concrete rising up and cracking the foundations. In therapy it is called your sub-conscious mind.

Self-Awareness training was the crucial part I was missing when teaching business and financial empowerment all those years ago and the reason I, and my students, repeated patterns of debt. No one can make you more self-aware. Only you have the power to study your behaviour and chip away at what you want to let go of and what positive parts of yourself you could expand upon.

In my business I noticed that the need to become more self-aware tended to arise after a huge shock, often the death of a loved one, a health scare or a financial crisis that triggered the need to self-examine life and work. No one who is managing to pay all their bills, healthy and happy will seek out to better him or herself at this deep level – unless that is you dear reader that has made the choice to get to this page of the book and resisted switching the TV on! Congratulations for reading further, you are about to discover how to see yourself and your life in a completely different light!

The Three Steps Towards Self-Alert!

Have you ever wandered from room to room looking for your keys, not remembering where you placed them last? Dare you ask the question, which part of yourself was in charge of your body and put the keys down and now you have no memory of where? Or, you receive your credit card bill at the end of the month looking at the items you bought and wonder what part of you spends money you do not yet have? Often those who committed acts of violence when questioned by the police will say they have no memory of doing the deed. How did they lose control over a part of themselves and allow 'something else' to step forward and take over their body and mind so powerfully?

In my own experience, through colour analysis, I discovered that 'something else' was a child devil spending my money and a victim devil in charge of my relationships. Using the steps I have shared in this book with you, I mastered both of them and never got back into debt again, and I attracted a wonderful, caring man who loves me unconditionally.

This book suggests three specific steps to study that will help you to be in self-alert mode when your debt devils take over your mind and body.

When you have studied the 3 steps and feel confident that you have gained an understanding of the ideas and philosophy offered, use the 8 colour tools to help you towards freedom from whatever has held you back from financial and personal empowerment. Keep this book close by so that you can reference sections and exercises. Bookmark the website www.8coloursofprosperity.com on your devices where free colour tools have been gifted, from me, to help you deal effectively with your debt devils' antics and to strive towards more of your true potential.

Steps to Prosperous Self-Awareness

Step A: The Universal Law of Attraction

There are many universal laws that govern the human existence on this planet, for example the Law of Gravity prevents you from drifting off into space. The Law of Polarity ensures everything has an opposite for balance. The Law of Cause and Effect gives every action a reaction, you reap what you sow.

The universal law that mostly applies to creative power is called the Law of Attraction, like attracts like. Each law has a specific purpose that allows you to explore and learn from a wide variety of life experiences. When you know the operating rules of these universal laws, you can begin to work consciously at designing a life that really works for you.

The Operating Rules of Like Attracts Like

The totality of who you are as a being acts as a magnetic force field that reaches out and attracts people and events that match you at a mental, physical and emotional level. The magnetic force field is your body and mind's archive where you have stored all your beliefs, fears, hopes, dreams, knowledge, memories and experiences.

If you tend to be a negative person and you have stored away being grumpy, unhappy and unable to see the gifts of your existence, then your magnetic force field will be attracting more opportunities to be disgruntled. If you have worked at storing 'the bright side of life' your magnetic force field will attract happier people and events towards you.

A study of the operating rules of the Law of Attraction is recommended to strengthen your ability to self-alert and stop the creating process instantly when you detect your debt devils doing the grumpier attractions!

There are 4 rules crucial to knowing how to attract love and get out of debt and back into positive cash flow:

Rule 1: Everything that exists around you, you attracted towards you.

Rule 2: Everything you desire will come to you.

Rule 3: Everything you do not desire will come to you.

Rule 4: You attract more of what you judge.

It has become popular amongst entrepreneurs to attend programs or read books where Rule 1 and 2 of the law of attraction are explored. Some of the exercises given to attract love and wealth may include: visualisations, meditations, setting good intentions, vision boards or positive affirmations and to take specific actions to help the creation process unfold.

These two rules operate from the *positive pole* of your body's magnetic force field.

Have you noticed that you also attract what you cannot recall desiring or ever wanting in your life? Learning how Rule 3 and 4 are utilised by your debt devils who reside in the *negative pole* of your magnetic force field, will help you to stop attracting the darker experiences where chaos, pain, fear and confusion results. It is therefore important to master Rule 3 and 4 so that you have the freedom of choice to work only with the easier Rule 1 and 2 to create rapid expansion and success.

The Universal Life Experience of Rule 3 and 4

Rule 3 and 4 have a specific purpose; for you to experience what it feels like to hand over your power to debt devils who create chaos so that you can, for a while, play the blame game – "Someone else did it to me." "It is the government's fault." "It is the economy that caused me to lose my job." "If only my parents saw the real me." So many stories where you felt powerless and unloved have their roots embedded by your devils in the negative pole of your magnetic force field.

That feeling of having no power over your destiny and not being valued is an important part of your human evolution. And then one day, you have had enough of this game and the law of attraction takes note and suddenly self-help books, life mentors and invitations to empowering seminars start appearing. You are now ready to master Rule 3 and 4. In metaphysics, this process is called 'mastering your shadow side'.

Mastering Rule 3: How to Stop Attracting What You Do Not Desire

You have to experience the bumps of life to grow in your human experience. You never learn anything powerful when life is a bed of roses.

During difficult times you learn:

- how to toughen up
- how to love
- how to forgive
- how to have faith
- how to be empowered
- what your true potential is

To gain these gifts, you will have needed to be born with negative forces already embedded within your magnetic force field to attract difficult events to learn from and grow in wisdom.

Accept that this is a normal part of your human emotional evolution and cease being angry with yourself and others, then you will stop feeding negative emotional or thought based energy to the debt devils. When their food supply of negative energy diminishes, so does their ability to create situations you are not fully aware of. You are then more self-aware of the stories they create and you have the power to cancel their agenda and most importantly, you then have the power to choose to use Rule 1 and 2.

As your self-awareness expands and you choose to feed positive energy to your magnetic force field, you will feel stronger mentally and emotionally. Your health and well-being will improve. Your debt will clear. You will fall in love with your life. You will be in bliss.

Mastering Rule 4: How to Stop Judging

This rule being utilized by your debt devils is a little easier to identify than Rule 3. Notice the people and situations that push your buttons because you have a judgment about how they do life. However, it is very difficult to stop judging.

Your negative magnetic force field is soaked in the need to judge from birth. When you are born you belong to a tribe, and are taught that anyone that does not act or look like your tribe, must be separated and feared. Anyone that has a different skin colour, speaks differently, dresses differently, worships a different deity; are to be avoided as they are not like you. You are right and they must be wrong and Rule 4 has you experiencing being the judge, the jury and the executioner.

This rule requires you to find humanity's common ground, which is the same spark of life within each human being. The more you work on accepting every person as already perfect with all their faults, including yourself, the less you will attract betrayal and human struggles.

As you begin to replace your judgements with acceptance and love for every living being, the law of attraction will note and begin filling your life with the most loving, kind and generous support to help you create miracles to get out of debt and into flow.

Identifying Your Life Experiences and Judgements

As you study each of the 8 colours of prosperity, you will be given the opportunity to discover which life experience and judgement could potentially be repeating a cycle of negative financial events and people being attracted towards you. As you begin to apply the colour frequencies to attract different situations – your job is going to be to say 'Yes' to all of it. Even if you doubt the way being shown or you dislike the person the law has firmly placed in front of you to communicate or interact with, there will be a reason and you will be called to action. Commit to:

SAY YES AND TURN UP
NO MATTER WHAT OR WHO PRESENTS!

You never know who or what the law of attraction has waiting around the corner to be the catalyst for new love, new prosperity and new hope! You are simply required to follow the breadcrumb trail, take action where asked and keep your intention on success.

Step B: Poverty Mind Set versus Prosperity Mind Set Habits

Poverty is general scarcity and lack of material goods and support

Prosperity is wealth, happiness and health

You are deeply conditioned to practice poverty habits as a way of life. Your family, community and global habits around love and money are practiced by 97% of the human population. And you are unaware that you are using poverty habits to create yet more poverty.

Poverty habits have become a part of your communication systems. You speak poverty by using the words CHEAP, BARGAIN and DEALS.

The advertising and marketing industry rely on you responding to their campaigns through your poverty mind set; 'two for the price of one'. Financial institutions encourage you to get into credit and 'reward you with air miles'. A poverty mind used in business can create pressure and stress; 'if you buy right now you will save 50%!'

When Enough is Never Enough

Poverty habits have their origins in the belief that you do not have enough. Not enough money, not enough love and not enough time. Your debt devils thrive on poverty habits and prod you with their pitchforks to actively seek out bargains and negotiate discounts so you can experience the stresses of not being in prosperity. They get a drug high every time you feel not enough, every time you feel in lack, every time you settle for sub-standard services or products.

The New Money Currency is Called Intention

If you are committed to quit being limited and poor, you can begin to powerfully change your debt situation – without working harder to earn more money! Poverty mind set has nothing to do with how much money you have. Even rich people may create their money from poverty habits of not enough by working non-stop and only doing business if there is a good bargain. They often become unhappy and the money being earned through a poverty mind set fails to give them meaningful love and joy in their life.

I noticed this poverty pattern being played out in 2015 in Toronto during an exhibition where my husband Paul was displaying products for our nutritional supplement business. A couple came over and enquired about the product and chatted for quite a long time with Paul. They ensured he knew that they were wealthy and semi-retired already at the age of 45 and had the luxury of spending time writing and going on vacations. Later I happened to pass by them in the restaurant and heard the husband very loudly proclaim to the staff that the price of the coffee at this event was extortion, making quite a fuss about just how much it cost him to buy one cup and then refusing to buy one for his wife. Considering how much wealth he claimed to have, he still appeared too poor to buy a cup of coffee for his wife.

Poverty mind set habits can be changed with the *power of intention*. Whatever you do, if you are clear about the intention that underpins your choices and actions, you can change your habits.

That means you can still buy items on sale, so long as the intention is clear that you just happen to like or desire the item, and not from the 'not enough' poverty habit motivating your purchase. Be very clear about your intentions and ensure they reflect that you deserve the best value at all times.

It is difficult when your cash flow is tight to just walk into a shop and pretend you have money to buy anything. However, the law of attraction is very specific – like attracts like. So, what if you INTENDED that you are prosperous and walked into the shop and tried on the best outfits as if you could afford them?

Perhaps by the time you get to the till, the salesperson will say the sale price did not get added and you find the item price matches what you can pay. What happened in the time between you intending you are worth more and the fact that you did not have the cash needed in your wallet, to suddenly being able to buy it?

Prosperity Births Within the Universal Void of Nothingness

When you pour your intentions into the void of nothingness – the space of time between your intentional wish and the fact that what you desire does not yet exist, that void is where the law of attraction creates miracles.

Stop and re-read that paragraph 3 times, type it up and put a memo on your fridge to read every day …. *When you pour your intentions* ….

The most often spoken phrase of a poverty mind is: "I can't afford it". The moment you say it, the law of attraction has to accept that as your true status. Yet there was a split moment in time when you desired the item to when your poverty mind kicked in and advised you that you did not have enough.

If you could self-alert when you are about to say "I can't afford…" and stop the words leaving your mouth and allow time, even a few minutes, for the law of attraction to take over, you may be surprised at what you can afford!

Your biggest challenge is not going to be to stop saying "I can't afford it", believe it or not, it is going to be your need to control or manipulate the law to deliver a result for you. So often when you wish for things, you stipulate *when, where* and *how* you want it delivered. You will have to let go of controlling outcomes and allow your prosperity mind to work with the law of attraction and deliver far more than what you can even possibly imagine.

A poverty mind set will always limit your dreams. What if you desired a bigger home? And you cut out pictures for a vision board that specified 3 bedrooms. The law of attraction will deliver a 3 bedroom home. However, the moment you move in, your parents become ill and also have to move into the new home that has nowhere near the space for the entire family. You actually needed a 5 bedroom home to accommodate parents and a carer, a situation you could not have predicted.

Whenever you feel the need to stipulate and control exactly what you want to manifest, remember that the law of attraction can work with your prosperity mind and because it operates in the void of nothingness, what we call time, it will know what your future needs are and can deliver the 5 bedroom home over and above what you thought you may need. Always be flexible and dare to dream bigger!

Eradicate Poverty and Activate Prosperity

Prosperity habits can help you get out of debt, and you do not need more cash to begin the process for you. You start by using intention and allowing that void where the universal laws get to work on your behalf to discover the solutions.

The universal law of attraction does not care if you have $2000 overdraft or a $20 bank balance or $20 million, universal laws only register how you believe and feel about yourself and that bank balance. Does the $20 make you feel poor or prosperous? Do you feel you have enough or not enough? Decide that you are enough and you already have enough and the law of attraction has to use your prosperity mind to bring you more.

Letting go of poverty mind set habits and embracing prosperity habits is like going to the gym for the first time and your muscles ache until they get fit. Literally, your head will ache when you start to notice and eradicate poverty habits from your life. The will to keep believing in the reality of not enough money and your debt consuming you, versus intending to act as if you are living life differently with prosperity will challenge you. Your debt devils consider your poverty habits their paradise playground and will try to use every trick on their pitchforks to prod you and make you doubt your prosperous intentions.

In each of the colour chapters you will be guided to a colour to help ease the process of change from poverty to prosperity habits. It is also recommended that you practice on a daily basis at least 3 of the prosperity exercises suggested, whichever you feel would be easiest to implement as a new prosperity habit that will activate the law of attraction to deliver the miracles and get you out of debt and into positive cash flow.

.

Step C: The 8 Debt Devils Running your Love and Money

Debt devils are hidden aspects of you, responsible for creating negative events around your finances and relationships. You tend to be unaware of their existence, however you will certainly notice the labours of their work as the fall-out that is debt and loneliness. These devils are perhaps your biggest inner teachers of knowledge and wisdom. Without the antics they get up to, you would have no challenges to test out your skills of creation and learn how to turn your life from struggle to freedom.

They exist in your magnetic force field's negative pole and you created them. There would have been times in your life where you struggled or were overwhelmed by certain feelings and fears, often pushing these emotions aside to deal with later. And later came and went and it became a habit to keep storing into your magnetic force field what you were unable or unwilling to face. Each time you added negative thoughts and feelings to your magnetic pole, the negative field grew stronger until it became autonomous and organized itself into categories to make sense of the energies you kept sending in.

Each category has a job, for example a category responsible for filing away your fears around being betrayed would file away your feelings of how you felt when you were betrayed or betrayed others. Another category may develop a job filing away your feelings of not being loved; this file may have already started when you were in the womb as your mother's pregnancy may have been unexpected and unwanted by her or her family. And every time you experienced not being loved or allowed yourself to not be loved, it fattened up that file.

The more feelings you have stored away, the more information was available to create your little devils, with their own personalities, behaviour responses and specific job functions. They grew in power as you kept feeding them their food of negative thoughts and feelings. When you added un-forgiveness, judgements, control, blame, fear, hate, abuse of power and guilt to the files, they could grow horns and prickly tails and sharpen their pitchforks.

It can take a lifetime of professional analysis to work through what you have stored away in your magnetic force field. If you have experienced, especially in childhood, traumas and shocks and were overwhelmed by circumstances, you will benefit from seeking out professional therapists and gain clarity on all your inner devils. In this book we are going to focus only on the 8 inner devils most commonly found to be responsible for love and money issues.

The Devil Made Me Do It!

As you were the creator of your devils, your first step in mastering them and diminishing their power of destruction, is to take responsibility for what you have created. That requires you to look at what is not working for you in your life and even if you cannot remember creating the chaos or thought someone else was to blame, work with the concept that an inner autonomous little devil created by you, without you being aware at the time, caused that situation to unfold. Once you take responsibility and become aware of their existence, you can begin working at:

a) not adding any more negative thoughts and feelings to the files

b) starting to clear out the files

c) turning your devils into angels by teaching them how to create only from the prosperity files in your positive magnetic force field

The Language of the DEbt DEvils

You can self-alert when your debt devils take possession of your communication system and use your voice to create more drama and negative situations. They use a specific language strategy to hook you into their games. You have given your voice to the debt devils when you respond with:

DEny

DEfend

DElay

DEflect

Negotiate

Justify

When you hear yourself begin to speak their language, stop and take a deep breath. No matter how hot under the collar you are to jump in and defend yourself – just clam up for one moment!

That single breath stops everything, and gives you that crucial moment to enter the void of nothingness where the law of attraction operates. In that breath's space of time, you have a split moment to decide whether you are going to give your inner devil access to use the law to attract more struggles or whether you are going to take your power back and use your wisdom to instruct the law to deliver a different outcome. Like attracts like!

The 8 colours in this book will each offer guidance and exercises to help you clear out the files where you have stored unresolved feelings and begin to respond differently in your communications. As the food stores of negative energy clears out, the debt devils will start to look for a new source of energy to survive. By practicing and speaking prosperity daily, these devils will turn their focus from creating trouble in your life, to helping you fulfil your dreams of a prosperous life and eventually become your angels.

Chapter 1

Pink Boot Camps

Pink Attracts: Romance, Money and Love

Pink Attributes: Affection, Diplomacy, Friendly and Charming

Pink Power: Pink is usually thought of as a feminine soft fluffy colour. Many cultures believe that the colour red is the most powerful colour for good fortune, money and masculinity. Pink is intensified red. When you add more light to red, it turns it pink. The frequency of pink is therefore stronger than red.

Pink and the Law of Attraction

In colour analysis the frequency of pink refers to both love and money. It is the first and most powerful colour tool you can use to attract a higher flow of income and the love of your life. It is also the colour that will rekindle the romance in an existing relationship.

By adding specific colours to your magnetic force field, wearing colours, decorating rooms, visualizing colours, or bathing in or rubbing coloured oils on your skin, even spritzing the colours into your spaces – you are changing your body's magnetic forces to attract a different experience.

Now adding pink to your magnetic force field may not appeal to everyone, especially men who may find wearing pink to work unsuitable, and pink walls in an office that caters to both male and female clients may alienate the male sector. However, the colour choice you add to your bath is no one's business but your own! So men, give it a go, pour pink oil into a bath and see what happens.

Because love and money responds to the same frequency when the law of attraction is at work, you will find that during times when you are experiencing cash flow issues, you will also feel undervalued by your colleagues or family. There is a distinct relationship between the health of your bank balance and the health of your love life.

Clients with cash flow issues are often appalled that instead of offering strategies for solving their financial crises, they are instructed to instead spend a great deal of time romancing themselves! When these clients begin to participate in activities they love, treat themself as if they are the most precious person in the room and dip into pink baths and spray pink essences into their spaces, the pink frequency generated by those actions and the help of the coloured bottles contribute towards increasing the law of attraction's power to attract more love and automatically more money.

Case Study of the Nurse in Pink

Nicky, a nurse working in the cancer wards of a hospital in North England was struggling with her job; she felt undervalued, overworked and underpaid. Her department head was a bully and she felt trapped because she loved nursing, just not the circumstances around her current position. She was instructed to go to work with a different intention and to wear pink underwear and bathe in the Colour Mirrors number 6 pink coloured bottle.

She set aside her old feelings of dread when going to work and replaced them with the intention that she worked for the perfect boss, earned the perfect salary and everyone loved her. She reported 3 weeks later that she was moved, without her having to request a transfer, to a different ward and received an increase in salary. Soon afterwards, her favourite aunt had a brain haemorrhage and Nicky says without the move to the new ward, she would not have had the knowledge to support her family through the shocking events that followed. Her boyfriend of 15 years also finally proposed and they got married.

Notice that with Nicky's intention exercise, she did not instruct the law of attraction specifically what to do to change her circumstances – she simply used pink and said 'I choose to love' in a reality that was not kind and loving. And the law moved her to a position where there was love to match that intention and had to simultaneously deliver more money as well. The law also knew ahead of time, because it operates in the *void of nothingness*, that the knowledge gained in that specific ward would serve her family during an event that Nicky could not possibly have known would occur.

The law when allowed to work with the added frequency of colour and without your control of *when, where* and *how*, will always over-deliver!

Pink Poverty Habit

Blocking the Flow of Receiving

There is a tendency during times of lack to go into hiding and not show that you need help, whether it is emotional or financial. Even when support is offered you may say no, so you do not appear vulnerable or helpless. The last thing you want your family and friends to see is you not coping and possibly becoming open to ridicule, being judged or seen as stupid for getting into trouble. This pattern of saying no and resisting asking for or accepting help is stronger when you have previously failed at a job, a marriage or maybe a business venture. Perhaps you see yourself as the black sheep of the family, and receiving help from them just affirms that they get life right and you always mess up somehow.

Using pink to end this poverty habit and intend accepting support, will result in the law of attraction using the pink frequency to bring you:

- a person that may be the catalyst for meeting the love of your life
- a person who is the love of your life
- useful advice on how to re-ignite passion in your existing relationship
- a person or organization that can help you sort out your financial issues effortlessly

You may even find that pink brings in new ideas for creating wealth that you could not have envisaged. For example, a business partnership. Even if you do not like the idea of working with someone else, remember to say, 'Yes', and turn up and follow the breadcrumbs, it will lead you to solutions where you will be both in love and have a positive cash flow.

When you are self-employed you may find you are working very hard, doing everything by yourself, perhaps doubting that no one else can do your job as well as you. You do your own books, marketing, sales, technology and research. You know that what you offer as your services or products are of high value, yet your market stays small and you cannot seem to figure out why your unique message or product does not grow.

This is quite common in small businesses where the owner is the jack-of-all-trades and has spread his or her time and resources so widely that they miss taking opportunities for expansion and success. If this is you, you could be managing your business from a poverty habit of not allowing support in.

Your poverty language will be 'I can't afford to hire anyone, I can't afford to contract in experts, I can't afford to get a professional to do it, and I can't afford to be mentored'. Or, 'when my business makes more money, then I will hire someone, then I will get a new website, then I will write the book, then I will take the time to attend the course'. This poverty habit is blocking you from receiving support to take your business to the next level.

Intend to allow support into your business and open yourself up to receiving without going into fear that you cannot afford the fees. The law of attraction will know exactly who to bring towards you and the cash or means to pay them. This philosophy goes beyond everything you have been taught about being sensible in business, earn the money first and then sign the contract. However, when you study the most successful entrepreneurs in the world, who discovered how the law of attraction works, you will notice a common thread – they all said yes and figured out how to make it happen later on. When you truly desire a change, the law will respond by sending you all the support you need and more, just be open to receiving it.

Pink Prosperity Habit

Activate the flow of Giving

The act of giving is an act of prosperity. When you start giving the law of attraction registers that you 'have' to give, and will send you more to have. Money is a value system as *currency* that is meant to flow. In a savings account, money earns interest and that interest creates movement and the account grows in value. The moment money becomes stagnant and you hold onto your last dollar with a fear of not enough, the law of attraction has to stop attracting the flow of money coming towards you. Your money ceases to be interesting!

Is it a leap of faith to spend or give away your limited funds when you yourself do not have enough to pay your bills? The law of attraction does not operate based on faith – it works based on intention!

Faith *believes the law* will work for you

Intention *is activating* the law to work for you

To activate cash where the flow is stagnant, set an intention that you are prosperous and can give or spend because you can. Be very careful and avoid a poverty habit where you justify giving the help or spending the money because you can get it back ten-fold or it will come back to you somehow, sometime. The moment you set an *outcome* or have an *expectation* attached to what you give, the law registers you as needy and can only send you more need.

Give without an expectation of return, give because you can and give because you love, and then the law will work miracles for you. You may even find that in the act of giving to a specific person, that the flow of cash that comes back to you because it is free to move *when, where* and *how*, may come from other surprising sources. When you set your money free to flow with love, the law will have it flow wherever it is needed to flow and has to ensure it flows your way again; and when it goes your way again, it arrives with added *interest* it picked up along its travels.

Debt Devil # 1: The Pink Victim

The main life experience being taught by the victim debt devil is to experience what it feels like to have no power and control over your own life. This devil will throw you into a set of circumstances that will frustrate you, anger you, and set you up to be rescued by others, adding to the humiliation and feelings of powerlessness. When this debt devil gains even more power to deliver a deeper life lesson, your anger can turn into the need to lash back and often you do not even realise you are practicing passive aggressive behaviour.

This devil has the power to act autonomously and will use opportunities when you are tired, stressed or in poor health, and take over large chunks of your behaviour, and each time you allow this devil to have control of your mind and body, it grows in strength until you identify yourself through the lens of a victim. From that moment on everything in your life will have a victim's response and belief system as the blueprint for love and money.

You know you have a victim devil in charge when you have a belief that other people or organizations have more power than you, that their power controls you.

In business it is common to hear the victim's voice during that time of the year when the tax is due. Or when the economy takes a plunge. Do you believe the tax system is out to make life difficult, or perhaps that your business will suffer during an economic recession? Your victim devil will try to justify keeping you in this belief system, that you have no power above the giants of government, and that everyone is in the same boat as you. Who do you blame for difficult times in business? If you have not yet realized that you are the power in your life and you can create the dream life and not have to be subjected to outside influences, you have a victim devil running interference tactics.

You cannot exterminate your devils; you can only re-train them. And the colour pink teaches you that love and forgiveness are the only weapons you can use to claim your power of creation back.

YOU CANNOT FIGHT IT RIGHT – YOU CAN ONLY LOVE IT RIGHT!

Can you love the tax system? See only the good intention of a system that gives you lights, water, sewerage, roads; a system that, even if flawed at some level, sees to the necessities of life so you are free to pursue your passions. Can you imagine if you started to send pink love vibes to your government, instead of judgment or feeling victimized, how would all that angry energy wasted by your debt devil be utilized to instead grow your finances?

Your victim devil will ensure that you have the opportunity to deflect your energy towards the law of attraction to attract more reasons for disliking the governmental systems resulting in more frustrating issues with your tax bill or garbage collection. It will all cease when you stop judging and feeding your anger and frustration as a source of food to the victim devil. What will the law of attraction bring towards you when you have intended to love instead?

Pink Action

➤ Take all your bills, print copies off if you use electronic systems, and put them into a pink box. Add copies of credit card and bank overdraft statements. Add anything that represents where you owe money. Put $10 on top or a larger amount, whatever you can put towards the debt right now.

➤ Set an intention that you have all the resources already available and have paid all these items. Spray pink essences; rub pink oil on pulse points or wherever it feels good. Send love to the box!

Repeat whenever you feel the panic of your situation begin to surface and keep your intention at the strongest thought, that it is already resolved. Hear yourself speak and self-alert when you hear yourself uttering words of:

"I don't have."
"My debt is crippling me."
"I owe ..."

Remove them from your language and replace with prosperous words as if your situation is already different. Use the 'I' to affirm your new intentions:

"I am prosperous."
"I am in an abundant flow."
"I am valued."
"I am loved."

And remember to say, 'Yes' to all the things that begin to turn up and follow the breadcrumb trail that may appear as new invitations, ideas, meetings, events, emails or phone calls. One of those leads could be providing you with viable solutions that may include debt consolidation, financial support from unlikely sources, a sale, a debt owed that you forgot about being paid to you, a new direction to grow your business into, or a new market. Clients who tried this exercise reported back that they unexpectedly inherited or won money; some had friends or family offer to pay their debt and gifted them a new beginning and the freedom from stress and suicidal thoughts. Be open to any miracle!

For additional pink support visit my website,
www.8coloursofprosperity.com where you can access
free pink empowering visualizations and purchase
Colour Mirrors pink bath oils and spritzer essences.

Chapter 2

Coral Sex and Toys

Coral Attracts: Sensuality, Creativity, Luxury and Courage

Coral Attributes: Leadership, Ambition, Independence and Expansion

Coral Power: When you mix pink and yellow, you make coral. Yellow is the colour of joy and pink is the colour of love and money. To achieve true financial freedom, you need to attain a state of both love and joy. When you have fun, your love and money has the capacity to expand beyond all limiting beliefs.

Coral and the Law of Attraction

Coral is often a colour you feel drawn to when you seek to break your glass ceiling. The glass ceiling is that line you drew that reminds you of the heights you believe you are capable of reaching. You will know this line very well; it represents the most money you have ever been able to earn. It is the most challenging goal you have set and achieved. It is the highest rank you will rise to in your industry or your job. And if you ever try to go above that line, your debt devils will take over and ensure you are reminded of your rightful place lower down the economy scale. You may have drawn that line when your parents expected very little of you and did not motivate you beyond the need to plan for your retirement at age 65.

If you feel that you are worth more, can achieve more and desire a vast expanse of spaces, people and experiences to explore in your lifetime, coral is the colour that will help you leave the road laid down by your ancestors and attract everything you need to lay down a new road that matches your vision.

The reason the law of attraction keeps delivering the 'sea of sameness' every day is your belief in that glass ceiling and how it reminds you of your perceived limited creative powers.

The colour coral says you can have it all, love, money and fun! No need to make sacrifices, no need to play small and hide the magnificent you that you secretly always knew existed within you. And if you believe that you are more than the sum of who you are now, coral is the colour to unlock your potential.

Using coral with your intention to break through the glass ceiling may require additional help from your physical body. Coral is a colour that loves to connect with the law by taking action and creating movement. The physical coral energy you generate when you move your body is used by the law to smash the ceiling and open up a fast track system to expansion, taking your love life and your business to new heights.

Clients who seek a method to break through their limiting beliefs at times have been advised to do something physically challenging and fun instead of applying business tactics. Try activities such as; join a dance class, learn to ski, go white water rafting, go up in a hot air balloon, sail a boat, parachute, climb a mountain, go ziplining, sing karaoke – something new that gets your adrenals pumping coral physical energy.

That extra dose of physical activity says to the law of attraction that you are committed to serious effort to do the work and break through the ceiling to reach new heights of success, and it in turn has to up its energy output to ensure you get what you desire and more.

Case Study of the School Prefect

In the south of England at an exhibition, a family, all dressed in black approached the table, mother and father were both in wheel chairs and the little girl went straight for the bottle colours that told a story of a family who had given up all joy, and how sad she was. I was so busy looking at her that I almost missed seeing her brother, head down, hands in pockets looking defeated with red skin in full acne crisis. I tentatively asked what I could do for them and the mother spoke for her son, saying that he wanted more confidence, was being bullied at school and was willing to try anything, even the strange coloured bottles. After his session, he took a coral spray home with the instruction to use before going to school every day.

Around 6 months later I was doing another exhibition in a different area and I noticed a man and a woman walking towards me, each with a walking stick. They looked familiar however without the wheelchairs I did not recognize them until I saw the little girl bouncing over and picking up bottles, this time happy colours, and I knew something had changed for this family. I wondered where the son was and was about to enquire when the mom pointed to a very tall young man next to her; I almost did not recognize him! His skin had cleared up and his stance was oozing with confidence. The mom explained that everything changed for him the first time he sprayed the Colour Mirrors coral bottle and the bullying never happened again. He in turn told me that he joined the rugby team and found he loved sports and recently had been elected as a prefect in his class. His mom said that they drove hours to get there, when they had heard I was at this event, just to come and express their gratitude for the coral advice I had given 6 months back.

I have long since unfortunately forgotten their names, but I never forgot the power of that one little coral bottle helping to attract joy and power back to a family, and activating leadership skills for a teenager.

Coral Poverty Habit

Money and Love Starvation

How you connect with others in your social environment and your beliefs about your physical body can reflect poverty habits without you being aware of them. You may even have habits around food that are based on a poverty mind set. These behaviours send out signals not only to the law of attraction, but also to potential clients who could be noticing and are influenced to avoid investing in your business. If you ever wondered why on the first date over dinner, they never called you back, it could be that the date sensed your poverty or neediness by observing what you ordered, how you ate and how you treated the staff.

A powerful poverty habit is where you starve your body by not feeding it regularly or don't drink enough water for hydration or avoid physical exercise, and allow your sex life to diminish. Not putting the needs of your physical body first tells the law of attraction that you do not value who you are and it has to respond by not regularly feeding value to your bank account!

The next time you have a business lunch, even with someone who claims or is known for being successful and wealthy, look out for the poverty signs, and also note here that these may be your tell-tale poverty signs on display!:

- Spending a long time looking at the menu, going over every item and changing your mind several times about what to order
- Commenting on the high or low prices
- Suggesting that the meeting should have happened in a better restaurant
- When the waitress appears you question the ingredients and have her run back and forth to the kitchen
- Asking for the special deals of the day
- Asking that if you eliminated an item from the meal, would the price change
- Keeping everyone waiting while you discuss your special needs order with the waitress and become the centre of attention
- Making a point to list what you do not eat
- Start moving the salt and pepper pots around, re-arranging the table
- When the meal arrives, you complain
- While eating, you complain about the meal or service
- Eating unconsciously, not enjoying the flavour, not chewing properly or not pausing between bites
- Your response to the meal leads to the staff being forced to offer a discount
- Asking to split the bill

- In larger groups, asking to have the bill itemized and everyone paying only for what they ordered
- When the other person offers to buy, you insist on paying your half, unable to accept their generosity
- Not leaving a service fee for the waitress
- Ensuring that everyone notices how much you are tipping

This behaviour hints that you are not the power in your life, that you struggle to get what you want, you have to fight for what you want and you are financially, emotionally and sexually starving.

If you want to accelerate the growth of your business, seek advice on nutrition, change habits around buying and eating food, start an exercise routine that is fun, try sex-therapy and use coral bottles to help you self-alert when you eat unconsciously. Any love you focus on your body's care is going to instruct the law of attraction to deliver more caring events and people to nourish your body and bank account.

Coral Prosperity Habit

Throw a Party!

When you plan a party it is an act of prosperity. Have you noticed that when you are in debt you stop visiting friends? Perhaps you stop going to the movies, eating out or meeting up for drinks after work? When you are at your lowest ebb, throw a party!

Your intention will propel the law of attraction into life instantly, working to ensure you are supplied with all the resources to make it a fun event; perhaps each person bringing a plate and bottle, someone offering a venue, the music.... lets leave the law here to get on with the party planning, you have already done your bit by setting the intention to have fun!

The law of attraction works so diligently to create your life experiences that it really appreciates when you take time out to celebrate that life. Have you ever considered what would happen if you threw a party when you got divorced, fired or lost a deal? What if you celebrated change as a positive event making your declaration to the law of attraction that you are ready for the new beginning and that it is perfectly okay to let the old ways go? How much extra time and resources would you have between the gap of the disaster unfolding in your life and what is, inevitably going to be a fresh start?

Celebrations are part of your cultural beliefs. You celebrate birthdays, national events, historical events; dates set to remind you of the passage of time and to take time out to remember. All such events, relate to time – and by now dear reader you know that the universal law of attraction operates in the void of nothingness that is called time!

Plan a celebration, find any excuse to throw that party and gather your friends, neighbours, and family and let the law of attraction be advised that you are ready to blast through that ceiling, I think there is a party song about that ... 'dancing on the ceiling'!

Debt Devil # 2: The Coral Prostitute

Earlier in the book under Pink Prosperity, the statement was made about the law of attraction that:

Faith *believes the law* will work for you

Intention is *activating the law* to work for you

The job of the coral prostitute devil is to undermine your faith. Faith in your own abilities, but mostly the faith in the silent workings of a universal law that you cannot see, feel, hear or touch.

This debt devil will remind you of the previous times you had faith in others and they let you down. The prostitute devil will especially dig into your childhood experiences where you were innocent and trusting and your parents failed to deliver your wishes. If your parents, whom you could see, feel, hear and touch, failed you, how can you have faith in something as intangible as the law of attraction?

You will notice this devil's antics in your life during the times you take control and force events to unfold exactly how you need them to be. You may already have triggered this devil within you by reading this book. This devil could be encouraging you to dismiss the sections in this book that advise you to leave the *when, where,* and *how* up to the law to decide when setting your intentions.

The need to control can be so severe that it is akin to going to a restaurant and ordering your meal, then getting up and entering the kitchen and cooking it yourself! There is no faith in place that when you ordered your meal it will arrive perfectly cooked.

To ensure you get your life delivered exactly how you need it, your prostitute devil will use whatever methods is necessary to stay in control of the creation process. This devil will have you following a rigid schedule, leaving no gaps of time for miracles to reveal themselves to you.

You will find that you may dismiss potential mentors or courses because they appeal to an open mind to test different strategies and your prostitute devil does not like you to try anything that feels you may not be in control of the environment, people or exercises offered.

This devil is called, 'The prostitute', because just before the miracle arrives, it takes control and sells its body on the street corner to get the money. For example:

At the end of the month a huge bill is due and you cannot figure out how to get the money on time. You follow the law of attraction's teachings and set the intention that you will be able to pay that bill. Half way through the month, nothing has happened and you begin to doubt and you take your focus away from the intention that the bill will be paid somehow. That is when your devil steps in, that moment you hesitate and doubt your faith. As the days go by your stress levels increase and your faith diminishes and this devil gets ready to act. On the second last day of the month, you are in full panic mode and rush off to the bank to arrange an overdraft or extend your credit card limit to cover the bill. You fail to make it to the last moment when the miracle is about to be delivered and you may not have needed to get into more debt.

There is another part of the prostitute devil that may influence your business. The prostitute devil likes material goodies and will try to steer the choices to instant gratification of material wealth and luxury rather than considering what is good for the greater community. This devil will have you design a marketing plan aimed at maximising profit and earnings and dismiss moral, ethical and spiritual considerations. You may offer your staff a below inflation rate salary increase pleading low profits, and at the same time they would notice you decorating the office in expensive and unnecessary artistic paintings and crafts.

Working with the prostitute devil in your positive magnetic pole will make good use of its creativity and ambition to raise your business to a whole new level of wealth, and your personal relationships to deepen in intimacy and fun. You will find time to enjoy what you create and remember to create luxury and share that around. You have to have faith ... I think there is a song about that too!

Coral Action

There are several coral actions you can practice to set the intention of luxury, wealth and opulence:

➤ Leave tidy notes of money lying around your home in places where you can see it and put some in drawers so that every time you open up the drawers there is money visible. This sends a message to the law of attraction that you are already feeling and looking prosperous.

➤ Open a new savings account, set the intention that this savings account is purely for you to save $1000 a month that is going to be your coral fun fund! It is going to take you on holidays and buy luxury items and allow you to surprise your partner or family with generous gifts. Then go to the bank and deposit the first '$1000' even if in reality you are only putting in $10. Every month go to the bank and as you take the 'time' and physical effort needed to drive to the building, intend that you are putting in your $1000 fun money into your coral fun account. The law of attraction has to catch up with you at some point! It notices that you intent $1000 and only $10 is going in, and it really wants you to have fun and make that intention true. Keep your faith and keep this monthly ritual going until you put your first $1000 in – at which point I would love you dear reader to email me and share your experience.

➤ Make an appointment right now with a hairdresser, a manicurist, a massage therapist, a beauty parlour, a spa; anywhere that will treat your physical body with attention. Repeat monthly.

➤ Go on a date night, taking time to dress up and feel good as if you are the sexiest person in the world going to meet the sexiest person to play with. Repeat monthly.

For additional coral support visit my website, www.8coloursofprosperity.com where you can access free coral empowering visualizations and purchase Colour Mirrors coral bath oils and spritzer essences.

Chapter 3

Gold Authentic Power

Gold Attracts: Alchemy, Potential and Transformation

Gold Attributes: Wisdom, Value, Authenticity and Wholeness

Gold Power: Yellow is the colour that represents the ego. When you add a fraction of pink to the yellow, it turns gold. To transcend ego-based power into authentic golden power, add pink love.

Gold and the Law of Attraction

Remember those times when everything just seemed to go wrong at once? That would have been a time when the law of attraction delivered golden life experiences as a string of events to propel you to transform your life. It is the deepest push you will get from the universal laws to get out of the old ways of doing life, and regenerate a different approach to how you do relationships with yourself and others. Your career or business will be triggered to evolve, your views on spirituality will be challenged; when a gold process unleashes in your life, there is not a single aspect of you that will not feel the shake up.

Gold is the colour that represents alchemy. Alchemy is the process that turns you from base metal human who feels no value, into precious gold human where you find your own truth and sense of self-worth. Although when you are in a process of alchemical changes it feels rough, the rewards when you are out the other side are phenomenal. Often you become clearer about your life purpose and make changes to your career, or you let go of a partnership or marriage that no longer works for you. As gold relates to value systems, the law of attraction will also be offering the life experiences of financial systems and you will learn the value of money, how it works as an energetic flow of currency and how it mirrors the value of your self-worth.

The Stock Broker on Lunch

In Toronto during 2016, I was attending an event for women speakers at which I was thoroughly bored. I always say 'Yes' and turn up to invitations when undergoing a golden transformational period to ensure that I don't miss any opportunities. However, I was wondering why the law had drawn this event to my attention as the speakers and subject matter were not inspiring and I was relieved when it was time to break for lunch. It was a busy venue and a man asked if he could join our group. As we approached our table, he told the waiter that we had a short break and to ensure our food came quickly. At that moment I knew we were never going to see our lunch – this event was getting even more disappointing!

Our lunch never arrived but how did I know before we even sat down and ordered?

Working with the law of attraction you become more aware of how you are constructing your magnetic force field and how that energy is projected out into the world. It is *who you are* and that emanation of your energy that attracts everything towards you. This man, who turned out to be a Wall Street investor, was still learning that lesson. His emanation was ego and therefore he needed to take control of his environment and instruct *when* and *how* he needed his lunch.

When you are in authentic power you would walk into the conference restaurant and sit and order your meal. You would know there is no need to remind the law of attraction, being represented by the waiter, that time is important. Your magnetic force field will emanate your 'knowingness automatically' and deliver all your needs. That authentic presence has been recorded as a state of grace with leaders such as the Dalai Llama, Ghandi, Mother Teresa, Sir Richard Branson, Tony Robbins and Oprah Winfrey.

8 Traits of Authentic People:

1. They are self-aware
2. They listen
3. They are consistent in everything they say and do
4. They are present in the now moment
5. They are not judgemental
6. They focus on leaving a legacy
7. They respect themselves and others
8. They hold themselves accountable for their choices

And did I get anything from attending the conference? Oh yes, in the presence of everyone I met, including the stock broker at lunch, I was reminded again and felt huge gratitude of how lucky I am to have discovered the power of colour and how much colour analysis helped to evolve my life and those of my clients in the quest to be more self-aware and authentic.

Gold Poverty Habit

The Enticing Deal

Do you offer discounts or special prices to lure clients into your business? Of course you do! Everyone else does it, and if you didn't you would not get new business – correct?

When you are in authentic power emanating that knowingness of your self-worth and that all your needs are always met and more by the universal laws, you may begin to question the habit of offering deals to ensure clients notice your business and invest.

What if you offered value instead of deals? Could your business still prosper and grow?

When you offer a deal, examine whether you are expressing value of yourself, your product, your service, or are you saying you are desperate for new business and income? What is your intention behind the special offers, to get more money or to add value?

Read these two deals and feel which is more authentic to you:

Deal 1:
For a limited time only you qualify for a 50% discount never to be repeated again offer.

Deal 2:
We appreciate your business and as our thank you, your next purchase with us is 50% less.

The client will feel whether you hold them in a prosperity value system (Deal 2) or whether you consider them in the same poverty value system as you (Deal 1). Offer specials with a value intention that enhances how clients feel about you.

Mentioned in the introduction of this book, the new way of conducting business is about being authentic with your clients and appealing to their value system as well as their heart. The client wants to love you, the person behind the business. That little drop of pink love power added to the yellow will ensure you create lasting relationships with your clients and they will pay you your golden value without the need for too many deals.

Gold Prosperity Habit

Marinade Sauce Source

When your debt or cash flow crises has been a long term issue and you have been marinating your magnetic force field in negative energy, the only ones who benefit from that process are your debt devils. It is vital that you spend focussed time to marinade your magnetic force field in a difference source of energy.

Who do you admire? Who inspires you? Who are the leaders in the world that you would love to emulate? Who is already authentic in their business? Find a way to connect with their story and teachings on a daily basis. Watch their videos, documentaries, read their books, leave images of them lying around your home and office. Speak about them, print out their quotes to put on your fridge door, and your notice boards.

You will soon find your physical and mental energy being elevated as well as how you feel about your difficult issues.

As you set the intention to marinade in the presence of authentic powerful leaders, the law of attraction has no option but to eventually find a way for your paths to cross. Maybe in person with the leader you admire, or with one of their prodigies or mentors, or even a family member, or their organisation, a book signing or a seminar. A link will appear over time as your frequency begins to match theirs. Like attracts like.

Debt Devil # 3: The Gold Saboteur

This devil you know very well, it does not hide but operates in full view and at times you can actually feel yourself self-sabotaging and powerless to stop it! This devil has a huge life experience for you to master – conquering the fear of your own power!

When you are attracted to the colour gold and looking for ways to achieve your highest goals in the shortest time, the gold says there is a serious glitch in the plan. The glitch is your fear of being successful and you may be unaware of that fear.

Do you wonder what would happen if you became successful? What that power will feel like?

You may have witnessed those who have abused their power many times, some unleashing destruction on the environment and some making rules to suit their own agenda and ignore the greater good. When they do that, you will have noticed that people stop loving them.

Remember the pink colour, the colour of love that turns yellow ego into gold authenticity? Pink also speaks of the hidden fear you have that when you claim more power, people will stop loving you. The saboteur devil knows this and will use several tactics to trip you up as you begin to climb the ladder of success. Here are some well known tactics used by this debt devil:

- The moment you start to focus on a goal, you allow yourself to become distracted by non-important things. Especially addictions will be used by the saboteur devil, it knows how to twist your will and put the TV on and get lost in hours of watching sports instead of completing your project.

- You divert your time and energy to other people's dramas. The saboteur devil loves you to justify your intrusion into other people's stories and the more you engage in their lives, the less time you have to focus on your own goals.

- When attending learning opportunities, do you allow the information in, or do you take over the class and undermine the teachings – because you know more! The saboteur devil loves undermining tactics, making you so busy taking over and hearing your own voice, that you will miss the very new gift you are meant to be receiving in that class.

- When the law of attraction has led you to an empowering moment, you switch your attention by focussing on a phone call or check your emails. The saboteur devil arranged for the distracting phone call so that you will miss the key message that would have benefited you.

- How often have you ensured you depleted your cash fund on trinkets that do not serve your intention to expand your business? When a program or mentor arrives and you absolutely know it is a gift from the universal laws and will propel you to success – you find you have no cash on hand to immediately pay for their expertise. The saboteur devil will influence your shopping habits and distract you with shiny objects.

- Have you resisted going into a partnership or signing a contract because you feared being betrayed? The saboteur devil loves to remind you of past events where you were betrayed and push aside your new feelings of trust and faith that the law of attraction will deliver a perfect partner. It will entice you to take control and even collaborate with the prostitute devil's ability to lose faith, all to ensure you stay in control and miss the life changing union that would allow you to soar to new heights.

When you work with the saboteur devil in the positive pole of your magnetic force field, you can engage its energy to alert you to new opportunities, help you instantly decide on which contract to sign and embrace power fearlessly.

Gold Action

➤ There is nothing that feels more powerless when you are in debt than getting to the till and having your cards declined. Always have a $100 note stashed somewhere in your wallet, firstly as a back up and secondly it helps to notify the law of attraction that you are prosperous. If you usually only carry cards, put money into your wallet as well to represent the currency of prosperity. Your cards represent a financial institution.

➤ Ensure your wallet is a good colour and in good condition. If you desire financial power your wallet has to look powerful. Choose a wallet colour from any of the 8 colours you explore for prosperity in this book. Men, I know that carrying a pink wallet is not going to float your boat, the fashion gurus have already said black and brown are your colours! Put a piece of card in the colour of your choice in the black/brown wallet where you can notice the colour whenever you open your wallet.

➤ Clear your wallet out regularly and ensure that notes are neatly stacked. When you open your wallet you want to visually evidence to others, but mostly to yourself, that you are organised and in power of your finances.

➤ On a weekly basis check your bank accounts!! It is imperative to keep your eye on the cash flowing in and out of your account – it is *interesting* to view! When you feel the flow is not in your favour, sit quietly and have a chat with the law of attraction and re-focus good intentions.

For additional gold support visit my website, www.8coloursofprosperity.com where you can access free gold empowering visualizations and purchase Colour Mirrors gold bath oils and spritzer essences.

Chapter 4

Olive Recalibration

Olive Attracts: New Beginnings, New Blueprints, Hope and Harmony

Olive Attributes: Optimistic, Panoramic Awareness, Trusting and Spacious

Olive Power: Olive is the body colour positioned between the yellow naval area of personal power and the green heart relationship area. Personal yellow ego power can be destructive and controlling. Mix yellow power with the green heart and it becomes a soft olive power that is creative and nurturing.

Olive and the Law of Attraction

Olive, more than any other colour is about a new beginning. The law of attraction loves a spring clean of your mind, heart and body. As you detox and clear out negative old stories, judgements and toxins, it creates a vacuum and the law cannot wait to fill these spaces with new people and opportunities whose frequency matches your newly polished magnetic force field.

The need to detox often arises after a period where you have simply burnt out, where you can no longer hold onto the old stories and ways of doing life, and the only option is to let it all go. Olive is a colour that will help the law of attraction to re-invent your entire life.

To attract a new beginning, set the intention first. Make vision boards with images that represent what your new future looks like and how it makes you feel. The law of attraction loves to connect with the emotional part of your body, ensure that you put words on your vision board that represent those emotions including; hope, joy, love, anticipation, satisfaction, fulfilment, bliss, ecstatic, peace and harmony. Do not worry if you are not yet clear as to a new purpose or direction, you do not need to be specific.

Also obtain a notebook and write on the first page in large letters:

SAY YES
AND TURN UP
NO MATTER WHAT

That tells the law of attraction that you are ready to receive and act upon instructions that may come as invitations or suggestions from other people; something an actor says in the movie that caught your attention, emails, social media posts, a neighbour walking their dog passing by with a comment – all could be potential instructions on your way forward and can come from anyone and any direction. As you start noticing them, write them down in your notebook so the law knows you caught the message, and when you have acted on it, write that down too. Over a period of time, sometimes weeks only, you will notice a pattern appear, a theme to the instructions. For each person it is going to be different as you have your own unique purpose and life path.

This system of intending your new beginning is based exactly on the steps I followed when I desired a new beginning during 2010 after my mom passed away and again during 2014. It worked both times. There were some odd things I said 'Yes' to that I would have normally dismissed or thought too bizarre, however I turned up and over time each message I acted upon revealed the reason they had appeared. In 2010 I was guided to start a new therapy business, the Love & Money Boot Camps and publish the *Colour Mirrors Oracle Cards.* In 2014 I was guided to get married and move to Canada.

On arriving in Canada, I again followed the system to see how the law of attraction would guide *where* and *how* my business needed to be established in a new country. I followed the breadcrumb trail that started as a suggestion by my husband Paul to attend a network meeting with him and then a post on Facebook for a live event caught my eye – all these signs I said 'Yes' to which eventually led to this book being created! As a bonus I met wonderful new friends and created a powerful team of colour entrepreneurs who also use the Colour Mirrors bottles as the tool of change in their businesses. Each time I, and the international graduates of the Love & Money Boot Camp, use this system of always saying 'Yes' and turning up, something new inevitably begins for us.

There may be a period of time where you are sorting through what you want to clear out, and receiving instructions to move forward in your new direction. That period of time is where you can sometimes get lost in the gap and doubt your decisions for change.

That gap is a vital part of your transformation, it is the space in time where the universal laws recalibrate your magnetic force field until it emanates fully the new vision you have intended as your future. For each person the timing of this change is different. The change in 2010 took a full year to evolve for me, the change in 2014 happened within 3 months.

Your magnetic force field systems have to be re-wired so that you never go back to where you were before. During the recalibration gap phase, you may feel slightly confused and cast doubt on your faith that the law of attraction has actually received your intention for change. Some tangible symptoms of change where you will feel the recalibration process may include:

- Losing the taste of previous types of food you used to eat, perhaps becoming vegetarian or vegan for a time
- Becoming sensitive to chemicals in foods or developing food allergies
- Being a bit forgetful, misplacing items and your ability to focus seems to have shorter time periods
- Needing an hour or more sleep a night and experiencing deep sleep states
- Joint pain or discomfort that the medical profession cannot explain
- Sore throats, sinus issues as it clears out old tears you never cried
- Buzzing sounds in ears that there seems no medical diagnosis for
- Increased sensitivity to noise pollution and smells
- Wanting to avoid being with crowds as it feels as if they drain your energy or irritate you
- Needing to drink more water

Always check in with your medical doctor! Be sensible. If there does not seem to be anything seriously wrong and you are going through a major life adjustment, it may just be growing pains as your body's magnetic force field adjusts to match the new expanded life vision you desire. Be gentle on yourself and investigate with a nutritionist a detox program and nutritional supplements, anything that can support your body as you are recalibrated for a new beginning.

Olive Poverty Habit

Material Possessions Possessing You

Have you noticed that often people with financial issues have an attachment to their material goods? It is possible to attach value to items to emulate feeling valuable when your bank account has no value in it. Your material possessions could however be owning you and draining your energy as they need regular maintenance and cleaning – creating time poverty – where you do not have enough time in the day to look after your goods and to focus on your intention for creating more cash flow.

Olive relates to your spaces, and what you fill those spaces with is very symbolic. When you are locked into a poverty mind set, your possessions may be reflecting that 'not enough' belief and it can delay the law of attraction to bring you your new beginning.

You can identify using colour analysis through the combination of the olive 'I have no value' and the gold 'I have no power' a serious hoarding issue. To stop hoarding you may require the intervention of a therapist as this issue could last for many years and effect mental health.

Go around your house with a sheet of paper and clipboard and answer these questions:

- How many glasses, cups and crockery is chipped, stained, cracked, ancient, not matching sets?

- How many items in the fridge and cupboards are past their 'sell by' date?

- How many items of clothes do you have in your wardrobe that you have not worn for over two years?

- How many items that you wear regularly are threadbare, fluffed out and stained?

- How many half or almost empty used bottles of creams, make up and toiletries are you storing?

- Are your towels fresh, fluffy and colour coded; or are they rags that exfoliate your skin?

- Check the linen closet, how many sets of bedding are stored that you have not used in two years?

Your debt devils will want you to hang onto items using the 'it has sentimental value' or 'I will never find that item again' to stop you from de-cluttering. Be clear that if you keep that sentimental stained mug, it is with the intention that it is not because you are poor and can't afford another mug!

Discard whatever you feel represents the 'you of the past'; the 'you' that struggled and felt you did not have enough. The symbolism of letting go of what is broken and old will help the law of attraction to notice your decision that you deserve better quality goods and begin working on matching items to your new value system.

Olive Prosperity Habit

Movement

To help start the flow of money in a positive direction, you can create movement in other areas of your life. Any movement you create will add energy to your magnetic force field and give the law of attraction more fuel to deliver what you need financially. You can, in the spaces you work and live in, create movement as follows:

- De-clutter what you have stored away in garages, sheds, basements, attics and cupboards. The stuff such as seasonal items that you need to keep put them into identical storage containers and label so they look professionally organised and tidy and there is a system in place. When your eye runs over these items it will not register chaos and clutter, instead your eyes will see order and structure.

- Examine all your ornaments and pictures, and thin out until you can see clean uncluttered lines. Only keep items that are attractive and serve a purpose or are of sentimental value. Look for the symbolism of items in full view, check that they remind you and visitors to your spaces only of happy days past and happy prosperous days to come. Once a week move one or two items around the home or office, do not allow them to stay in one place permanently and stagnate.

- If at all possible, rearrange furniture to new spaces. Moving the bulkiest of items in your house will result in bulkier movement of energy being reflected towards your cash flow. If you cannot move them, add new colour cushions and throws to freshen up the areas. Clean the dust bunnies underneath the furniture.

- Throw away plastic flowers or anything that is artificially made and replace with fresh living energy where possible.

- Spring clean your home, removing all items from shelving and put back into different spaces or in a different order – anything that creates movement.

- Clean the light fixtures as they need to shine brightly on your future. Put in daylight bulbs for the brightest lighting if possible.

- Repair anything in the house that does not function properly, tighten loose doorknobs, railings, and touch up with paint and varnish where needed. Where extensive repairs are required and the cash flow does not yet exist, lovingly place your hand on that item and promise that the makeover is coming soon. Add a picture of the completed new look to your vision board.

- Make a commitment that when the seasons change, you will be sorting out the weeds in the garden, a tidy green garden reflects a tidy green heart! Gardens are often neglected when the heart is not feeling loved enough, let go the poverty of the heart by setting the intention to make your garden great. If you do not have a garden, arrange potted plants if possible to symbolise your healthy loving heart of the future. ·

- Fill up all your coffee and tea containers, so when visitors pop in they see you are abundant and brimming over with prosperity. This symbolism is very important for the law of attraction to match that prosperity action of full containers to a full bank account.

- File away your papers in the office at work and at home, create a neat system with labels. A tidy office reflects a tidy mind! You do not want visitors or clients to symbolically see the confusion in your current mind where you are still grappling with changes that is symbolised by a messy office.

- Clean your car until it looks and smells as if it is brand new. Your car is the symbol of the direction in where your life is going to head to next. Does your car reflect that new life as poor and clouded with grime or is it prosperous and sparkling clear?

Debt Devil # 4: The Olive Envy

There is nothing more forceful to keep you out of authentic power and success than for the green-eyed debt devil of envy to divert your focus to want you to be like someone else.

This debt devil's tactic will have you constantly make comparisons between your life and someone who appears to be doing better than you. It will have you believe that the very people whose love and validation you seek do not even notice your efforts because the person you envy's light is so bright that you fade into the background.

The envy devil's life experience for you to master, is to propel you to seek out your own uniqueness and to find that spark within you that only you can polish up and shine into the world. Everyone has a talent, a natural ability that is yours alone and while you desire someone else's ability you are missing finding and nurturing your gift to the world.

Your envy devil will also have you believe that you are not good enough, strong enough, and clever enough compared to the idol version you have of a successful person. This will prevent you from writing the book, starting a business and feeling fulfilled. It may have you develop thoughts of 'why bother, they have done it so well, who am I to speak/write/teach on that subject, no one would want to listen to me'.

This envy devil lurks in the business world as well, disguised as 'beating the competition'. Entire industries, political campaigns and TV shows have been built out of the envy debt devil's jealousy and need to be better than someone else, earn more than someone else and be more famous than someone else.

As mentioned in the introduction of this book, there is a shift in how businesses are marketing themselves if they want to stay in business to serve the new generations that demand high ethical standards. The new marketing movement is from competition to co-operation.

Advertisements that depict how poor the product of another company is and naming them, then justifying why your product is better, is a marketing strategy based on poverty mind set. An advertisement that focuses only on the value being offered and how happy the outcome will be for the client if they use this product or service is based on a prosperity mind.

In the businesses of the future, the only race that you will be running to win is the one against your own set of standards, not against others achievements or failures in your industry. Strive to be the best you, not the best version of someone else. Develop your product and service to a standard that makes you happy, not a standard that is set by someone else.

The act of being competitive is an act of fear. It elicits the need to exterminate or steal someone else's market so that you can be noticed first. It needs you to invest a huge chunk of your time and resources to prove that you are better than anything else out there. What if you used those resources and instead diverted it to serving your clients to the highest ability you have? You may find that what was previously considered competition becomes an ally and new affiliations may evolve, you may even begin to share discoveries and innovations.

Olive is the colour of war; soldiers wear olive as their camouflage and invade green spaces on land. Remove the envy devil's olive camouflage of competition and decide to stop taking your business to corporate warfare. You will be setting your business up for longevity and serve the new generation that desires a more peaceful approach to life.

When you have chosen peace instead of war, you can use the envy devil in your positive magnetic pole to help you unearth your unique gift and position your business in the perfect market.

Olive Action

➤ Create an olive coloured gratitude journal. Find the most beautiful book or cover a book with beautiful olive paper. Every morning before you do anything, before you even get out of bed, write down at least three things with a beautiful pen that you are grateful for in your life – even if they have not happened yet.

GRATITUDE is the engine of Generosity

GENEROSITY is the engine of Prosperity

Being grateful is a state of prosperity and will attract even more prosperity to be delivered by the universal law of attraction.

For additional olive support visit my website, www.8coloursofprosperity.com where you can access free olive empowering visualizations and purchase Colour Mirrors olive bath oils and spritzer essences.

Chapter 5

Turquoise Dragons

Turquoise Attracts: Heartfelt Communication, Emotional Freedom and Technology

Turquoise Attributes: Intuitive, Idealistic, Enquiring and Artistic Creativity

Turquoise Power: Mix the body's green heart with the blue throat and you have turquoise heartfelt communication. This is the most powerful colour to help you speak up and say what you feel.

Turquoise and the Law of Attraction

Entrepreneurs will often say that their biggest fear is speaking in public. Does the thought of standing in front of people and delivering a presentation make you weak at the knees? There is one underlying reason why public speaking is considered one of the biggest fears; it makes you visible and therefore requires you to be in your personal power. Being in your personal power is when you have a sense of your own value and believe in the value of your message. The level of value and power you take on stage is the level of return you will get from the law of attraction.

Attend communication courses and be mentored to speak using stage techniques until you become proficient and comfortable in front of an audience.

To connect with your audience at deeper levels and become a sought after speaker, you can enhance your personal power to authentic power.

Traits of Authentic communicators:

- Have no fear of rejection. You know that whoever responds to your message is enough, and those that did not are not an issue.

- Have no need to be validated or applauded. The fact that you turned up and delivered a message will be enough.

- Believe that who you are is enough. Your presence on stage makes a difference before you have even said one word.

- Motivation for speaking is based on your life purpose and your legacy.

- Genuinely love people and desire to inspire them by making a positive impact in their lives.

The colour turquoise will help you achieve that connection between *what you desire* to communicate through your message and *how you feel* about your message. When the two are conveyed together, your audience will feel the authenticity that you believe and care about everything that is coming out verbally; and they in turn will believe you and care enough to invest in you.

The law of attraction is very clear when it comes to communication, every word you speak is an instruction to the law. And it listens and does not miss one word. However, have you listened to what you say with that much care and focus, aware of every word that it is going to be used to attract that outcome towards you? Add that to the emotions you have around those words and the law has enough instructions to deliver your next bite of reality.

YOU SPEAK AND FEEL YOUR REALITY INTO BEING

It is almost impossible to keep track of every word you speak and every emotion you feel every minute of the day. You can however spend time on affirming your intention and ask that it over-rides any negative words or feelings you may have let slip into the law's creative system. Also you need to train to self-alert when you hear yourself speak poverty and as you hear yourself speak it, just say:

CANCEL or THIS IS NO LONGER MY TRUTH.

Another way to strengthen your powers to speak with more awareness is to really listen to other people, and notice how many times they have allowed their debt devils to speak through them and you will soon gain clarity on why they attract so many difficult lessons towards them. Observing how others communicate will be a strong motivator for you to put greater effort into speaking with more self-awareness and loving intentions.

Before you fall asleep every night, review your day's conversations and feelings, cancel out the parts you do not want to become reality tomorrow and re-affirm the parts you really want to attract.

Turquoise Poverty Habit

Poverty Letters

How you read and write all your correspondence, whether they are emails, short text messages or posts on social media, will reflect whether you are in a poverty mind set or feeling prosperous.

- The length of time you take to answer correspondence reflects time poverty, not enough time or I am too busy.

- Glancing through and skipping words and then replying to what you have perceived the message to be, often results in you having missed the real question or issue. And when you send a half reply it may result in several communications to establish the correct message.

- Not spelling words correctly.

These habits send a message that you do not value the person you are communicating with and in turn others are sensing that you do not value yourself.

Read all messages *three times* before replying, and read everything you write *three times*, and say it at least once out loud if possible before you hit send or post it. Over time you will become more aware of your communications and reduce the time you need to spend reviewing correspondence.

This discipline in communication is also useful as it gives you time to become aware whether one of your debts devils has taken over the communication process and is using your writing to start dramas and create stress to once again divert you from using your energy and time to focus on prosperity.

The colour turquoise relates to communication using technology; social media, webinars, computers, videos and broadcasting. When you are in a poverty mind set, you will use the excuse of not understanding technology to avoid expansion in your business. You do not need to know how it all works! There is an entire new generation that seems to have been born with a microchip in their brains that could assist you.

Attend courses to discover the basics of on-line marketing and using social media to attract clients. The law of attraction cannot bring more clients to you through technology if you have not placed your presence in the devices. Using technology is going to be the fastest method of expanding your client base and attracting new cash flow. There are many courses for on-line marketing where you will either learn to use the systems yourself or meet someone who can do it for you. The law of attraction will notice your desire to learn technology and the perfect solution will appear.

When you do not feel valuable enough, you will feel your message and presence is not of enough value to put in front of a camera and will in turn, cause you to avoid offering your work through the medium of videos, webinars or live broadcasts. Turquoise is a colour that says 'what you communicate comes from the heart'; decide on the aspect of who you are or what you offer that you feel is genuinely authentic to you, and put that part of yourself or your business in front of a camera. Take courses and practice being comfortable speaking in front of your computer or phone camera.

Turquoise Prosperity Habit

21 Days

To help you emerge from the depths of drowning in debt and begin to feel prosperous without having yet earned more money, you can begin to work on the intention of prosperity by writing and speaking a prosperity language.

- Acquire a beautiful colourful book that fits in your bag to accompany you on your daily commute and let it be visible on your desk every day.

- Write down on one page a list of affirmations of what you are experiencing as your prosperous life, even if it has not yet happened. Here are some examples:

I am an asset to everyone I meet
I add value to everyone I meet
Money flows in huge quantities effortlessly towards me
All my clients love and respect me
Every day new opportunities arrive
I am supported by a team of people who love and respect me
My book is changing many lives each day
I love my neighbourhood and kind neighbours
I love my life
I am grateful for my supportive family and friends

- Write the same set of affirmations for 21 days in your book. It takes 21 days to break old habits. After each page is written, read each sentence out loud to yourself so you can hear the words as well as see them.

- When you feel overwhelmed with debt issues or slow cash flow, or have problems at work, open this book and read the affirmations again to re-align with the intention of a good life.

- At the end of 21 days, review the set of affirmations and adjust or add to them where needed and repeat the new set for 21 days, keep this process going until it becomes a routine habit to communicate with the law of attraction using correspondence.

Debt Devil # 5: The Turquoise Child

The child devil is perhaps the most self-destructive of all the debt devils. It will be intent on interfering where you are most vulnerable. If your biggest fear is to be sick, this devil will attract serious bouts of poor health. If your biggest fear is not having money, this devil will work very hard at keeping you in financial struggle. If your biggest fear is being alone, this devil will create chaos with relationships until you feel abandoned. Whatever your worst nightmare is, this child devil will hone in on that fear and take charge.

The reason this devil has such power is that it has been storing up a supply of food since you were in the womb. Every time you felt angry and frustrated and did not express the emotions, lacked the emotional wisdom to know how to respond or you were bought up to be seen and not heard, you fed the inner child's negative magnetic pole.

Over time the child devil will have created its own system of categorizing the negative emotions and you will by now have one very big fat file labelled "The Dragon". A dragon symbolizes to a child the ability to keep the angry fire within its body until it is provoked, at which time it unleashes such hot flashes of flames that it has the capacity to singe everything and everyone in its path. Remember the times you lost your temper? Experienced road rage? When you want to make friends with the child devil, you need to first make friends with its playmate, the dragon.

All the old emotions your child devil has stored in their dragon you have the power to clear out and turn the dragon's power into your own power animal. When you do that, you will have a resource of energy to propel you towards your goals of high performance and top achievement while having the most fun.

Here are some reflections of a child and its dragon playing out their games:

- Do you run your finances like a child, spending what you do not yet have?

At the age you received your biggest wound as a child, you will have registered your value and it is that limited value system that could be operating your money. For example: If your father left the family when you were 9 years old, you may have registered that you were not valuable enough for him to stick around. A 9 year old will buy sweets with pocket money without the thought of how to go out and earn the money, as earning money is the job of the parents. As an adult, you could therefore have a spending pattern that says someone else will pay for me; but someone else does not appear and you have to apply for more credit cards, loans and overdrafts to keep up with your inner 9 year old child's spending habits.

- Do you know how much money you have or the total amount of your debt?

A child will not pay attention to details and keep you from setting up accounting systems and keeping track of the flow of money in your accounts. It will distract you with the help of its dragon mate to go out and do fun stuff instead, meeting up with friends, dancing, drinking, going to parties and staying up all night. It will do whatever it takes to keep you sleepy and away from being a responsible adult.

- Do you interrupt others mid-sentence, because you have to be heard right now?

The child devil will speak at inappropriate times, and really loves a captured audience. You will notice this behaviour on courses or at seminars, or meetings. It is the person who has to add something to everyone else's communication, often irritating the group.

- When you need attention, do you set up dramas to get noticed?

As a child you may not have had the emotional wisdom to say what you needed and quickly learned that you get attention when you are sick. As an adult that behaviour repeats when your inner child wants attention, it may affect your health to get the needed attention from family and doctors.

- Do you go shopping and buy inappropriate clothes or items for an adult?

An inner devil child loves to shop and buy pretty things, often because that may have been a method used by the parents to reward good behaviour. Depending on just how deep the wounds were growing up, this devil has the power to take possession of your mind and body and use those times to have you buy items that are not age appropriate. Notice when you have been shopping and try on clothes that suits someone much younger or you come home with clothes you know you are never going to wear. Children love clothes with slogans and images. Have you been tempted to wear that t-shirt with glittery dragons and fairies on it?

- Does your appearance reflect an adult or a child?

Case Study of the 'Sixty Six' 6 year old

A client, who had written a book for children aged 6 to 10 years of age, came for a session. She wanted to know why her book was not selling. Without her selecting any colour bottles, I knew instantly just by her appearance what the problem was. She was a 66 year old woman with her hair parted into two ponytails at the nape of her neck and tied with children's elastic bands, one colour on one side and another colour band on the other. She then selected her first bottle, the Colour Mirrors Turquoise Dragon bottle.

The people who are in a position to buy her books are parents and bookstores, all adults who cannot help but feel they are looking at a 6 year old in an older woman's body trying to do business. It does not make business sense to do deals with children.

- Are your relationships adult to adult?

Case Study of the Living Dolls

A student in my course shared that the intimacy in her relationship had died years ago and she could not understand why her husband no longer initiated physical relations with her. I asked her to describe their bedroom. The description sounded very neat and grown up, until she mentioned that she collects antique dolls and they are displayed on the bed nestled amongst the pillows. I asked how her husband felt about the dolls and she replied that he often moaned at how long it took him to carefully remove the fragile dolls before he could get into bed. A grown adult man knows not to sleep with a child! Her husband at some level felt uncomfortable as their bed was decorated to please a child and not adults. Once she removed the dolls to another room, she reported that their relationship changed.

I have often had clients identify and then clear the childish items in their bedrooms and offices that are inappropriate for adults or business, such as teddy bears, angel wings, pictures more suited to children's rooms and children's toys.

The most powerful antidote to stop your child devil from feeding its fiery dragon is to allow yourself to feel and acknowledge your emotions in the moment. How often is your response to ignore or be polite and nice, when someone has insulted you? How often when someone frustrates you do you also respond with nice or polite?

You are mostly afraid to speak the truth because if you really verbalized your feelings, others may not love you anymore. What tends to happen when you find the courage to speak up is that they will apologize, perhaps unaware that they had hurt your feelings.

Self-alert when you recognize yourself being 'nice' and use turquoise colours to grow in courage and say how you feel right in the moment, instead of later on admitting 'I should have said...'

Tame the child's dragon and win them both over to work for you in the positive pole of your magnetic force field by embracing the life experience they are trying to teach you – to have fun and not be so serious all the time. Incorporate into your lifestyle times when you go out for ice cream, times to splash in puddles and times when you enjoy a Disney movie. Those child-like moments feed joy to the child devil and its dragon.

Turquoise Action

➤ Commit to a weekly play date with your friends or family where the activity is focussed to feed love and joy to the inner child. A healthy inner child leads to a healthy responsible adult and together can create a business or project that makes working fun and easy.

For additional turquoise support visit my website, www.8coloursofprosperity.com where you can access free turquoise empowering visualizations and purchase Colour Mirrors turquoise bath oils and spritzer essences.

Chapter 6
Platinum Seekers

Platinum Attracts: Unlimited Potential, Peace and Universal Purpose

Platinum Attributes: Unity, Commitment, Gratitude and Perfection

Platinum Power: The soft yet steely hue of platinum enables you to complete any task effortlessly in record time. Platinum lets you see the bigger picture and dissolves procrastination.

Platinum and the Law of Attraction

The previous sequence of five colours will have shown you how to master several life challenges and you have learned more on how the law of attraction operates. The colour platinum has the ability to help you escalate your powers of creation to the next level and dissolve resistance as you go through the gateway of opportunity to a new beginning.

- *Pink* taught you about the power of love and money and how, if you focus on more love, automatically more money arrives

- *Coral* taught you to break through the ceilings of limiting beliefs, and to add joy to the creation process

- *Gold* encouraged you to be more authentic, and raise your value systems to attract prosperity

- *Olive* taught you how to instigate a new beginning and strive for setting your own higher standards

- *Turquoise* taught you how to communicate prosperity and the benefits of healthy emotional expression, oh and how to tame a dragon!

Working with platinum is akin to realising you have come as far as you can on your own and having become the big fish in your pond, so big, you have to relocate to a bigger pond. However, arriving in your new pond, you find you are really just a guppy at the bottom and swimming above you is a multitude of larger more powerful fish. The law of attraction will have succeeded in getting you to this pond where you now swim in the magnetic force fields of the inspiring people you have set your intentions to connect with.

In business it could be a position you attained at a company you never thought you could achieve; as an entrepreneur it may be clients in a higher income bracket seeking your expertise; or it may be offers to appear on TV or share the speaking stage with celebrities. Initially you may feel overwhelmed with the added work required or responsibilities or still doubt if you even deserve to be there and concerned you may not yet have enough know-how or tools to work in this new level.

Platinum asks you to look up from the bottom of that pond, do some stargazing and pick out the colour fish that mostly appeals to you and ask them to mentor you.

I cannot stress this point more strongly, if you want to reach the pinnacle of success that you aspire to, the fastest and easiest route is to find someone that has already achieved that and can share their blueprint with you. The law of attraction will ensure you are connected with mentors whose own life purpose and motivations match yours.

Open up to being mentored by several people, each within their own field of expertise, you may find use for a business mentor, a physical fitness coach, a spiritual teacher, a relationship mentor, technology mentors – any area of your life that you still need to become a master at, or any area of your life that you want more from; use your intention and work with the law of attraction to bring them and the financial requirements needed so you can invest in their guidance. Investing in mentors is the most profound investment you will ever make in your business as it adds value to you, and you are the biggest asset of your business.

When I wanted to write this book, I sat down and made several attempts over 3 years to start, and it did not become a reality until the law of attraction led me to a book writing program and a mentor! Examine whether you have reached that stage where you cannot teach yourself anything new or exciting, and are possibly frustrated at repeating the same routine and eager for more.

SEEK OUT A MENTOR

You may be unable to see your own potential clearly and a mentor will extrapolate all your highest abilities and see the bigger picture of what you can create. The most successful athletes, entrepreneurs, musicians, artists, actors – they all had several mentors coaching them to achieve their ultimate potential.

Mentors do not have your fears or feelings of 'not enough' clouding the view of the future you. A mentor's guidance may even surprise you by helping you re-define your life purpose and business goals.

Platinum Poverty Habit

Escalating Negative Frequencies

The more you grow in power the more you need to be aware that the law of attraction is going to speed up the delivery and the size of the intentions you have set.

Platinum, as with all the other colours, amplifies both the negative and positive poles of your magnetic force field. Whatever you place your focus on, will expand and by the time it has a run through the law of attraction's system and comes your way again, it can pack a punch if you focussed on negative energy. You may even be adding to global negative events without being aware of it.

Facebook deliberately at the beginning chose to have one button, the LIKE button and made a decision to not add a thumbs-down dislike button. That presents a challenge – you have to be more on the alert as to which post you click LIKE on! How often has a friend posted pictures of starving or beaten animals and you hit the LIKE button. What did the law of attraction just notice you do?

Your LIKE on the post results in the law having to create more of the situations that featured in the post. Be acutely aware of what you LIKE and judge on the posts made in social media. You will attract more of what you judge and add energy to the cycle of struggle in the world. Your LIKE is a very precious commodity of creation energy, give it to the law of attraction with reverence.

Platinum Prosperity Habit

Meditate

Everyone has a 6th sense, an inner knowing that adds to the human senses of touch, smell, sight, hearing and taste. You however tend to ignore the importance of this sensory emotional and spiritual gift and often choose to follow the mental body's systems of proven logic and statistics.

When you want to follow a path of prosperity you will discover times where you need to set aside logical and tangible rationalizations, and perhaps follow the intangible gut feeling instead.

The law of attraction uses your 6th sense to alert you to follow a path you may not have considered before, but it could just be the path leading to that prosperity miracle. A miracle you will miss out on if your mind first requires evidential proof or a probability outcome.

There is a powerful exercise you can do to hone the power of your 6th sense and have ready to use as a prosperity habit – Meditation. For five minutes a day, still your mind and slow your breathing and allow your thoughts to leave and deeply relax. You can learn how to mediate, or use music or guided meditations, do some research and find out the best method and time frame of meditation to suit your schedule.

Meditation is often referred to as a dose of daily mental hygiene. Added benefits of meditation include:

- Reduction in stress levels
- Improved concentration
- Increased self-awareness
- Promotion of happiness
- Influence of optimum physical health

Experiment with the 'colour meditations' on my website, www.8coloursofprosperity.com

Debt Devil # 6: The Platinum Duty

The duty devil delivers a life experience where you may feel confined by a set of circumstances or beliefs and feel you are sentenced to a lifetime of doing what is expected of you. You become a prisoner of your own life.

This devil will have you follow the path of what is expected and negate your dreams of freedom. Often this devil will use strong cultural and religious beliefs or the fear of survival to keep you locked into a system that you feel is your duty to stay committed to.

The fear of alienating your family and friends if you dared to be different can be a frightening prospect. What could happen if you decided to be brave and make courageous choices?

Case Study: A Different Choice

Gursharan had to leave her family in England for a country she did not know in an arranged marriage. She followed the cultural duties expected of her for many years despite being very unhappy. When her three children decided to further their studies in England, she saw this as her opportunity to leave her marriage and live in the country she loved.

All financial support for her and the children stopped and they were excluded from activities and the support of their cultural community. The children worked to put themselves through University and Gursharan took on whatever jobs she could find, also studying part time with the goal to start her own business. Her bravery inspired her children to follow their own choices.

Her eldest daughter became a psychologist working in research for the government; the second daughter became a sports psychologist working for England Rugby and leading campaigns to empower young women through sports. Her son went home to visit his father and was shown what financial security he could have if he decided to stay and be dutiful. He declined, instead desiring to follow his own path working in politics at the House of Lords. He is also a successful poet and playwright.

The duty devil could also be using a self-imposed duty that you put into place based on a belief that you have to do that job because it gives you a sense of purpose and value. You can become fanatic, overzealous and focus all your attention on this one purpose to the exclusion of all else. Your devotion to the project, charity, cause, person or job blinds you to the signs that the law of attraction sends you to let go and move to a new beginning. Judgements are a huge part of what will hook you into this process and drain you until you burn out and can no longer sustain the energy needed to stay dutiful.

The law of attraction will facilitate a break away from the duty devil's claws. Often the first response is panic because it may be an unexpected change, for example: getting fired or forced into early retirement or retrenched from a job or project with funds no longer being available.

Over time you would look back at the event that appeared so devastating at first, and realize that it was the catalyst that propelled you to a new beginning where you have more choices around creating and living a prosperous life.

When you read autobiographies of entrepreneurs and how the law of attraction delivered severe blows to their lives, you will notice that the blow often led to them fulfilling a much higher global purpose with their skills. Do not underestimate the power of 'blows' in your life, you could just be the person an entire nation is waiting for to lead and inspire them!

Platinum Action

Platinum is the colour that depicts gifts in music and sound. Music has a profound effect on your mind and body, it has the power to uplift you and change your moods instantly.

Dr Masaru Emoto's experiments with water crystals, showed how beautiful ice crystals grew when music was played. Your body is made up of 70% water and your water will respond and be influenced by the frequencies of music.

➤ Each day listen to five happy songs. Songs that make you want to get up and dance and move your body. Create a playlist of songs with only positive words and messages, songs that celebrate life and prosperity and reflect the future successful you. Already two songs have been hinted at in this book to get your playlist started, Dancing on the Ceiling and Faith!

For additional platinum support visit my website, www.8coloursofprosperity.com where you can access free platinum empowering visualizations and purchase Colour Mirrors platinum bath oils and spritzer essences.

Chapter 7

Magenta Leadership

Magenta Attracts: Bridging Opportunities and Evolutionary Leaders

Magenta Attributes: Human BE-ing, Highest Presence and Authentic Authority

Magenta Power: Magenta is a mix of red, the lowest frequency colour and violet the highest frequency colour. Magenta is the colour that helps bridge the red material survival world with the violet spiritual service world.

Magenta and the Law of Attraction

You have been divided into two separate worlds, the human do-ing and the human be-ing.

The human do-ing has to actively be in control and make things happen, plot and plan, scheme, push and pull to get what you need, tapping into the resources and information learned in one lifetime. You rely on facts and figures, statistics, records, evidence and proof as the foundation of all your choices, experiencing life in a red world of survival.

To get out of or make sense of your world when you no longer find fulfilment and seek something more meaningful, you may begin to seek out the violet spiritual side of yourself. It happens that some people leave the red material world behind completely and enter the violet world of service; starting up alternative or complementary therapy businesses, doing humanitarian or environmental work, setting up or working for charitable organizations, re-newing a connection with religious beliefs or studying new age spiritualism.

Whether you have been in either world; in the material red world working hard to earn and where money is important, or in the violet world striving to help others and where service is the motivator – you will have been a human do-ing.

Judgements between the two worlds are fairly common as the red material world views those in the service violet world as woo-woo and unrealistic. The violet world views those in the red material world as being over-focussed on money and stuck in systems that stress and control. The new generation is here to teach you how to bridge the red and violet world, turning it into a magenta world of higher aspirations. In the magenta world you can have both the red financial freedom and the violet universal service. This is where you become a human be-ing.

When you have worked in the red business world and burned out from overwork and stress, become ill or had the shock of losing a loved one you may start searching for more meaning to your life. Often you will feel drawn to study subjects including; NLP, EFT, Reiki, Mindfulness, Meditation, Yoga, Sound therapy, Spiritual Principles, Hypnotherapy, Astrology and so on.

By adding these metaphysical tools to your old business skills, you can set up a 'magenta' business that offers a universal approach on how to have a good life and do purposeful work.

You then become part of the new self-help evolutionary advisors and mentors being sought out to uplift businesses to higher standards, higher financial success and higher authenticity, while maintaining optimum health and work-life balance.

When you are mentored by leaders who themselves have bridged the red material and violet spiritual worlds, you will gain a deeper understanding of the law of attraction and its one universal truth:

Your activities in the material DO-ING world do not create your life

Your spiritual BE-INGNESS creates your life

Working harder or longer hours is not going to change your life. What is required is for you to become aware of yourself and adjust at the core of your being; your feelings, your beliefs, your habits, what you communicate and your intentions.

Those who have managed to bridge the material and spiritual world become evolutionary leaders. You can recognize them by how they have bridged their ethics with traditional business strategies and developed unique business modules. For example:

- They are authentic authorities in their field; their expertise is based on personal life experiences and they share their failures and successes with clients.

- Evolutionary leaders construct their business around their 'why' and not 'what' they sell. They base all their marketing on their belief systems and not what their product can do.

- Teach or implement business systems that do not restrict or control; instead offering systems only as guidelines to assist their clients or staff to stay focussed on achieving goals while maintaining their uniqueness.

- They do not require you to pass tests, when they issue your certificate it will be in recognition of who you are, and not what you have done for them.

- They will reflect their high value systems to you as if you are already at the same prosperity level as them, and therefore tend to avoid offering discounts. Evolutionary teachers will not validate your 'I can't afford' or 'I need it cheaper'. Instead they may offer systems of payment that remind you of your power to create prosperity by working with the law of attraction.

- They value their time and energy and therefore choose who they want to work with. The motivating factor is not to earn the highest income and have the highest sales statistics; instead it is to work with those who have the highest potential and desire to achieve their goals. They will respond to your commitment.

- They choose to co-operate and do not teach competition strategies, their focus is entirely on how to be fulfilled doing what you love while attaining financial freedom.

- Balancing work and home life is a high priority, as well as physical and mental health. Family has priority over business, always.

- Evolutionary leaders build relationships with their clients and staff that feel deeply personal. You will feel genuinely cared for, valued and loved.

- At the forefront of every business opportunity is 'how can you add value' and not how much money can be made.

- They prefer wherever possible for the old fashioned handshake to seal the deal. Evolutionary leaders know how the law of attraction works, what you intend on a contract will attract that outcome. Contracts not worded carefully can be construed by the law of attraction as a potential betrayal and retaliation outcome desired by the signing parties. When there is no option and a contract is required, they will ensure their intention underpinning the contract is free from fear when signing.

- Evolutionary leaders will not 'do it for you'; instead they will use their systems to empower you. They pass on their techniques ensuring you know that they expect you to eclipse them as you combine their teachings with your talents and blaze a trail that is uniquely yours.

Magenta Poverty Habit

The Confined Mind

When you make decisions based only on what you personally know and believe, you will have a confined outcome. To be truly successful requires you to investigate or research everything that turns up with an open mind. When you are challenged with a new concept or a different belief system and you reject them instantly because you have a judgement on the person or how they operate, you may have closed the door on your miracle.

If you are facing a problem in your life, and a friend makes a suggestion for you to go see what you perceive as a weird, wacky, hippy-dippy, incense smelling, away with the fairies crackpot; open your mind, put a peg on your nose and do it! Say YES and TURN UP.

If you are facing a problem in your life, and a friend makes a suggestion for you to go see a specialist in business systems in the city and you resist because you don't like to follow the structures of the booted and suited city folk, preferring to be a free spirit; slap on the tie or lipstick and get your butt to that appointment! Say YES and TURN UP.

Do the research before closing the doors on your miracle because you have fear, resistance or judgments.

An open mind will open the flow of prosperity and accelerate your steps towards financial freedom. Treat every step you take towards that freedom with a sense of exploration and adventure.

Magenta Prosperity Habit

60-Minute Prosperity Time

You are at your peak capacity early mornings. Do you spend your precious first 60 minutes fussing with the chores of the day, catching up with what you missed the day before, reading emails, returning phone calls or on social media? The first 60 minutes of the day where you sit down for work, is the highest peak time for setting intentions that will affect your future.

Use the first 60 minutes of the day for activities that are exclusively going to add energy to your magnetic force field for future attractions. Anything that is about maintaining what you have already created and experiencing in your daily life can begin in the second hour of the working day.

Focus your 60-Minute Prosperity intention time on:

- Researching items and ideals you intend incorporating into your life

- Writing your book

- Writing your 21-Day Affirmations

- Reading and studying and immersing your energy into books and stories for inspiration and new ideas for the future

- Work on the designs or concepts that are your future products or services

Debt Devil # 7: The Magenta Servant

This debt devil loves to play havoc with your life when you have set the intention to be of service to others. The servant devil especially loves to influence those who have chosen careers and businesses in the industries of nursing, health care, charities, religion, mentoring, alternative therapies, environmental and animal welfare, rescue services, social and civil service – the type of industry where you feel a calling to work in and want to make a difference.

When you start off in these industries you are filled with idealistic visions of how your contribution and effort is going to help others. You are happy because you are doing what you love. Often you will work long hours with low income. The moment you begin to feel that this work is a struggle, the physical effort required is too much, the lack of effective results, not enough income – anything that has you feeling negatively about your work, this is the moment your servant devil from your negative magnetic pole increases the downward spiral.

The servant devil wants you to feel you are a martyr and it wants you to feel abused and it wants you to feel powerless to deliver results. You will find this debt devil active in your life when you no longer feel of service and instead feel like the servant. It may even happen to you as the person who has chosen to stay at home and raise children, or the person who has committed to care for elderly parents.

Your debt devil will have one goal in mind, to burn you out mentally and physically and have you question your self-worth. When you feel you are not valued enough by your industry or by the people you have tried to help, you will question who you are and the meaning of your life.

This debt devil's life experience is for you to master the intention that underlies your need to be of service. Examine whether your decision to help others is based on a judgement that someone got the plan wrong and you have to step in and fix everything.

Working in the service industry without burning out and being valued for your contribution, needs to be without any judgements as the motivating factor. When you are clear about the work you offer, that you are simply doing it because it feels good and it is fun and you are putting your talents and skills to work because you can, then your chosen path will feel effortless, the results will be higher and your financial return will be more satisfying.

Case Study: The Royal Servant

Lise gave up her full time successful corporate job to pursue a business in the field of astrology as a personal development tool. She shared in a course that she felt drained after sessions with clients who constantly demanded more of her time and knowledge without being willing to pay more. The service work she thought would be more meaningful than the corporate job, instead felt difficult and financially challenging and she was contemplating the thought of returning to a corporate job.

While in the course, she explored the idea that she was allowing herself to be treated by clients as their free servant instead of a valued authority and leader in her field of service. With the help of the colour analysis she realized that she held a belief that anyone in powerful positions such as royalty, often were not liked or given authentic respect. Her belief said that royals were so far removed from their subject's reality, that they never truly understood or empathized and often abused their power. Her servant devil had her convinced that this belief is true and that if she dared to raise herself up to a leadership position, she would not make a connection with her clients and end up not having a business.

Magenta Action

Activate the magenta evolutionary leader within you who wants to be of service by sharing what you have already mastered.

➤ Become a Trainer. Research a teacher trainer program that offers skills on how to motivate, inspire and support others who desire the same results you achieved in your business, personal life or finances.

➤ Become a Speaker. Consider sharing your story of successful change by offering to speak at events. You may even decide to become a professional sales speaker selling your own programs from the stage.

➤ Become a Mentor. Attend coaching programs and learn how to offer one-to-one or group support where you can combine your experience with new skills on guiding clients to achieve their highest potential.

➤ Become an Author. Create a self-help book that uses your unique life experiences as a guide for others to transform their lives.

➤ Become a Broadcaster. Use technology and social media to share your message.

For additional magenta support visit my website, www.8coloursofprosperity.com where you can access free magenta empowering visualizations and purchase Colour Mirrors magenta bath oils and spritzer essences.

Chapter 8

Diamond in your Heart

Diamond Attracts: Global Clients, Pure Clarity and Respect

Diamond Attributes: Philanthropy, Uniqueness, Perceptive, Dignified and Honest

Diamond Power: Diamond light amplifies and intensifies whatever you choose to focus on. It reflects all the colours in the rainbow and reminds you of your unlimited potential to change the world. When you gaze into Diamond light you can only see how precious and perfect you are.

Diamond and the Law of Attraction

Diamond light is clear, white, silvery and reflective. As it holds all the colours of the rainbow, it will shift your focus from serving a small community to finding ways to be of global service. The law of attraction will use diamond light to activate the philanthropist within you and the desire to leave a legacy. Your focus expands from creating wealth for yourself to creating opportunities of prosperity for everyone. This is the colour of successful leaders who have mastered the law of attraction, such as Warren Buffet, Bill and Melinda Gates.

There are 8 universal principles linked to each colour, and as you integrate them into your life, you too can activate that precious diamond in your heart with all the potential to make a difference in the world.

These principles are the highest standards you can set for yourself and your business. As you integrate these philosophies, your magnetic force field will expand and in turn your powers to create prosperity. Each universal principle is based on a prosperity colour:

PINK: Judgements

Judgements are the root cause of all the problems you have in your life. If you stopped judging others and made the choice to instead focus on how to make a difference, you can become living proof that change is possible. Not judging yourself will be an even harder concept to master as by now in your life you are already deeply ingrained in the habits of criticizing how you look, speak and act. Try to become kinder to yourself and others and when you feel the need to judge by deciding what is right and what is wrong instead choose to feel compassion.

Everyone has deep life experiences that they are mastering and at times they will not be doing so great. It is those times that you tend to judge the most, maybe masking your judgement with the appearance of trying to help.

When you notice yourself judging, try to not judge the judgement! Accept that you are simply in the process of becoming more self-aware when you split your opinion into right or wrong and then make a note to be more compassionate in the future.

When you judge you lower your magnetic force field's frequency to its lowest vibration - Fear. All the other universal principles can only work at turning you into a precious prosperity diamond if you end the need to judge.

"If you change the way you look at things, the things you look at change. How people treat you is their karma, how you react is yours. When you judge another, you do not define them, you define yourself." *Dr. Wayne W. Dyer*

CORAL: Forgive Everyone

The concept that 'the person who hurt you may be your most powerful teacher' is a tough one! You live in a reality where there are legal systems and institutions to take care of those who cause you pain. What if what they did to you was the catalyst that propelled you to master your life experiences? What if your parents failed you in some way and you were able to forgive them because you know that without their poor or lack of parenting you could now not be the person you have become, knowing all that you do? If you fail to forgive yourself or others, you stay in judgement and the lowest frequency of fear. And that fear will attract more teachers to deliver life experiences until you let go of the need to judge and instead choose to forgive.

"It's one of the greatest gifts you can give yourself, to forgive. Forgive everybody." *Maya Angelou*

GOLD: Be Authentically Powerful

When you no longer judge and are able to forgive, you will emanate the energy of authenticity. You will also understand that no one else has a value higher or lower than you. As you emit the belief that everyone has equal value, your power will grow. Maintain authenticity by affirming, 'I am the power in my life'.

"The characteristics of an authentically empowered personality are humbleness, clarity, forgiveness and love."
Gary Zukav

OLIVE: Love Unconditionally

Choose to love unconditionally without attachments and expectations on having your love returned. Love is a choice. Love has always been that for you and for others. It was never automatic, love has gears that shift up and down and you control the gear lever.

Love may be the balm that soothes the need to judge. If you love, you will have no need to forgive anyone. When you add love to your authenticity, your magnetic force field will expand to begin to attract others who themselves have learned to hold the frequency of love. Those that still go into fear-based judgements will simply recede from your life. Unconditional love for yourself and others is the magic potion of prosperity.

"Love sought is good, but given unsought is better."
Twelfth Night, William Shakespeare

TURQUOISE: Speak Impeccably

Each word you speak carries the vibration of creation and moment after moment, unfolding before you, is what you have uttered an hour, a day or a week ago. When you speak with judgements you will attract more fear-based dramas, choose to instead speak your reality into being with impeccably chosen words of love. Especially to yourself, say only kind words that nurture you and keep you feeling authentic and powerful.

"Be impeccable with your word. Speak with integrity. Say only what you mean. Avoid using the word to speak against yourself or to gossip about others. Use the power of your word in the direction of truth and love." *Miguel Ruiz*

PLATINUM: Hold the Perfect Vision

Focus your outer and inner visions on views of perfection, even if what in reality you are seeing appears to be chaos. Avoid going into judgements of the chaos and hold a vision of the prosperous future that is unfolding perfectly before you, both the dark and light threads weaving your tapestry of life. Love what you see and speak pure words of appreciation, compassion and understanding.

When you no longer judge what you see, the gift of what is actually happening can reveal itself to you and you will see further afield into the panoramic plan for your life, beyond the few dark stitches you may have been tempted to judge. Without those dark stitches your tapestry would not be complete.

"Your vision will become clear only when you look into your heart. Who looks outside, dreams. Who looks inside, awakens." *Carl Jung*

MAGENTA: Universal Mind of Unity

You are part of a universal mind and you have a unique contribution to add to the greater experience that is ultimately spiritual beings having an individual human experience.

When you still see yourself as having separate origins from everyone else, you go right back down into judgment and fear based frequencies. You come from the same source and return to the same source. Everyone is born and everyone dies.

While having your individual human experience, you go into separation dramas to learn how to get back to the universal mind of unity by; judging each other, not forgiving, claiming superior power over one another, selecting who to love or hate, using your voice to harm and not seeing how everyone weaves together as a collective universal force.

If you were to remember the truth that you are universally connected and chose to separate into individual human bodies to experience separation, then you will never judge again. You will have nothing to forgive. You will be automatically authentic. You will love. You will speak purity and see perfection always. And then you will share magnanimously everything you create.

"We are travelers on a cosmic journey, stardust, swirling and dancing in the eddies and whirlpools of infinity. Life is eternal. We have stopped for a moment to encounter each other, to meet, to love, to share. This is a precious moment. It is a little parenthesis in eternity." *Deepak Chopra*

DIAMOND: No More Guilt

Examine where you still carry guilt, for what you did or did not do. You are the only one still judging the collusion of what was ultimately a life experience. The universal mind has always known exactly what you needed and everything you ever did was simply to experience your individual power of creation as an individual human mind. To help you learn about your individual mind, the universal laws had to create both pain and love. They were your life experiences and you used both pain and love to offer life experiences to others.

All of it was simply life being experienced to discover how it feels to be a human. There is nothing to be guilty about, or to guilt others by judging them. Ending your guilt will end the need to start again with fear. Your life is perfect and it always was and will always be perfect.

"All pain and suffering is guilt looking for punishment. Guilt is the biggest misunderstanding of all." *Melissie Jolly*

Diamond Poverty Habit

The Poor Hero

Are you very passionate about making a difference, setting up projects or charities to help others, perhaps playing the hero to others when it is you that actually needs to be rescued?

Maybe you have lost someone you loved and the only way for you to cope is to feel useful by helping others, even if you do not have adequate resources. Or perhaps you have suffered in some way and feel guilty for the help you received and immediately need to 'pass it on'.

Trying to establish a healthy foundation for your own relationships and finances while diverting some of your energy and time towards a cause – no matter how dear to your heart – is a poverty tactic. If you are committed to make or be a difference in the world, your attention would be better served in strengthening your own situation until it is stable and flowing so that you can genuinely serve from a place of stability and prosperity.

On airplanes the safety instructions are clear, 'put your oxygen mask on first and then help the person next to you'. A prosperity hero is someone who has resources such as support teams, multiple streams of income and established networks and connections with other powerful leaders who will add their value to help with causes close to your heart.

For now, temporarily put aside diverting your attention to rescuing, perhaps add to your 21-day affirmations and vision boards the cause or charity you wish to add value to in the future, and use all your resources towards studying, implementing and living prosperity for yourself. When you are in a positive strong cash flow, have investments, feel joyful and fulfilled, you will have so much more power to make an effective heroic difference in the world.

Diamond Prosperity Habit

Add Value

A diamond is the hardest natural occurring substance in the world and a useful industrial cutting tool; it also represents value and beauty. When you gift someone a diamond you are affirming that person's strength, value and preciousness in your life.

You have the opportunity to utilize the diamond's symbolic power to attract more prosperity with new habits:

- Share your profits with those in your business and community, whether they directly or indirectly ensured your success. Acknowledge their contributions financially or through symbolic rewards such as celebrations and ceremonies.

- Build a team that believes in what you believe in and reward them for their loyalty and ability to hold and work towards the same vision as you.

- Create affiliate programs for your clients and your suppliers. The more they know you value them, the higher they will value and respect and support you.

- Share your clients, let go of the need to say 'my clients' and allow opportunities to add value through other organization's services and products to ultimately increase results for your clients. Your clients will not leave you for someone else, instead they will appreciate that you put their interests above your need for exclusive market share.

Debt Devil # 8: The Diamond Soldier

This is a tricky devil as it has you acting and responding as part of a unit and makes you feel as if you are in danger if you dare to step out of line. The soldier devil will have you follow orders, question nothing and march you into old age when you may be rewarded with a pension. Any attempt to be unique or different, will be swaddled with fear of change.

Over the years you will stop offering resistance and feel you will have found your spot in the unit and like the comfortable feeling of fitting in with the unit. When they surround you, you feel safe. Achieving anything more than a sense of routine and safety will seem unattainable. Anything new and adventurous that may lure you away from the unit will be met with scepticism and resisted by your soldier debt devil. If it is seriously attractive, your debt devil will recruit the unit's devils and over a barbeque or lunch your colleagues and family will convince you to stay and not break up the team.

And then one day, you find courage and you flee, taking perhaps a backpack and travelling to the furthest regions of the world hoping that you will find something to make you feel alive. Or at least you dream of doing this while marching with the unit's collective hut-two-three!

Fleeing is not always the answer. When you begin to feel restless and desire more from your life and you want to offer more of yourself to the world, it begins within you. The soldier devil lives within you, not outside of you; if you are going AWOL you are still going to take it and all your issues with you.

The life experience to master through this soldier debt devil is to dare to be you no matter what your unit is saying or expecting from you. Can you drop all judgements of who you are marching with and love them fearlessly while discovering what makes you happy?

For example: As a wife and mother you may have helped with the family financial income by working at a job you have no passion for. Then unexpectedly you discover a business that excites you. Your family however resist by telling you they do not believe in this type of business, it is too risky to be self-employed or you will never make money. The more you become convinced that this is what you are meant to be doing, the more they fail to support your idea and you may feel judged for wanting more in your life. In extreme cases I have had clients in distress feeling that the only option is to get divorced and break up the family so they can pursue their dreams.

Fleeing and breaking up the family unit is exactly what this debt devil wants you to do. Instead, can you love your family anyway? Regardless of their criticism and doubts, can you stay and prove them wrong? Would it not be satisfying to become so successful that you end up employing your entire family to work with you?

Dare to be uniquely you and become the innovator that experiments and explores new ideas, designs and concepts that ultimately improve the lives of your family and the rest of the world. The soldier devil will allow you to recruit it to work for you in your positive magnetic force field once you show your courage. It will add discipline and enhance your new projects and ideas through networking and teamwork.

Diamond Action

The highest life achievement you can attain is to leave a legacy, something you have created or become known for that is passed down through history long after you have left the world. Your legacy can be left within your family, your community, your region or it can be a legacy that is world-renowned. However, you have to begin to work on it immediately!

When you know what your legacy is, you can use that as the ultimate goal and motivation for achieving success in your businesses and relationships. Your legacy can become the 'why' you do what you do. Your belief in your legacy can be woven into your marketing campaigns and propel you to success as you share your values and philosophy.

Example of Apple's beliefs that became their marketing message during 1997:

The belief:

"We believe that people with passion can change the world for the better."

The Think Different Campaign:

"Here's to the crazy ones. The misfits. The rebels. The troublemakers. The round pegs in the square holes. The ones who see things differently. They're not fond of rules. And they have no respect for the status quo. You can quote them, disagree with them, glorify or vilify. About the only thing you can't do is ignore them. Because they change things. They push the human race forward. While some may see them as the crazy ones, we see genius. Because the people who are crazy enough to think they can change the world, are the ones who do."

If you could effect change or make a difference in one or many people's lives what would it be?

For additional diamond support visit my website, www.8coloursofprosperity.com where you can access free diamond empowering visualizations and purchase Colour Mirrors diamond bath oils and spritzer essences.

References and Further Study

Four of the Debt Devils are derived from the terms used by the author **Caroline Myss** as the Survival Archetypes of Victim, Prostitute, Saboteur and Wounded Child and feature in her deck of cards called: *Archetype Cards*

Dr Masaru Emoto wrote several books on Water Crystals and they are interesting to study as he demonstrated with his experiments how prayer, music and the intention of words placed on water bottles influenced the formation of water crystals.

My business partner, mentor and friend **Melissie Jolly** has written about spirituality with more elegance than I ever can. Her book *What the Seeker Found* is perhaps the most understated yet powerful book I have read on why we should not be judging others and striving to love unconditionally. In her book she answers all the big questions in life.

In Chapter 5, the turquoise prosperity habit of 21 days written affirmations was inspired by the teachings of friend and mentor **Rachel Elnaugh**, a UK ex-Dragon's Den panellist, author of *Business Nightmares* and *Prosperity*, and co-founder of SourceTV.

My clients would be surprised if I did not mention somewhere in this book, a person who has inspired me with her work, and whose videos I shamelessly 'force' my students to watch – **Oprah Winfrey**. We share the same birthday (29 January) and I believe that Oprah has shown women how to serve fearlessly, powerfully and tread a path where others fear to go. Her *OWN* Channel with programs such as *Super Soul Sunday* and the *Believe* series – all are worth watching more than once.

Several books have been written about the Colour Mirrors system, for a list of authors visit **www.colourmirrors.com**

Please visit my website **www.moirabush.com** for details on upcoming Colourful Live Events, Boot Camps and Master Retreats.

And remember to visit **www.8coloursofprosperity.com** for your free bonuses!

About Moira Bush

Born in South Africa Moira studied business, marketing and facilitation; specializing in developing training programs for entrepreneurs and community projects. She also studied drama; acting, writing and is an award-winning author and director.

In 2002 Moira moved to England where she worked with an organization that helped women and refugees to get off the welfare system and into self-employment.

Moira works with the South African Colour Mirrors system of colour psychology as her tool for business, financial and personal transformation. She has helped to establish international centres of colour training and product distribution, and creates powerful teams of exclusive and highly specialized Colour Entrepreneurs.

Moira educates and empowers through Live Events, On-Line Courses, Boot Camps, Master Retreats, Colour Conferences and Mentoring Programs.

Moira is featured on SourceTV as an Evolutionary Leader.

She moved from England to Canada during 2015 and lives in Oakville, Ontario with her husband Paul Valade.

International Speaker

Contact Moira to speak at your next Event

www.moirabush.com/contact

Moira has many years experience speaking at international events where with colourful humour and audience participation, she draws on her experiences in establishing and working in entrepreneurial businesses that included:

- Slick Ice-Cream: Ice-Cream Packaging Franchise
- Business Outreach: Community & Corporate Entrepreneurial Training Centre
- Traditional Craft Centre: Website and Training Centre
- Colour Mirrors Colour Training and Product Distribution: Colour Psychology
- Silver Spheres System: Alternative Therapy
- Love & Money Boot Camps: Business and Personal Training and Mentoring
- NewGen Superfoods Plus: An All-in-One Nutritional Supplement

You can discover more about colour analysis through her websites, Facebook group and YouTube channel.

YouTube Channel: Moira Bush

Facebook Group: Entrepreneurs in Colour

www.source.tv

www.moirabush.com

www.8coloursofprosperitycom